For Mom:
    The Kellys were
among the few blacks
in Greenwich: one was
the model for "Stones
Jones" in ~~the~~ ~~Epilogue~~
chapter of Fits & Starts.
            Love,
            Andy

Dr. Sam

Soldier, Educator, Advocate, Friend

An Autobiography

Dr. Sam

Soldier, Educator, Advocate, Friend

An Autobiography

SAMUEL E. KELLY

with Quintard Taylor

UNIVERSITY OF WASHINGTON PRESS

Seattle & London

University of Washington Press
PO Box 50096, Seattle, WA 98145 USA
www.washington.edu/uwpress

Library of Congress Cataloging-in-Publication Data
Kelly, Samuel E. (Samuel Eugene), 1926–
Dr. Sam, soldier, educator, advocate, friend : an autobiography /
Samuel E. Kelly ; with Quintard Taylor.
p. cm.
Includes bibliographical references and index.
ISBN 978-0-295-99061-3 (hardback : alk. paper)
1. Kelly, Samuel E. (Samuel Eugene), 1926– 2. African American college
administrators—Washington (State)—Biography. 3. College administrators—
Washington (State)—Biography. 4. University of Washington—Professional
staff—Biography. 5. African American soldiers—Biography. 6. Soldiers—
United States—Biography. I. Taylor, Quintard. II. Title.
LD5752.8.K45A3 2010
378.797'77—dc21   2010014165
[B]

To my wife, Donna,
without whom this manuscript or my life
would not have been complete.

Contents

Foreword, by Governor Daniel Evans *ix*
Acknowledgments *xi*
Introduction, by Quintard Taylor *xv*

Part I: Childhood

CHAPTER 1   A Connecticut Childhood 5
CHAPTER 2   Thirty Minutes from Harlem 19

Part II: Soldier

CHAPTER 3   A Segregated Army 37
CHAPTER 4   In Occupied Japan 52
CHAPTER 5   Integrating the Army 62
CHAPTER 6   Korea 78
CHAPTER 7   A Career Soldier 99

Part III: Educator

CHAPTER 8   Community College Instructor 121
CHAPTER 9   Coming to the University of Washington 136
CHAPTER 10   Building the Office of Minority Affairs 159
CHAPTER 11   Final Years at the University of Washington 180

Part IV: Advocate

CHAPTER 12   Starting Over 199
CHAPTER 13   The Vancouver Years 211

Epilogue: A Life of Service and Friendship 225

Chronology 227
U.S. Army Awards, Citations, and Commendations, 1945–65   231
Index   232

Foreword

The late 1960s and early 1970s in the United States were times of strife and conflict and glimmerings of hope. Growing opposition to the war in Vietnam collided with forces seeking environmental protection. The biggest struggle was the unending drive for equal rights for all citizens.

I was inaugurated as Washington State's sixteenth governor in 1965 with little experience in coping with civil unrest. The euphoria of a new administration and growing economy soon evaporated in a rising tide of protests, usually peaceful but increasingly intense. Many were centered on college and university campuses, and I spent an increasing amount of time on those campuses seeking information and solutions to our troubling problems.

That is when I first met Sam Kelly. He stood ramrod straight as the soldier he was and as a black man who personally experienced the sting and shame of discrimination. He told me in blunt terms of the growing frustration of young African Americans. Many had fought in an unpopular war in Vietnam and returned to discover job and educational discrimination. In his quiet but incisive way, he said, "This cannot continue." I was deeply impressed by his intensity and determination as he spoke and thought to myself, "Here is a man I can learn from."

Sam was a pioneer in opening the doors of higher education to all minorities and the poor. His trailblazing work at Shoreline Community College showed what could be done, and soon educational institutions throughout the country started to emulate his innovative and creative approach. Leaders at the University of Washington, recognizing Sam's success at Shoreline, asked him to create a similar program at their institution.

Here was the focal point of ferment, and Sam quickly formed a powerful partnership with President Charles Odegaard.

He also became an important mentor to me. Sam gave me valuable insight into the goals behind the bluster of young protesters. Progress was not always easy, since most citizens saw only the rant and occasional violence of protest. Most were pressuring me to react with force, but Sam Kelly and President Odegaard counseled patience and a positive response when grievances proved real.

The results were spectacular. Minority enrollment at the University of Washington climbed rapidly. Many of these students were the first in their families to attend college, and their presence created a powerful incentive for the next generation to pursue education. The assistance programs Sam devised helped produce a growing number of diverse graduates, and today these UW alums are providing professional and educational leadership throughout our nation. Many would never have entered college but for the vision and determination of Sam Kelly.

After Sam left the university, he moved to Vancouver, Washington, supposedly to retire, but he was soon deeply involved in advising and teaching some of the most difficult teenagers in the minority community in Portland, Oregon. I lost touch with him for a dozen years until he returned to the Seattle area to be close to his family.

A few years ago, at a University of Washington function, I heard this deep voice call "Dan," and as I turned, I saw this familiar figure approaching. Now white-haired but still ramrod straight was Sam Kelly. We embraced and spent the next several minutes exchanging stories about our experiences since we had last seen each other. It was a joy to learn that neither of us really believed in retirement.

I last talked with Sam shortly before his death when he asked if I would write a foreword to his autobiography. He said he was having a few health problems but was feeling pretty good. We both laughed when I told him that he was a lot faster on his autobiography than I was on mine. I said I would be honored to do so for an old friend. After I hung up the phone, I sat for a long time thinking back on those tumultuous days and the many times I had turned to Sam for help and advice. He played an important role during a critical period in Washington State history. He was a giant protector of the rights of all citizens and the integrity of the university. We should thank the U.S. Army for sending Sam to Fort Lawton, and thank Sam for falling in love with Washington. Sam Kelly helped make us a far better state.

Daniel Evans
Washington State Governor (1965–77)

Acknowledgments

A number of people have helped me tell the story of my life. I want to acknowledge my military colleagues who jogged this old soldier's memory and reminded me of both the honor and the sacrifice that comes with wearing the uniform of a U.S. Army officer. I think specifically of Brigadier General Steve Stephens, Colonel Jim Manning, and Colonel Sam Jones, who over the phone shared memories about life in the army. I want to especially acknowledge my dear friend, Lieutenant General Julius Becton, whom I met when we were in Officer Candidate School at Fort Benning, Georgia, in 1945. Our sixty-five-year friendship and the memories we shared of our intertwining army careers were invaluable in helping me write my story.

My friends and colleagues at the University of Washington helped me recall details about my twelve-year history at that institution. Many of them visited Donna and me in our Redmond, Washington, home or at a favorite restaurant, where we reminisced about that period. Often they didn't know that our conversations over great food and drink, and interspersed with lots of laughter, helped me think about those UW events with a fresh perspective. Among those guests were Bill and Dorothy Hilliard, Eddie and Andrea Rye, Aaron Dixon, Larry Gossett, Emile Pitre and his wife, Barbara McCants, Dr. Millie Russell and her late husband, Ed, Gertrude Peoples, Bill Baker, Dr. Karen Morrell, Jim Ryan, and Drs. Thad and Lois Spratlen. Washington State senator George Fleming and his wife, Tina, and Dr. James Goodman were generous in sharing their recollections and helping clarify the course of events during the late 1960s through the 1980s. I particularly want to acknowledge Emile Pitre's tremendous help in providing nearly forty years of statistics on the students of color who have graduated from the University of Washington with the assistance of the Office of Minority Affairs.

My dear friend Dr. Dick White and his wife, Jean, shared memories of my transition from the military to the academic world when I worked at Everett and Shoreline Community Colleges. One of my oldest friends, Bob Woodard, and I often chuckled over our recounting of the changing Seattle social scene from the 1950s to the 1990s.

Sometimes help for the manuscript came in indirect ways. During 2005 and 2006, our Vancouver friends and neighbors helped enormously by recalling the efforts of the Friends of Portland OIC/Rosemary Anderson School. Also, when both Donna and I had significant health issues including multiple surgeries, they stepped forward to provide assistance that allowed us to continue the work on the manuscript. We especially want to thank Bob and Dawn Nesbitt, Dick and Gwen Michalek, Rod and Ingrid Hoover, Jennifer Ellsworth, Dave and Holly Patton, Pat and Kathy Carpenter, Dave and Debe Palmer, Chris Kane, and Bo and Jeffra Schultz-Andersen for the errands they ran, the food they provided, and the laughter that kept our morale high and ensured our continuation of the project.

Mrs. Rosemary Anderson and her grandson, Joe McFerrin II, who succeeded me as president and CEO of Portland OIC/Rosemary Anderson School, generously provided reference materials regarding the nearly fifteen years I spent working with the faculty, staff, and students and mentoring Joe.

I am especially grateful to Casey Nichols, Quintard Taylor's research assistant, who spent hours in the University of Washington Libraries seeking valuable collaborative information for this manuscript. I also want to thank the History Department at the University of Washington and especially department chair R. Kent Guy who obtained crucial funding to support this project. My gratitude also extends to the University of Washington Press and especially to acquisitions editor Marianne Keddington-Lang for believing that my story should be told. I also want to thank the anonymous reviewers of the manuscript, our copy editor, Laura Iwasaki, and other members of the UW Press production team, including Kathleen Pike Jones, Veronica Seyd, and Tom Eykemans.

Since our reconnection in 2005, Dr. Quintard Taylor has grown to be like a younger brother to me. A passionate academic with a heart of gold, he is one of the most gifted scholars with whom I have ever collaborated. We found the ability to laugh and fuss together during the hundreds of hours we spent on this project. Our interviews were always candid and sometimes rambling; all of them, however tangential, added breadth, depth, and flavor to this manuscript. I am deeply indebted to him for his perseverance and scholarly pursuit of excellence.

My children, each in his or her own way, have provided valuable assistance. Whether through conversation, memory-jogging, or reading drafts, Bill, Brenda, Sharon, Heather, and Sam Jr. have been an integral part of the writing of this story. I only wish I could adequately describe the joy each of them has brought to me over the years.

My son, Sam Kelly, Jr., has made some of the most stalwart contributions to this work. His quick mind makes him a consummate critic. It has been a personal joy to have him by my side so much of the time during the evolution of this writing process.

Finally, my wife, Donna (Schaplow) Kelly, spent countless hours at my side, listening to my stories and providing key "bits" of information that I had hidden away too deeply in my memory bank. Donna possesses a keen intellect and is a superb writer and editor with a gift for finding just the right word to make a point. She is also a beautiful wife, mother, lover, and friend; my love and respect for her are boundless. Moreover, she demonstrated consummate love and dedication that resulted in the smooth blending of our families more than twenty-eight years ago. During the ensuing years, she has remained my constant companion, best friend, and the finest caregiver one could hope for as my health has declined. Our life together has been filled with animated conversation, romantic interludes, and various challenges, which we have faced side by side, hand in hand, with a sense of great joy and gratitude for the many blessings we have received.

I have described the events and people mentioned in this book to the best of my recollection. Others may have different perspectives on various matters; those expressed herein are from my unique personal viewpoint and memory.

SAMUEL EUGENE KELLY
June 14, 2009

Introduction: The Sam Kelly Saga

On Saturday, January 28, 2006, more than one hundred people gathered at the Riverside Golf and Country Club in Portland, Oregon, to celebrate the eightieth birthday of Samuel Eugene Kelly. As his children performed the songs of his youth, his grandchildren brought forth handmade expressions of love, and adults from various phases of his long careers presented their own tributes, which included a surprise call from the White House, I realized that we were witnessing the summation of the full and rich life of an extraordinary individual.

This summation on a cold, blustery January afternoon was hardly the end of the Kelly story. Sam Kelly and his family would continue to experience life's drama in the years following his milestone birthday. Yet that eightieth birthday celebration was an opportunity to pause and reflect on the broad sweep of history that had changed his life and the course of a nation. It is a story of enormous triumph punctuated by frustration and agony. Through it all, Sam Kelly remained robustly optimistic about life, ever ready to urge those around him to strive for their own personal best, to be aware of the barriers but also mindful that obstacles can be overcome. His own story, after all, is a powerful testament to overcoming barriers.

Samuel Eugene Kelly was born when Calvin Coolidge was president of the United States and when the vast majority of African Americans could not cast ballots. He lived to see the election of the first African American president, Barack Obama, who was in many respects a personal fulfillment of Dr. Sam's lifelong efforts to help craft a nation that recognizes both the rights and dignity of all of its citizens. Thus his personal story is a prism through which we can look at a variety of major events in twentieth- and now twenty-first-century U.S. history.

Whether it is his firsthand account of class and race dynamics in Greenwich, Connecticut, one of the wealthiest communities in the nation, his youthful explorations of Harlem, his personal struggles against racial segregation and discrimination in the U.S. Army, his creative leadership of diversity efforts at the University of Washington, which helped thousands of underrepresented students earn college degrees, or his dedication throughout much of his retirement to educating the children of the underclass in the 1990s, Sam Kelly always followed his parents' advice to help others and especially African Americans. When Paul Robeson asked a teenage Sam Kelly, "What are you doing for the race?" that question became a challenge that would inspire him to devote his life to helping others and, as he would say, especially "those who looked like me."

Dr. Sam's story captures his youth in a close-knit family of five brothers in overwhelmingly white Greenwich and his visits to virtually all-black Harlem thirty miles away, where he was initially exposed to the richness of African American culture and where his identification with the destiny of black people was first forged. He describes his fifteen-month rise from high school dropout and private to second lieutenant in the army between 1944 and 1945, his bitter encounters with Southern racial segregation while wearing the uniform of a U.S. Army officer, his participation in the U.S. occupation and transformation of Japan, and his role in the integration of the army in 1948 while stationed at Fort Lawton, Washington. As a rare African American plans, training, and operations officer in the 1950s and early 1960s, Captain, Major, and eventually Colonel Sam Kelly helped create the post–Korean War rapid deployment army that would fight in Vietnam and Iraq. During the 1950s, Captain Kelly, airborne officer, trained his troops to engage in combat using the most advanced tactical nuclear weapons, yet he and other black officers were not allowed to accompany his unit, the 101st Airborne, when its white troops were deployed in Little Rock, Arkansas, in 1957 to protect the nine black teenagers who integrated Central High School. In the 1960s, Major Kelly helped develop plans for the suppression of urban uprisings, and yet, before the end of the decade, educator Sam Kelly earned first the respect and eventually the admiration of the Black Panthers who took his African American history courses.

Sam Kelly entered a different combat arena when, on October 1, 1970, he became the first vice president for minority affairs and the first major African American administrator at the University of Washington.

For the next six years, he would develop and lead one of the strongest programs in the nation dedicated to integrating students of color into a major U.S. university. Here Dr. Sam (he received a PhD from the University of Washington in 1971) would, through the university's Office of Minority Affairs, help thousands of students graduate from that institution. Simultaneously, he would help educate the university—its administrators, faculty, and staff—as well as the general public on the school's obligation to meet the needs of those who had by race, culture, or economic status been excluded from the state's flagship institution.

At sixty-five, an age when most people enter retirement, Dr. Sam began a fifteen-year career as a teacher and administrator at an alternative school, helping teenage women and men build new lives. Embracing his commitment yet again to "do something for the race," Sam Kelly plunged into an effort to assist students that many in the community had written off as impossible to teach. Dr. Sam taught them, and inspired them, but he also carried their story to those vastly more fortunate and persuaded them to support the efforts of these young women and men to turn their lives around.

The autobiography also addresses the many personal and family issues in Sam Kelly's life. The birth of his special-needs son in 1952, his second wife's long, unsuccessful struggle with breast cancer, the age discrimination he faced in the late 1980s, and the challenge of creating an interracial blended family are reminders of the profound pain and anguish that accompanied his extraordinarily successful careers.

Through it all, Samuel Eugene Kelly remained committed to his core values of duty, honor, country. For him, these words were not simply a slogan blindly recited for public consumption. They had a deeper meaning. They reflected a commitment to support and, if necessary, defend with his life the nation he loved. His values also included an obligation to critique, challenge, and change what was unjust in the nation he cherished.

I had the distinct honor and privilege of working with Dr. Kelly and his wife Donna on this autobiography project. I encountered Dr. Kelly for the first time in Olympia, Washington, in 1972, when he was the keynote speaker at the statewide Black Studies and the Academy conference at a time when I was an assistant professor in Black Studies at Washington State University. I was one of dozens in the audience; he did not remember me. Our paths diverged, and I became reacquainted with him again in 2005. In the 1970s and beyond, I knew of Dr. Sam the icon, the man who was already legendary in statewide circles that focused on minority students and minority programs, as they were called at that time. In 2005, I met Dr. Sam the man, who wanted me to assist him in telling his story to the world. While I had respected the icon from afar, I came to know and admire the man who willingly shared the details of his life with me.

I signed on to the job of helping Dr. Sam with his autobiography assuming that my role would be that of modern-day scribe, recording the recollections of one man's life. Initially, I marveled at his powers of recall, his ability to, through memory, reconstruct in rich detail the events that had shaped his life. I also came to admire what I will call his "historical sense," that is, his foresight in saving government records, personal papers, photos, and memorabilia that supported his amazing memory. As time passed, I came to realize that I was not simply recording one man's story; I was viewing, at least vicariously, African American and U.S. history through the experiences of a remarkable individual. By the end of the project, I had come to have enormous respect and admiration for Dr. Kelly's courage, tenacity, and wisdom. I also developed a richer understanding of the nation's past and how all of us, through our individual choices and actions, help chart the course of history.

The Samuel Eugene Kelly story is one of hope and caring, friendship, loyalty, duty, and devotion. It is a reminder of what can be accomplished in the United States even as it recalls the obstacles one man faced and the difficulties he overcame to achieve his goals.

QUINTARD TAYLOR
Seattle, Washington
June 14, 2009

Dr. Sam

Soldier, Educator, Advocate, Friend

An Autobiography

"My life has been a continuous quest for balance."

PART I

Childhood

"I was the colored kid from Cos Cob."

THE HOUSE WHERE SAM KELLY WAS BORN IN COS COB, CONNECTICUT, IN 1926. COURTESY OF THE KELLY FAMILY.

CHAPTER I

A Connecticut Childhood

I was born to a poor family in one of the wealthiest towns in the nation. My earliest memory goes back to when I was three, riding my tricycle on the front porch of my house in Cos Cob, an area of Greenwich, Connecticut. The neighborhood was named after John Coe, who in the 1640s built the first cob, or sea wall, at the mouth of the Mianus River. Coe's cob eventually became Cos Cob. Place mattered, and my childhood experiences there would profoundly shape the rest of my life.

Cos Cob was on the southeastern side of Greenwich, close to Long Island Sound. Its residents were generally poor working people—some Greeks, a number of Italians, some poor Jews, Scandinavians, Germans, Irish, and a few "colored" families. The wealthy people, mostly "Yankees" and some Jews, lived in estates surrounding Greenwich proper and abutting Long Island Sound; most were successful businessmen who commuted to Grand Central Station by train. Almost all of the less well-off women and men in Cos Cob worked directly or indirectly for the area's wealthy families, although there were some shop owners who lived with their families above their small stores. Some of the people were kind; others were openly racist. Most were somewhere in between.

My ancestry spans three continents: Africa, Europe, and North America. My grandfather, Albert Kelly, was the son of Thomas Kelly, who was born in Ireland in 1804 and migrated to New York probably during the time of the Irish Potato Famine, which sent tens of thousands of Irish to the United States, where they could get food and jobs. My grandfather was born in New York in 1852. Although we don't know why or when, he moved south to Virginia and settled in Gloucester County, on Chesapeake Bay, about sixty miles east of Richmond. That's where he met my grandmother, Hilda Cheatham, who was born in Virginia around 1865. She was visibly African American and had some Native American blood.

Albert and Hilda owned James's Store and Post Office, a small grocery and hardware store at a crossroads in Gloucester County. It was tobacco country, and one of the first areas settled by the English in the early 1600s. This was where Pocahontas saved Captain John Smith's life. It was also the birthplace of Walter Reed, for whom the Walter Reed Army Medical Center in Washington, D.C., is named, and of Rev. Jack Yates, a former slave who in 1866 founded Antioch Missionary Baptist Church, the first black church in Houston.

My father, James Handy Kelly, was born on May 26, 1889, the youngest of four children. I don't know what it was like for my biracial father and his siblings to grow up in Virginia in the 1890s. Nationally, it was a period of growing segregation, and Virginia seemed to be one of the leaders in that movement.

My mother, Essie Matilda Allen, was born on March 19, 1890, in Dunn, North Carolina, about halfway between Raleigh and Fayetteville. She had one brother and two sisters, and by her early teens she had decided she wanted to become a schoolteacher. Training for black teachers in North Carolina was limited, however, and she worked as a domestic servant during the day and attended school at night. Eventually, she moved to Virginia.

My parents met in church in Gloucester. My mother caught my father's eye, so I am told, and they fell in love. They were married in 1912 and eventually had five sons, the first three born in Virginia and other two in the North: William Allen (Bill), born on May 7, 1913; John Edward Alexander, born on March 26, 1917; James Thomas Bland Kelly, born on April 16, 1920; Robert Wade Allen, or "Tot," as we called him, born on September 23, 1923; and me. I came along on January 26, 1926.

MOVING NORTH

My father was an itinerant Virginia preacher who had been called to the ministry while digging a well in Gloucester County. He became pastor at Rising Valley Baptist Church and Mount Ebenezer Baptist Church, both in the county, but he became so disenchanted with the rancor at Mount Ebenezer that he moved north to Connecticut to look for other opportunities. My parents were likely influenced by the "great migration" rhetoric of the time, when more than 500,000 blacks moved from the South to the North during and immediately after World War I. "Go north, child," was the expression. "You can get yourself a good job, paying good money, you know?"

In 1921, James and Essie and their three sons left Gloucester County, Virginia. They had a number of choices for their northern destination. Black folks from Virginia and points farther south headed by car, by train, and by coastal steamboat to Washington, D.C., Baltimore, Philadelphia, and New York, with a few traveling as far north as Boston. My parents avoided the big cities and decided to join Wade, Essie's brother, who was working for a wealthy family in Greenwich, Connecticut. Greenwich was not the destination for many African American migrants. There were few industrial jobs, and the only work for our people was in manual labor and domestic service.

Greenwich, founded in 1640, was one of the oldest towns in the United States. It had only a handful of blacks, about five hundred, just 2 percent of the population, when my parents arrived. Most of those who were born in the town or who settled there in and after World War I did domestic work, earning twenty-five dollars to thirty dollars a month. Single women worked as maids and single men as chauffeurs or butlers. If a married couple was lucky, the husband and wife worked for the same family. I remember the domestics having every Thursday off—"Pot Slinger's Day Off," as it was known, although the butlers and chauffeurs usually got the day off as well. They also got every other Sunday off unless they had to work a special party.

My father escaped that type of work. Like many ministers, Rev. James "Pop" Kelly held a second job. As a stonemason, he built dozens of rock walls in typical New England style and worked for many years for Ernest J. Drenkhaun, a local contractor who constructed dry rock walls out into Long Island Sound near Cos Cob. These rock walls, some of which remain standing, were built to protect private boats in Cos Cob Harbor and on the Mianus River.

Nine months out of the year, at least in the 1920s, Pop Kelly seemed to do very well. The winter months, however, were hard on my family; it was very difficult to put food on the table.

Despite her training as a teacher, my mother did domestic work and took in ironing throughout my childhood and until her death in 1933.

She was frugal, and, as they used to say at that time, she could "squeeze every nickel." Somehow, however, even with my father's day job, the modest income from his preaching, and my mother's work and frugality, the wolf was always at the door of the Kelly household. We were poor, and our situation seemed to get worse in the early 1930s. Everyone we knew was in the same situation.

Our house was at 113 Mill Street. It was an eight-room apartment building, large enough for us to take in a few boarders. We lived on the bottom floor and rented out the upper floor.

REV. JAMES KELLY

James Handy Kelly was proud and compassionate. Like many Baptist preachers who lived in communities with small African American populations, he did not have a regular church. Instead, he preached at several churches in southwestern Connecticut and neighboring Westchester County, New York. On more than one occasion, he had twenty-five people in the living room of our house for Wednesday prayer meeting.

In 1932, Pop settled at Mt. Zion Baptist Church in Port Chester, New York. The Kelly kids regularly attended Sunday school at Mt. Zion, and we stayed for the regular service, where black folks would often get up and testify. When I was about eight-years-old, I remember I was so moved by the Spirit that I got up and testified. My brother Bob followed me. My father was very happy and very proud of us that day.

Pop Kelly was slightly over six feet tall, and I don't ever remember him weighing less than three hundred pounds. He was a broad man with very large, strong shoulders and arms. I called him a gentle giant. I recall him once asking my older brothers and me to help him repair a flat tire on our old Studebaker, which didn't have a jack. Pop took a tree branch about five inches in diameter and twelve feet long, fairly green but strong, and stuck it under the axle. We loosened the lug nuts, and then he told us, "When I say 'hup,' snatch that tire off and put on the other wheel."

My older brothers said, "OK, Pop, we're ready."

JAMES HANDY KELLY IN 1969 IN STAMFORD. COURTESY
OF THE AUTHOR.

With a "hup," he put his shoulder under the limb. Up came the car, and
the tire was off the ground. While Pop held the branch on his shoulder,
my brothers changed the tire. We thought he was the strongest man in
the world and drew a great sense of security from that notion.

As strong as he was, Pop was a tender and caring father. He never
cursed. He never laid a hand on any of his children. He was a hugging
and kissing dad, refusing to leave the house without picking me up and
kissing me good-bye. I always felt safe and warm. When we did something improper, he would never raise his voice.

"Samuel, I am so hurt that you did that," he would say and then add,
"Samuel, you're my son. You are a Kelly, and Kellys don't do those things.
Kellys don't lie. They believe in God, and they help their neighbor." I
loved my father; we all did. He was a man of great patience and wisdom
who gave us many life lessons—how to treat women, including your
wife, and how to look at your disadvantaged situation and turn it into
an opportunity.

Although he had limited formal education, my father was an expert
on the Bible. On Sunday afternoons and sometimes on Saturdays, after
work, he would discuss the Bible around our kitchen table with a local
Jewish rabbi, a Catholic or Greek Orthodox priest, and a Protestant

minister. Young men in the neighborhood often sought Pop's advice, and he resolved disputes over the Bible. He was, in his own way, a biblical scholar and taught himself to read Greek.

For a brief period in my childhood, I saw myself following in my father's footsteps, not just being a preacher but also becoming a scholar of the Bible. Eventually, I just settled for being a scholar. What I do know is that during all of my childhood, my parents always encouraged me to think about attending college.

MOTHER

My mother, Essie Matilda Allen Kelly, died on July 27, 1933, when I was seven years old. We were both in the Greenwich Hospital, on the same floor but in different wings, so I could see her out my window. I waved at her every chance I could, and I recall her waving back. I was there for a tonsillectomy, and sometimes when my oldest brother, Bill, visited us, my mother would have him bring me the ice cream the hospital gave her with her meals. Seeing her in the window of her hospital room is my last recollection of my mother.

One day, after I returned home, I was on the front steps of our house playing marbles with Jimmy Luxey and Billy Dewey, two of our little neighborhood gang of kids. Our boarder, a Mrs. Ellison, came down the steps and said, "Sammy, Sammy, go get your daddy. I have bad news. Do you know where he is?"

My father was at his sister's house, two blocks away, and I ran to get him.

"Mrs. Ellison, Sister Ellison, wants you, Pop. She wants you, Pop. She said she wants you to come home right away."

We walked out of my aunt's house, and as we got about a third of the way down the stairs, he stopped me. "Well, what's wrong, Samuel?" He always called me Samuel.

"Well, Mom died, Pop."

"What?"

"Yes, Pop, Mom died."

"Is that what Sister Ellison said?"

"No. But I know she did."

Then his pace quickened. We finally found my oldest brother, who had the family car. Pop got in the car and told Bill, "Go to Greenwich Hospital. Just open it up."

As we pulled up the hill, through East Port Chester and Greenwich, we flagged one of the motorcycle policemen and told him we needed to get to the hospital. The policeman, who knew my dad, said, "OK, Jim, follow me."

He led our old Studebaker to the hospital with the sirens blaring. My dad reached my mom's room in time to witness her last breath.

The months and years following the death of my mother were very difficult. For the first time, I hated going to school. My clothes were no longer neat and clean, and I had difficulty concentrating. My school, New Lebanon Elementary in East Port Chester, routinely divided kids in the first, second, and third grades into groups based on their academic performance. Group 1 was composed of the brightest kids in the grade, group 2 was the middle group, and group 3 was for the "slow" children. I qualified for group 3.

My first-grade teacher, Mrs. Casey, was very strict. On more than one occasion, she said to me, "You can do better than that," but I didn't, because I didn't care. Even though I was at the bottom level for reading and writing, Mrs. Casey passed me on to second grade. I didn't do very well in that class either.

By third grade, I began to have some great teachers. Mrs. McCune was tall, slender, and very attractive, and I would read anything and study hard for her. I was selected to play the lead in a play about the Native Americans who first inhabited the Connecticut coast, and I did love acting. I ended the school year as one of her top students.

Mrs. McCune passed me to Miss Flaherty, who had a wonderful capacity for telling stories, especially historical ones. Miss Flaherty made history come alive, and it was through her class that I began to love history. I particularly liked her account of the Battle of Hastings in 1066, and I started learning about major historical events in western Europe. No one discussed Africa, Asia, or Latin America at that time, but we learned about the history of the French, English, Swedes, and Italians in great detail.

LEAH HOCKADAY

It took two years after my mother's death for me to find my way in school. It did not take that long for me to find my way out of the grief I felt for my mother. About a year after the funeral, my father began dating. His "dates" consisted of bringing some ladies from his church by to have lunch or visit us on a Sunday afternoon. There were three or four ladies who were very interested in him, but there was one that I liked very much—Leah Spencer Hockaday. She had been married before, and when she and my dad met, she lived in Harrison, New York, between Port Chester and Mamaroneck.

I now realize that Pop's goal was to find a mother for Bob and me, the two youngest brothers. We were eleven and eight, and I don't think Pop felt he was capable of rearing us without a woman's influence. Which woman was the question.

Pop brought Leah Hockaday to a few Sunday dinners, and Bob and I fell in love with her. After a series of dinners with all of the women, Pop quizzed us. "Well, boys, which one of those ladies would you like to be your new mother?"

I jumped up and blurted out, "Mrs. Hockaday!"

I liked her because she brought us peanut brittle, and she sent us out to get ice cream. We'd sing together and have a fabulous time. So my brother Bob and I voted for Mrs. Hockaday.

Pop came home about three Sundays later with Mrs. Hockaday. After we had dinner, he turned to us and said, "Well, I have some news for you, Sammy and Bob—Mrs. Hockaday is coming to live with us." I hugged her and so did Bob. I will always miss my biological mother, but Mrs. Hockaday soon became our mother. Because I was so young, it didn't take long for me to begin calling her Mom.

Leah Spencer Hockaday married my father in 1934. My stepmother loved me and I loved her, but she was a rigid disciplinarian. I sometimes joked that she was the one who prepared me for life in the U.S. Army. If we lied or did something else that was bad, she inflicted the wrath of God, and she didn't mind using the strap on our young behinds when it was needed. She was meticulous in speech and dress and taught us to be the same. She also taught us the value of money and proper money management.

LEAH SPENCER HOCKADAY, SAM KELLY'S STEPMOTHER, IN GREENWICH, CONNECTICUT, IN 1934.
COURTESY OF THE KELLY FAMILY.

Leah Hockaday Kelly was a divorced woman during a time when very few women were divorced. As far as I can recall, she worked as a domestic for most of her life, including the period after she married my father. She was a firm "race woman," a term we used to describe one who was proudly African American. She believed we should be proud of and loyal to black people, and she taught me the first African American history I ever learned. "These are your black heroes," she told me.

She used the word "black," which back then in the 1930s had a bad connotation for many African American people. Negroes didn't like to be called "black." If you called someone that, you might have a fight on your hands. But Mom used "black" proudly and consciously. Eventually, so did the rest of my family. My brothers and I began to say to each other and then to our black and white friends, "We are black. We should be proud of our skin." I don't know what our friends thought of that, but no one ever challenged the Kelly brothers for saying we were black.

Mom was a light brown–skinned woman. She was not light enough to pass, but she clearly had considerable "non-black" ancestry. She talked about how African Americans would rate hair and use it as a marker of status. Black people back then would say, "So-and-so had 'good' hair, meaning wavy hair, which looked like the white man, and someone else had 'bad' hair," which I always thought was the description of my nappy hair. She challenged those distinctions. "As long as hair grows," she proclaimed, "it's good hair."

As I look back today, I know that I was blessed and really far ahead of my friends in Greenwich in my understanding of and speaking about race. I kept those attitudes for the rest of my life, and I owe my stepmom for making me racially conscious in a positive way. Mom also understood the power of education. I consistently heard her say, "Get yourself an education. The only way you will escape discrimination is to get yourself an education." Respect for education was one of her core values. It would remain one of mine throughout my life.

THE KELLY BROTHERS

From our Mill Street house, we moved with my father and our new mom to 336 Hamilton Avenue, a home owned by a black couple, the Wrights. Soon, that home became known as the Kelly boardinghouse.

I loved that house. Across the street was a large open meadow, perhaps three to five acres of land where cows grazed. My brother Bob and I felt that the cows shouldn't have all of that land to themselves, so when I was about eleven, we got together with some Italian buddies and made a three-hole golf course. With three hills, the area that we cut out had a perfect natural formation for our course. The longest drive, the first hole, was about three hundred yards, and we had a short hole over some rocks that jutted out of the terrain. We made a short hole there and then a third short hole over a drop-off. We spent hours playing on that makeshift course, using a club we had found in the basement of our new rental home and two others we had picked up from caddying.

While boys in Harlem grew up playing basketball and boys in Georgia played baseball, we Connecticut boys grew up with golf. There were dozens of golf courses, public and private, within a fifty-mile radius of my home. By the time I was eleven, I had started playing golf regularly on Mondays, the traditional "caddies' day." I caddied virtually every weekend. We caddied at the Westchester Golf and Country Club, where the annual Westchester Tournament was played, but we got most of our jobs at our home course, King's Ridge Golf and Country Club, which was owned by a Jewish family. We earned a dollar for eighteen holes and often got a quarter tip, although we were required to pay the caddy master ten cents out of that quarter. Normally, we'd go two loops, or thirty-six holes, and we would bring home two dollars each. We were allowed to keep our fifteen-cent tip and spend part of that for a slice of pie and a soda; the rest of the money went home to my stepmother. We thought this was pretty good income for young boys in Depression-era America.

My third brother Jim was in many ways my lifelong mentor. He read the Harvard Classics when he was in high school. He always excelled in his classes, even ranking above classmates from much more privileged backgrounds. When James graduated from Greenwich High School at the age of sixteen in 1936, he finished as an honor student, and he was the first in our family to go to college.

Jim, who wanted to be a minister like our father, received an AB degree in theology and philosophy from Eastern Nazarene College in Wollaston, Massachusetts, in 1943. He then enrolled at Howard University School of Theology, where he earned a bachelor of divinity degree in 1946. Jim took his first teaching post the same year at all-black Florida A&M University in Tallahassee. From there, he moved to Storer College, a small black college in Harper's Ferry, West Virginia. He quickly became dean of chapel and chair of the Department of Philosophy and Religion. In 1948, he became chairman of the Department of Philosophy at West Virginia State College, in Institute, just outside of Charleston. West Virginia State began as a black, state-supported college, but it integrated with the U.S. Supreme Court's *Brown v. Board of Education* decision in 1954. Both West Virginia State and Bluefield State University at the southern tip of the state became, along with Lincoln University in Missouri, examples of reverse integration in that large numbers of white students entered the university although its faculty and staff remained predominantly African American.

Jim worked for eighteen years at West Virginia State and eventually became the dean of personnel. In 1966, he left West Virginia State for Washington, D.C., where he became associate director of the National Institute for Advanced Study in Teaching Disadvantaged Youth under the National Defense Education Act (NDEA). In 1968, he entered the graduate program in the College of Education at the University of Pittsburgh. Jim received a PhD from the University of Pittsburgh in 1972, the second of the Kelly boys to earn his PhD (I was the first), and was dean of the College of Education at the University of Pittsburgh from 1973 to 1985.

I was proud of my other brothers as well, although they all took very different paths in life. My oldest brother, William Allen (Bill) Kelly, finished Greenwich High School and immediately went to work. He was a chauffeur, butler, and waiter in posh restaurants throughout southwestern Connecticut. Bill worked for one restaurant on Greenwich Avenue that wouldn't serve black people; at the time, he didn't have much of a choice. Although blacks could eat at most of the working-class restaurants in Greenwich, the "better" restaurants discriminated against African Americans.

Bill met a woman named Miss Winslow, who befriended him. Miss Winslow was a tall, attractive Caucasian woman who had a large, shiny black car. Bill was her chauffeur, but she always sat up front with him. Once, I actually saw them embrace. That was the first time I saw a white woman and a black man in each other's arms. That made me believe their relationship was rather personal.

I recall Miss Winslow coming by our house shortly after my mother died in 1933. She brought food and clothing and cookies for Bob and me. Just days before the funeral, Bill and Miss Winslow came by and picked up Bob and me. They took us to Nizener's Five and Ten Cents store in Port Chester. She outfitted me with trousers and a little jacket and shirt and bought Bob a sweater. I thanked her, and she hugged me. I sobbed both out of gratitude to her and because I realized my mother wouldn't be back. That was about the third or fourth time Miss Winslow had hugged me in a warm, almost motherly way. On other occasions, she came by our house and always sought me out. Miss Winslow had great compassion. She treated me as if I were her smallest son or grandson.

I don't know what happened with Bill and Miss Winslow. Shortly after that time, he married a tall, light-skinned black lady named June. They settled in Mamaroneck, and although they never had children, they were married until he died on December 26, 1998.

I do recall that Bill was ambitious and that working in a restaurant and driving for wealthy people were not career goals for him. When the United States entered World War II, Bill joined the army, rising to the rank of corporal. He later became a police officer in civilian life.

John Edward Alexander Kelly, my second brother, dropped out of high school when he was sixteen. John was in his own way very inspirational. He married his church sweetheart, Myrtle Brown from Rye, New York, and they had seven children. Myrtle Brown was the choir director in my father's church, Mt. Zion Baptist.

John went to work at the Suburban Awning Company next door to the place where my father worked. In fact, the store was no more than half a block from the house we were living in when I was born. John often found part-time jobs for me when I needed money. Once, he arranged for me to work the night shift at a plant that ground horsemeat. It was not a fun job, but it gave me the money I needed.

John lived in Connecticut all his life. He had a wonderful singing voice and often sang hymns on the local radio station on Sunday mornings. His work in the awning business led him to a career as a sailmaker. In the early 1980s, my wife, Donna, and I visited him at his workplace, a beautiful brick building with a huge expanse of hardwood floor where tall sails could be laid out and measured to fit custom yachts. I have never seen a more fascinating workplace; it is widely believed that he was the only black professional sailmaker on the East Coast. John died on February 2, 2001, in Stamford, Connecticut.

Then there was brother number four, Robert; I was really close to Bob. We spent the first twelve years of our lives sharing a bed. We occasionally fought, but we were united when we faced the world. You had better not hit either one of us by yourself because you'd be in trouble. Tot was his nickname. All five brothers had family nicknames: in birth order, we were called Willy, Bub, Tee, Tot, and Sammy.

Bob was born to be an artist. He entered Howard University with plans to become a doctor. He married Roxana Greene instead and dropped out of Howard, returning home to Greenwich. Bob and Roxana had one daughter, "Little Roxana." Bob put himself through New York University while living in Greenwich Village, where he worked with black artists such as Romare Bearden, Jacob and Gwendolyn Knight Lawrence, and James Washington. Bob also taught in the South Bronx, one of the toughest neighborhoods in New York. He taught art there but soon realized he wanted to create art as well as teach about it. Because he had formerly worked as a welder, he began working in metal sculpture and in 1963 created *Ode to Marcel,* which was inspired by and dedicated to one of his mentors, Marcel Duchamp, who painted *Nude Descending a Staircase* in 1912. *Ode to Marcel* was Bob's wedding gift to Donna and me many years later.

Bob eventually relocated to Seattle, where in 1980 he was selected to create the metal sculpture that is now the centerpiece of the city's Martin Luther King, Jr., Memorial Park. Bob's work was so promising that he received a grant from the National Endowment for the Arts two years before his death. Robert Wade Kelly drowned on April 5, 1989, in a swimming accident off Kauai, Hawaii, which he was visiting with his fiancée, Lola Barkley.

CHAPTER 2

Thirty Minutes from Harlem

All the schools I attended in Greenwich were predominantly white. Of the four hundred students at Mianus Elementary, my brother Bob and I were the only ones who were black. Another black family moved into our Cos Cob neighborhood while we were in school but quickly moved out. When my family moved to the section of Greenwich called East Port Chester in 1932, I entered New Lebanon Elementary School. Eventually, we returned to Cos Cob and, in 1940, I completed the eighth grade at Hamilton Avenue Elementary School.

Because Greenwich had so few African American families, I was always the only black student in my classes until I got to the eighth grade. In 1940, I began my freshman year at Greenwich High School. Some of the teachers had PhDs, which, I would later learn, was almost unheard of in a public high school. Most of the two thousand students at Greenwich High were well-to-do and were drawn from the city and surrounding suburbs. On any day, you could count up to twenty chauffeur-driven limousines, usually with black men behind the wheels, dropping off white kids at school.

There were no more than thirty black students in Greenwich High School, and no black students in most of my high school classes. The high school curriculum was split into general studies for average students, commercial studies for those with a business orientation, arts curriculum for those so inclined, classical college for those with literary aspirations, and general college for those bound for some type of higher education. I was often the only black student in both the classical and general college courses. Later studies showed that the students who finished Greenwich High School in the general college or classical college curriculum had little difficulty getting into Ivy League universities, including Yale, which was less than thirty miles from my home. Harvard was only about six hours away by train or car, and Brown University was even closer. In nearby New York City, there were many colleges and universities, including City College of New York, Columbia University, and New York University. Competing with students who were planning to attend these institutions gave me the sense that I could more than hold my own academically. Pop and Leah Kelly had college plans for their youngest son, even if they lacked college money. I don't think the black kids who were assigned to the general curriculum program felt as self-confident.

One Greenwich High teacher, Miss Chalice, my history instructor, was a superb lecturer and a great storyteller. Occasionally, when she left the classroom, she asked me to take her chair and lead the discussion on the historical topic of the day. Some of the rich, snobby kids didn't like that, and one or two would challenge me, but I held my ground because I had a firm grasp of the material. Through Miss Chalice, I learned not only about European and United States history but also how to defend myself intellectually. I developed a set of four rules, which served me both in the military and in every college and university setting where I have worked:

1. Don't open your mouth unless you know your information and unless you know more than the challenger knows.
2. Prepare what you want to say long before you say it.
3. Don't fire all of your verbal ammunition at once; hold some in reserve.
4. Be confident because you are sure of your information. Then stand on firm ground; don't back down, and don't be intimidated.

Those rules, developed in high school, continue to serve me well in most situations.

We had excellent schooling, and I learned more than I thought I did at the time. Fortunately, because of that training, I was able to do things that many Southern-born blacks could not do. As I would come to learn, my Connecticut education gave me a huge advantage in the army and beyond.

RACE AND CLASS IN GREENWICH

As early as elementary school, I knew that black kids were treated differently in Greenwich. The custom was for students to invite classmates home for birthday parties, but I only watched with sadness when the invitations were handed out to everyone but me. Afterward, I would hear about the parties, but I was the only black kid in the class, and I was ignored, year after year. Early on, I understood that as a dark-skinned young boy, I was different from my schoolmates.

Because my parents did not give birthday parties, I can recall only one celebration, when I was sixteen. I remember it so vividly because I gave it myself. I arranged for a few friends to gather at the Crispus Attucks Community Center, essentially an all-black facility. Named after the part-black, part–Native American patriot who was killed during the Boston

MARY GARRISH SLOAT AND SAM KELLY IN A SCHOOL PLAY AT NEW LEBANON ELEMENTARY SCHOOL IN 1936. COURTESY OF THE AUTHOR.

Massacre in 1770, the center was a branch of the Boys Club of America. The all-white Boys Club had operated the facility until a wealthy Greenwich woman gave the club money for a huge new building. The old Boys Club became the Crispus Attucks Community Center.

The center had tennis courts, basketball courts, and an Olympic-size swimming pool. It was a great place for young black kids in the community. My family, including my mom and dad and some of my brothers, and a few others gathered on January 26, 1942. We played games and cards. It was the only birthday party I had when I was growing up in Greenwich.

I had a few white friends, such as Billy Dewey and Jimmy Luxey. While we were close, I don't recall ever being invited to their homes. The only kids I remember visiting were George and Bobby Partlow, German Americans who lived in a five-room apartment above Larsen's Delicatessen. All of us neighborhood kids were out playing sandlot baseball, and I heard Mrs. Partlow yell out, "Come on, Sammy, come on, Robert, come on, Bobby, come on, Georgie. Come and have some cookies and milk." That was the only time I set foot in the house of one of my white buddies.

Harvey and Jerry Howse were other neighborhood buddies of mine. They were black. Their family was from Ohio. Harvey and Jerry lived with their mom, a single parent, who worked as a maid, cooking and cleaning for wealthy families in the High Ridge area of Greenwich. The Howse boys in turn learned to cook, clean house, and take care of themselves. Their mothers may have worked for wealthy people in Greenwich, but the Howse brothers and the Kelly brothers went to the same school as the elite kids.

Few racist incidents involved me, but I do remember one situation. When I was walking home from Mianus Elementary School on a snowy afternoon, I passed an open-air fruit and vegetable market about half a block from my house. Several unemployed Italian men were standing there, and three of them grabbed me, took off my hat, and rubbed my head for luck. They didn't hurt me, but they did humiliate me. I kicked them and swung at them and ran home crying. My father was at home that snowy day because he had no work. I told him what had happened.

"Where are they, Samuel? Take me to them." He put his sweater on, and I led him to the market.

"There he is, Pop," I said, as I identified one of the men.

My father waded through the group of men and grabbed the one I had pointed out. He picked up the man and held him over his head. "Don't you ever, as long as I'm living, put your hand on one of my children," he warned. "If you do it again, I'll kill you."

When Pop said "I'll kill you," the man was shaking like a rag doll.

He tried to talk. "Mr. Kelly, Mr. Kelly, don't hurt me, don't hurt me, Mr. Kelly."

Pop threw him against the other men and said, "All right. Come on. I'll take all of you."

They just ran away.

Pop's actions that day taught me another life lesson. I had always felt a sense of security around my father, and now I understood that when I had a family, it would be my duty to protect them with the same determination my dad had shown in my defense. The Kellys may have been poor in a financial sense, but we were millionaires in terms of our love for family members. We were always there for one another.

The Mitchell brothers were my closest black friends. Herman and I were the same age; his older brother, Napoleon, was my brother Bob's age. We created a basketball team called the Sepia Flashes. Two sets of brothers, Herman and Napoleon Mitchell and my brother Bob and me, along with Jimmy Ward made up the core of the team. We had a few more guys to round out the number to ten. We won the Greenwich YMCA division a couple of times, playing out of the Crispus Attucks Community Center in town.

Frequently, we played "target ball," a game we contrived because the ceiling of our small gym was too low to arch the ball toward the basket; instead, we shot straight on at a target basket attached horizontally to the wall. "Finger pool," or carom, was a popular game as well. By winning the local finger pool tournament, I earned my first trip to Yankee Stadium.

I dated one or two of the handful of black girls in town, and I was especially smitten by a light-skinned young lady named Mildred Douglas, whom everyone called "Dolly." Dolly had auburn hair that fell past her shoulders and was quite popular among our circle of black boys. I met Dolly at a small party given by some friends. I expressed my interest in her, and she indicated she felt the same. I got her phone number, and within days of meeting, we were going steady, as they used to say in those days. She aspired to go to college, something rare among my friends. Her aspirations lifted my sights as well. My parents had always wanted me to go to college, but it was Dolly's conversations that made it seem tangible, something I could achieve.

PAUL ROBESON

Dolly introduced me to the world of culture. When I was seventeen, she and I went to see Paul Robeson in *Othello*, which was then playing at the Schubert Theater in New York City. I will never forget that late fall evening in 1943, when Dolly and I, along with two other couples, packed ourselves into my 1939 four-door Buick sedan to go to the theater. Robeson was magnificent and received twenty-five curtain calls.

Dolly thought we should try to go backstage to see Robeson. The girls hatched a plan—Dolly would claim to be his cousin and persuade the guard to let us in. I didn't think this was a bright idea, but Dolly and the other girls insisted.

The huge guard at the stage door looked like a mountain, but Dolly charmed him, and he opened the door to six eager teenagers. We made our way to Robeson's dressing room in time to see him removing some of his makeup. An aide told him that his cousin was outside with some of her friends. I suspect Robeson had heard these stories before. He was good-natured about it all and came out and greeted each of us, shaking our hands with his gigantic hand very affectionately. Before we could sit down, he bellowed in his deep voice, "Now, what are you going to do for the race? Where are you going to school?" Four of us said we planned to go to college.

I was very impressed with Robeson, and not just with his fame as an actor and singer, or even his huge size, which no one in his presence could ignore. Most impressive was his commitment to racial advancement, summed up in the question he had asked all of us, "What are you going to do for the race?" That question stayed with me the rest of my life. I would later see Robeson perform again, but it was his commitment to our race that I would always remember. Dolly and I continued to date for the next year until I went into the army.

HARLEM

Greenwich might have had only a handful of African American families, but we were hardly isolated from black culture. My family's house
was thirty miles from Harlem. I went there as often as I could and felt
comfortable on its streets even as a kid. Harlem was a different place
then. The "New Negro" that Howard University professor Alain Locke
had described in the 1920s was still in vogue there. Harlem had successful,
wealthy Negroes and glamorous nightclubs. The people of Harlem weren't
all shining shoes or doing a tap dance for white folks. Many of them were
in the upper strata. That too inspired me.

Even if Harlem had not been so close, my family, mainly because of
my mother, was inextricably entwined with racial issues. Prominent
black speakers lectured in Greenwich, and we put on plays about black
history and sang religious and secular songs. We participated in many
activities that helped teach us black history and culture. We also came
to know black artists such as the New York playwright Powell Lindsey,
who was a boarder in our home. Lindsey was famous for two plays, *The
Big White Fog* and *Young Man of Harlem*. He had a son, Raymond, by
a Polish woman whom he never married. The son stayed with Lindsey
at our home. Lindsey had moved to Greenwich to serve as the drama
director at the Greenwich Playhouse, which was funded by the Works
Progress Administration (WPA). The Greenwich Playhouse often gave
performances especially for local black kids. Many of us also performed
in those plays, such as *Dark Cavalcade*, which told the history of African
Americans in dance, song, and story. Lindsey's presence in our home
worked out to my benefit, not only because I saw his plays but also because
he introduced us to New York's entertainment and intellectual elite.

Beginning in 1938, Powell Lindsey took my mother and me into
Harlem to see his plays. After the performance, he often invited us backstage, where we met some of the leading African American actors of that
era. Once, we saw the well-known concert pianist Hazel Scott backstage.
She later became the second wife of future Harlem congressman Adam
Clayton Powell, Jr., who, along with his father, led the Abyssinian Baptist Church, which had more than ten thousand congregants in 1935.
Abyssinian was by far the largest church in Harlem and, for that matter,
in the entire nation.

REV. ADAM CLAYTON POWELL, SR.

When my mother and I went to see *The Big White Fog* in Harlem, there were more than a thousand people in the audience. It was there that I met Rev. Adam Clayton Powell, Sr. He shook my hand and patted my head, which I didn't like. Then he asked me, "What are you going to be when you grow up?"

I said, "Well, I don't know. I think I'd like to be a teacher."

He said, "Well, remember the race."

After he left, all I could think to say was, "Hey mom, who's that white man?"

She said, "Hush, child! He's not a white man. That's Rev. Adam Clayton Powell. He's a Negro like you."

"He is?" I asked, responding with a question.

Because of my mother's black history lessons, I knew enough to realize that I had met someone important, one of the great "leaders of the race," as she would say.

Just like Paul Robeson's "What are you going to do for the race?" Rev. Powell's question infused me with a sense of identity and purpose that would sustain me during my most difficult days in Korea and later at the University of Washington. That question continued to inspire me even when I was in my seventies and serving as director of education at the Rosemary Anderson Middle and High School in Portland, Oregon.

I met other great leaders of the race on subsequent trips to Harlem, including Dr. W. E. B. DuBois and Carter G. Woodson, who established the Black History Month observances. Almost always, these distinguished men and women were courteous, well-spoken, and well-dressed. I noticed that the men always wore coats and ties. All of them were proud of their race and ancestry. That was new to me. Except for my parents, I hadn't encountered many blacks who seemed proud of their race.

My life of learning about and rescuing people who looked like me began with my childhood exposure to black history and culture. Later, I would learn that African Americans who hailed from places where there were significant numbers of black people, particularly in the rural South, often had less knowledge of black history and culture than I did. I was surprised. Certainly, growing up in Greenwich, Connecticut, did not deprive me of black culture.

MY WORLD IN THE 1930s

Greenwich and neighboring Stamford, along with Port Chester, New York, were the three cities that made up my childhood world. All three were on an eight-mile stretch of the old Boston Post Road, also known as U.S. Route 1. By the time I was a teenager, I was traveling easily by car between all of them.

Greenwich was the first town you entered when coming east across the New York–Connecticut state line. By the 1930s, Greenwich, with a population of about 33,000, had already become a suburb of New York City. Greenwich residents could hop commuter trains on the New Haven and Hartford Railroad and be in downtown Manhattan in forty-five minutes. In fact, when I was a teenager, I remember that you could stand on the shore of Long Island Sound in Greenwich and see the Manhattan skyline in the distance.

The difference between Greenwich and the two communities on either side of it could be summarized in one word—money. Greenwich had it; the others didn't. As an exclusive bedroom community for executives who worked in New York City, Greenwich was one of the wealthiest towns per capita in the entire country, replete with millionaires and multimillionaires, industrialists, and corporate executives. Only about 800 African Americans lived there in the early 1930s.

Stamford, about two miles up the old Boston Post Road, was more industrial and working class, with a population of 56,000, including 2,100 blacks as well as other groups such as Irish, Italians, and Scandinavians. The city also was home to the Yale Lock Company and steel rolling mills. During World War II, Stamford became a major war production center.

Port Chester, New York, a town of roughly 16,000, including about 200 blacks, was right across the state line from Greenwich. It was famous as the home of the Lifesavers Candy Company and television entertainer Ed Sullivan. In my day, you could roll a ball down the hill from Greenwich at the corner of Mill and Water Streets, and it would cross a bridge and land in Port Chester. We kids didn't think much about the state boundary. My family went to church in Port Chester, and we had friends in Port Chester just as we had friends in Stamford.

Going southwest from Port Chester to New York City, you passed through a series of towns—Rye, Harrison, Mamaroneck, Larchmont,

SAM KELLY IN 1940 AT AGE FOURTEEN IN STAMFORD, CONNECTICUT. COURTESY OF THE KELLY FAMILY.

and New Rochelle—before entering the Bronx in New York City. All of these towns were within a ten-mile stretch. You just went from one to the other. In fact, I could leave my house on most days and get to 125th Street and Seventh Avenue in the middle of Harlem in about thirty minutes by car.

THE GREENWICH KELLYS

The Kelly family was well known in Greenwich, which probably kept my brothers and me out of trouble. None of the five Kelly boys ever spent a night in jail. My father knew the policemen who patrolled our neighborhood. On occasion, an officer would see me walking to school and say, "Young Kelly, jump in," and I would ride to school in the patrol car.

Once, I was in the car with my teenage brother, Bob, who should have gotten a ticket because he was driving without his license and registration. All was well until Bob ran a red light. The neighborhood policeman pulled us over, then asked, "Where are you going? What's your name?"

Bob gave his name.

"Bob Kelly. James Kelly and Bill Kelly are my older brothers."

The policeman responded, "Well, I went to school with Bill Kelly."

The whole scene was strange. We were pulled over because Tot ran a red light, and he and the policeman were having a casual conversation about our oldest brother, Bill.

The policeman abruptly stopped smiling and said, "You turn this goddamn car around, go home, and get your driver's license and registration. Watch those lights when you go through. And tell your dad I said hello."

That happened any number of times. None of the brothers drank and drove. But we did go over the speed limit from time to time. Stuff that was just a little over the edge like that. Yet we didn't have the sense that we were always being watched or that the police would treat us differently because we were black. We didn't fear the police, and they never mistreated us. I cannot speak for what happened to other blacks in Greenwich, but the Kellys had what I would later term "limited acceptance."

My early experiences with the Greenwich police and other law enforcement officials created a problem for me when, in the late 1960s, other blacks and white radicals began calling the police "pigs." I never understood it, I never liked it, and I never did it.

MRS. LOUISA HARVEY BOHN

My sophomore and junior years at Stamford High were important in shaping my life and values. In 1941, we moved from Greenwich to Stamford, where I entered Stamford High School as a sophomore. The teacher I remember most at Stamford is Mrs. Louisa Harvey Bohn. She was one of the people, besides my mother and Mrs. Flaherty, who influenced me to study history in college.

Mrs. Bohn was my tenth-grade history teacher. She seemed intrigued with my comments about slavery and was moved by my strident pleas against racial discrimination. Once, she asked me to make a fifteen-minute presentation for the class on slavery and post–Civil War racial discrimination, including the situation blacks faced in the North and especially in Connecticut. I gave the talk, which she liked so much that she arranged for me to visit other Stamford High classrooms to give the presentation. Through those talks, I became, at age sixteen, a minor celebrity.

I eventually got my 1944 high school yearbook in 1948. The caption underneath my photo was a variation of the statement Patrick Henry made during the American Revolution; it read, "Give my people complete liberty, or give us death." As I look back on my life, that statement seems representative of what I fought for throughout my various careers. I could not have chosen better words for that caption.

THE KELLYS AND THE GREAT DEPRESSION

I didn't realize that we were as poor as we were during the Great Depression. Pop didn't work steadily, and when we were on relief, he didn't work at all. Mom rented out some of the rooms of our nine-room Hamilton Avenue house. I helped out with chores related to running that house. My brothers and I went behind the Great Scott Supermarket across the bridge in Port Chester and loaded our bicycles with discarded food. Then we'd bike to the local bakery, where we'd buy day-old bread and pastries. If we waited for two days, we could get bread and pastries or a bag of jelly doughnuts for a nickel or a dime. We'd bring the food home to share with the family. We canned as much food as possible during the Depression. Wealthy Greenwich residents often allowed us to pick pears, apples, peaches, squash, and other fruits and vegetables from their estates. My mother would then can them for the winter months. The canned goods were especially welcome during the five years in the 1930s when we were on relief.

Bob helped out by washing dishes at Homestead Hall, a retirement home in nearby Belhaven. I remember one woman who worked at the retirement home who apparently took pity on me and my brothers. She asked Bob, "What do you want for Christmas?"

Without hesitation, he responded, "A bike!"

She gave Bob twenty-five dollars. We were grateful to receive it and thanked her. For a time, I called her "Homestead Hall" until we finally learned her name.

All the work we brothers did was intended to support the entire family. During this period, Pop bought used clothes for himself and the rest of us. Like many other black or working-class people, the Kellys had the hand-me-down system of clothing, which meant that when older brothers outgrew their jackets, pants, or shoes, these items went down to the next younger brother. As I was the youngest of the Kellys, my entire wardrobe consisted of hand-me-downs.

One brown suit was passed down through three Kelly brothers. It was Jim's suit, and he had a green shirt that he wore with it. The suit and shirt got passed down to my brother, Bob, who wore them for a while, and then they came to me. I thought I was really dressed in that suit. Of course it was so shiny by that time that you could see your face in it, but I didn't care. It was mine, and I thought I was sharp.

I never had a new suit until I joined the army, and that was a uniform. I never had a new civilian suit until I got out of the army in 1948. I was twenty-two, and I went down to Crawford's Men's Store in Port Chester, which sold new suits at bargain prices. I bought my first "Crawford suit." It was a big deal. The suit cost me only eighteen dollars and fifty cents, but I was as proud of it as of any clothes I would later have. I thought I was really very, very important when I wore that new suit.

A TEENAGER'S WORK

I worked from the time I was nine years old. Part of the reason was sheer necessity. My family needed the money, and my father was never in a position to give me a dollar or two for spending money. He gave all of us much love, but there never seemed to be any cash. I also worked because having a job gave me a sense of independence. If I earned my own money, it seemed I was more in charge of my own life.

My first job was delivering newspapers. My dad bought a bicycle for me for two dollars and fifty cents, and I had to repay him at fifty cents a month from my paper route. I also shoveled snow and raked leaves to pick up extra income. At age eleven, I started caddying at King's Ridge, the local golf and country club. I loved golf, and I especially liked working at the club in the summer when there were more golfers and the tips were bigger.

At thirteen, I began working part-time at Gene Freccia's Auto Body Shop on the Boston Post Road in Greenwich. There were usually about eighty to one hundred automobiles at the shop at any given time. My job was to wash and clean all the cars on the lot and to maintain the bathrooms. I was paid thirty dollars a month, which was a huge salary for a thirteen-year-old. Some adults in Greenwich weren't making that much money in the middle of the Great Depression.

In 1941, I worked as a chauffeur even though I was fifteen and didn't have a driver's license. My employer, Jacob Feldman, was a prosperous Greenwich merchant. I was his unofficial chauffeur as he and his wife, Hannah, sat in the backseat of their 1940 Plymouth. In addition to driving the car, I was expected to keep it clean. Once a week, I washed and waxed the Plymouth. I liked driving the car, but I hated waxing it.

Mr. Feldman talked and talked and talked while I drove. He discussed his business, local and national politics, and, since this was the early 1940s, the war in Europe. He had traveled extensively and knew all about the places that were being bombed. He'd tell me stories about those cities. He would always say, "Sam, I believe in democracy. I believe in democracy." One day, I got tired of hearing him say that and decided to challenge him.

"Well, Mr. Feldman, you really don't believe in democracy."

"What do you mean, Sam? I believe in democracy. Everybody is free to do as he pleases in a democracy."

"Well, if you believe in democracy, Mr. Feldman, can I take your seventeen-year-old daughter to the movies when she comes home from college for spring break? Can I date her?"

"Oh no, no, no, Sam, no, Sam. No. I don't believe in the mixing of the races."

"Well, you're just proving my point. You are not democratic, and you don't really believe in democracy." Mr. Feldman was chagrined, but we still continued our open conversations. We never agreed on interracial dating, but I think he respected my ability to think and reason.

I was pretty quick to judge people who claimed to be liberal but actually accepted discrimination. I pointed out the contradictions when I was fifteen, and I would continue to do so for the rest of my life.

By the time I was sixteen, my hours and responsibilities at Gene Freccia's Auto Body Shop had increased. I worked at the shop every day after school for five hours and all day on Saturday. I didn't have time to caddy or chauffeur any more.

Cars were a big part of our family life. My dad violated Connecticut law by letting me drive in 1937 at the age of eleven. I was not a very good driver, but I was proud of Pop Kelly for letting me get behind the wheel of the family car.

I practiced on our 1931 Studebaker, which had its idiosyncrasies. Normally, a driver would depress the clutch to shift a car from first to second. We had to learn to double-clutch that old car, that is, to depress the clutch about halfway, let it out, and then depress the clutch again to get from first to second, and do the same thing to get to third. I didn't care how hard it was to drive that old car—I loved to get behind the wheel.

I got my driver's license when I was sixteen. In fact, I drove myself to the test. Before then, I borrowed my brother's license when I wanted to drive. Soon after, I bought my first used car from Gene Freccia, a 1931 Chevy Roadster for which I paid thirty-five dollars. It had isinglass curtains and a rumble seat. Around the same time, my father bought a 1932 seven-passenger Nash.

PEARL HARBOR

The worst of the Depression was over by 1940, when I was fourteen. Things were getting better for the people we knew and particularly for the Kelly family. My father was employed steadily, and my brothers and I had "man-size" jobs. We also had a steady flow of boarders, whose rent checks reduced the financial pressure on our family.

The last major memory of my Connecticut childhood is Pearl Harbor, which occurred just before I turned sixteen. As news of the attack reached the nation, I was working part-time as a janitor and parking cars at the Palace Theater in Stamford. Before the movie began, the theater announcer said that army trucks were rolling through the back streets of Stamford on their way to Fort Devens, Massachusetts.

I will always recall the day of the attack on Pearl Harbor because of the anxiety and frantic activity in the streets. Crowds gathered in the streets yelling, "Kill the Japs, kill the Japs."

No one except my parents and my teachers used the words "Japanese" or "Japanese Americans"; the people were always "Japs" to the adults and kids I knew.

There were only a few Japanese in Connecticut at that time. Most seemed to run restaurants and laundries. The ones I encountered were always quiet and courteous. I especially remember the Fujitami brothers, Jimmy and Bobby, who played football on the Stamford High School team. I knew there were many more Japanese in New York's Chinatown.

On December 7, 1941, the mob chanted loudly until I felt as if I was stone-deaf. People were hugging each other and shouting for men to go to war in defense of our country. While I felt a surge of pride at the time, I would learn in later years that I was witnessing a demonstration of the virulent nationalism that ultimately led to such horrors as internment camps on U.S. soil. Nonetheless, I got caught up in the fervor. I knew at that moment that I would join the U.S. Army and fight to defend the United States.

PART II

Soldier

"The Lord's been good to me, but the army's been better."

CHAPTER 3

A Segregated Army

In 1942, I dropped out of Stamford High School to go to work for Northern Warren Cutex Corporation. Many students dropped out because they were not performing well academically, because of family or personal issues at home, because they needed to support their families, or because they were no longer motivated. None of those reasons applied to me. I left because I saw an opportunity to make a good sum of money and because I was given enormous responsibilities at my job.

I had started working for Northern Warren as an after-school job. I was assigned to the nail-polish compounding lab, where I cleaned floors, sinks, and cabinets. At night, while I mopped, the foreman, Mr. Fleming, mixed the compound, and I asked him questions. I had enjoyed my one class in chemistry, so I couldn't pass up the chance to learn the process.

Three weeks later, a worker spilled a fifty-gallon drum of nail polish on the floor, requiring a major cleanup. He was fired, and I was immediately promoted to his position based on the quality of my work as a janitor and Mr. Fleming's recognition of my interest in chemistry.

I had a car and a great job making eighty-five cents an hour, and I was dating. Life seemingly could not be any better for a teenager in 1942. Yet, there was a war going on. My older brothers, Bill and Bob, were already in the army, Bob at Fort Hood, in Texas, and Bill, a corporal in the transportation corps, was stationed in New York. I thought it was my duty to serve. I felt mature enough, and I was built fairly ruggedly. I was also swept up in the war fever gripping the nation in those years, the desire to punish the Japanese for the attack on Pearl Harbor.

In 1943, when I was seventeen years old, I attempted to volunteer. The recruiting sergeant said, "Kelly, why don't you just wait? In a few months, you're going to be eighteen." People at the local draft board said that as soon as I turned eighteen, they would immediately send me my papers.

My mother was not excited about my going into the army, especially since she already had two sons in the military. She was resigned to the inevitable, however, and told me, "Well, son, I guess we'll have to face it. We'll have to have a third star to put on the flag in the window. I'd like to keep you home as long as possible, but if you want to go before the call comes, that'll be up to you."

So I waited, out of deference to my mother. I got my draft papers just weeks after I turned eighteen. On May 18, 1944, less than three weeks before the D-Day invasion of France, I was inducted into the United States Army.

My first post was Fort Devens, Massachusetts, and my first military assignment was peeling potatoes for three weeks. It wasn't what I had expected. After two months, I was herded together with about five hundred black troops onto an all-black troop train. It was my first real encounter with the segregated army. In fact, except for my trips to Harlem and the time I was in Pop's churches, it was the first time I had been around more than a dozen African Americans at one time.

We traveled three or four days with the windows blacked out. We didn't know where we were or where we were going. We arrived at our destination—Harrisburg, Pennsylvania—on D-Day. I didn't know or care anything about what was happening in Europe that day. I was focused on my own situation. I said to the soldier sitting next to me, "Why in the hell did it take us three days to do this?"

The white officers herded us into trucks and buses and transported us out to Indiantown Gap Military Reservation. I was assigned to the 445th Port Company, part of the transportation corps, for basic training.

Most of my basic training was geared toward learning how to unload ships as part of the newly organized U.S. Army Transportation Corps. We had some advanced individual training, and we mastered the basics every soldier learns—how to run, shoot, and march, a little bit of bayonet training, some infantry training, and army organization. Eventually, we learned about military justice and how to conduct ourselves as soldiers, including how to properly salute a superior officer. We called that training the "school of the individual soldier." We learned how soldiers marched without bearing arms. Eventually, we learned to handle a rifle while marching and the various positions of the rifle.

SERGEANT 'SEED

Only two companies of the entire training regiment were commanded by black officers; the 445th Port Company was one of them. It was led by Lieutenant Peter A. Silva. I had some outstanding black noncommissioned officers. My platoon sergeant, James Turnipseed from Tennessee, is the one I remember best. He taught me more about men and leadership than just about anyone else I encountered in the military.

I remember when I was a private and didn't want to get out of bed, and Sergeant Turnipseed came into the barracks while I was sleeping. When he woke me up, I said, "Sergeant Turnipseed, I have a stomachache. I can't drill today."

He said, "Oh, is that right, Kelly?"

So he walked around my bunk bed, reached up to the top, where I was lying, flipped my mattress over, and dumped me on the floor. I hit the floor on all fours and came up ready to fight. He coolly said, "No, don't do that, Kelly, because if you fight with me, I'll probably kill you, so you might as well get dressed and get your butt out in the ranks."

I dressed and picked up my little hurt feelings, went out to the field, and started soldiering. He put me in charge of a five-man detail to take on an assignment that I can't now remember. But I drilled the detail up to the mess hall and drilled them back, and he said, "You know, Kelly, if you get serious, you could be a good soldier."

"Sergeant Turnipseed, I'd like that."

"Just do what I tell you to do!" he quickly responded.

To this day, I give him credit for providing me with the fundamental tools I needed to become a professional soldier.

CORPORAL KELLY

Five weeks after I entered the army, I was promoted to corporal. With that promotion, I learned for the first time that I could compete successfully against both officers and enlisted men. I also observed the consequences of segregated education. Most of the men I competed with were illiterate, and with a shortage of noncommissioned officers, I rose quickly in the ranks.

In July, I was sent to machine gun school, which had fifty men in training—thirty officers and twenty enlisted men. I fired expert, which meant I was very proficient with the .30 caliber and .50 caliber machine guns, and scored second in the final examination.

The instruction at machine gun school was quite good, but I got into a row with one of the instructors. He put a formula on the board, which he had probably done hundreds of times before, for calculating windage adjustment for rifle marksmanship.

I had taken algebra and knew the formula didn't look right. I raised my hand and said, "Sir, I don't think your formula is correct."

He said, "Oh-ho! Would you like to come and change it?"

"Well, sir," I responded, "if you want me to, I'll come and change it. I think I can correct it."

So he laughed at me as I walked to the chalkboard, told him what was wrong with what he had done, and then said, "Here's my formula."

He stared at me, and the captain who was in charge of instruction came over. The captain whispered to the lieutenant, who sat down in front of the class. As he took his seat, he said, "Well, Private Kelly is right. I made a mistake."

The troops rolled in laughter. That didn't settle too well with me. I never intended to humiliate a lieutenant in front of his men; I just wanted to give him the correct information. Sergeant Turnipseed talked with me right after that incident.

"Kelly, don't ever disagree with an officer in front of the troops. That is one of the main things you need to know in the U.S. Army. Talk to him aside, away from the troops. Never embarrass your commander."

It was another powerful lesson from Sergeant 'Seed.

Following that incident, I was given command of twenty-four soldiers. For the first time in my army life, I felt I had a serious responsibility.

FOX HILLS

Our unit shipped out to the Fox Hills Cantonment on Staten Island to continue advanced individual training. I didn't realize it then, but this would be the routine for me, and for all soldiers: training, then transfer, then training interspersed with occasional combat.

We were a transportation corps, and our job was to load and unload ships for the U.S. Army. We learned how to do this as quickly as possible. We learned about the five holds of a military cargo ship and how to use the monstrous stevedore equipment. I also learned that this work was very dangerous. Just a few months earlier, 320 sailors, mostly black, had been killed in a single explosion while loading an ammunition ship at Port Chicago near San Francisco. Other soldiers had been court-martialed for refusing to return to their jobs after the explosion. It may not have been frontline combat, but it was hazardous work.

The Fox Hills Cantonment was not a dock area. We had to drive about ten minutes or march twenty-five minutes along city streets to get to the pier area. The Fox Hills Cantonment was a very fine barracks area for five thousand troops just outside a civilian residential neighborhood. A fence separated the barracks from the adjoining civilian community.

I made an interesting acquaintance at Fox Hills, a five-striped technical sergeant named Joe Louis. The world heavyweight champion was in the U.S. Army in 1944 and assigned to Special Services, which meant he ran the office of sports services for troops. He also trained the boxing team.

I did a little boxing and thought I was pretty good. I got in the ring with Sergeant Joe, who quickly knocked me out. Nonetheless, Joe and I became friends. Once, when we were both off duty, we caught a bus and then the nickel ferry to lower Manhattan. From there, we took the subway uptown to Harlem. Once we got to Harlem, everybody recognized the great Joe Louis.

We visited the Braddock Bar on the edge of Spanish Harlem. I was surprised to encounter our former boarder Powell Lindsey working there as a bartender. As Joe and I crossed street after street, I realized that I was in the company of one of the best-known African Americans in the world.

I respected Joe Louis and learned a good deal about being a soldier from him and other noncommissioned officers. Apparently, I learned quickly and well, because I was promoted to sergeant on August 7, about three weeks after arriving at Fox Hills. Within three months of joining the army, I had gone from private to a three-striped sergeant.

A THREE-STRIPED SERGEANT

My first assignment as a sergeant was to lead twenty-four soldiers, two squads that had responsibility for loading and unloading a cargo ship, day or night. We trained with dummy weights. We did some specialized loading of bombs and artillery rounds at Raritan Arsenal in New Jersey.

Before long, I was called into the orderly room by my company commander, Captain Silva. With him were two African American lieutenants, platoon leaders Maurice Burke and Ronald Williams. "Kelly," the captain said, "we want to groom you to go to Officer Candidate School. We think you ought to try it."

I was only six months into my military service, and I had just gotten my sergeant's stripes. I didn't know it, but they had already begun preparing me for Officer Candidate School.

"You need to know everything," Captain Silva cautioned. "You need to know about the school of the soldier without arms, how to march, how to drill. Then you need to know the school of the soldier with arms."

They had me drill the platoon, in effect, half the company, and then the entire company. They mentored me by exposing me to much of what I would be expected to learn in Officer Candidate School.

I had never expected any of this and did not yet envision a career in the military. True, I always admired the uniform. I also knew that my brothers and a cousin had risen to the rank of corporal, and I was always competitive with my family. Thinking of them just before my promotion, I had said to myself, "Oh, I bet I can be a sergeant."

I worked diligently to rise in rank, but I was also fortunate to be in a company that was commanded by exceptional black officers. They believed that I could succeed in Officer Candidate School even though I was barely nineteen-years-old.

I also believed in myself. I knew that not having a high school diploma was a potential problem. Yet when I started successfully competing with officers in some of the training classes, I thought, "Boy, I can sure do this."

I took the officer candidate test in January 1945 and failed to qualify by three points. I was determined to study even harder to learn everything I would need to know for the second exam. After all, some very fine officers had placed their confidence in me. I was not about to let them down. I took the test again about thirty days later. This time, I passed.

The test was only the first hurdle. I then had to go up for the first of two board examinations. The board was composed of five officers who would determine my fitness for command. One officer asked, "How did you manage to shoot expert in infantry rifle weapons when you have never been an infantryman?"

I said, "Well, sir, I'm fairly good with arms."

The officer, who had been wounded, had just returned from operations in Europe. He looked directly into my face and said, "Well, how would you like to be an infantry officer?"

"Sir, I think I'd like that."

After about an hour, I went back to my barracks, where I learned that I had passed the first board examination.

Three weeks later, I got the call to appear for the final board exam. This time, the wounded officer questioned me further about infantry. He asked me why I thought I'd be a good officer. And I told him, "Sir, I like weapons far more than loading and unloading ships." I told him I did not like the quartermaster or transportation assignments because they reminded me too much of the subservient work that most Negroes performed in the civilian world. Then I added, "I want to be a combat soldier."

My candor must have impressed the examining officers. They declared that I had passed the second board examination.

OFFICER CANDIDATE SCHOOL

I entered Officer Candidate School at Fort Benning, Georgia, in a company of two hundred cadets. Three of us were only nineteen-years-old. I was assigned to the School of Infantry. I had spent six weeks in pre-ocs training at Fort McClellan, Alabama, with eleven other black cadets who lacked prior infantry training. We cadets were assigned as platoon sergeants and assistant platoon sergeants for black troops who were going through basic training, advanced training in heavy weapons, and machine gun and mortar training. We also trained them in artillery observation for 105mm howitzers. The army apparently wanted us to have a solid foundation in weapons before we went to Officer Candidate School. We used this training as an added opportunity to help us excel.

Although the U.S. Army was racially segregated, Officer Candidate School was integrated in both living arrangements and training at Fort Benning. Black and white cadets slept side by side, which was unusual anywhere in the United States, in both the military and civilian world.

There were three Kellys in my training unit, but I was the only African American. Albert Kelly, which was my grandfather's name, was from Rhode Island, and Mark Kelley was from Macon, Georgia. Soon after I arrived at Fort Benning, he told me, "You're the first 'Nigra' I ever slept with in the same room in my life." We had a big laugh about that. Unfortunately, Mark Kelley didn't make it through training; he washed out.

I consider my time in Officer Candidate School to be one of the most profound experiences in my life. The leadership training was superb, although it took a tremendous amount of mental and physical energy. We had tough physical training tests as well as difficult combat training course tests and rigorous academic tests on weapons and weapon systems, tactics, organization, and organizational theory.

THE IRON MAJOR

There was one training officer I encountered at Officer Candidate School whom I will never forget. We called him the "Iron Major." He was built like a spark plug—five feet ten inches, broad-shouldered, with huge arms and biceps. He was amazing. He could take a fourteen-pound rifle and hold it parallel to the ground for an interminable amount of time. By his size and abilities, he gained everyone's respect.

He was German, a former member of the German Army who had joined the U.S. Army. He was "clean," which in the parlance of the military meant he had no Nazi affiliations. The army must have trusted him because they gave him this crucial assignment, training future officers, when we were still at war with Nazi Germany. The Iron Major "wrote the book," as we cadets used to say, on the bayonet, and now he was teaching ocs cadets at Fort Benning.

The "Iron Major" stood on an elevated, fifteen-by-eighteen-foot platform while instructing cadets in the proper use of the bayonet. He used a microphone and was assisted by a couple of enlisted men. He demonstrated a series of movements, long thrusts and vertical and horizontal strokes, that each of us had to perform without falling off the platform.

One day, I was in the middle of this training, feeling pretty good and literally throwing myself into it. I was about sixty-five feet from him, in the right front, but he looked directly at me and said, "You, beeg Negro soldiah, I want you to come to the platform."

I looked at him out of the corner of my eye, and he said, "You!" And then he pointed at me. "Beeg Negro soldiah! Come here!"

I jogged up to him at port arms and saluted with my rifle.

"You do a good job," he said. "Come up here on the platform."

So I got up on the platform and saluted, and he took his microphone again.

"You are goddamn good soldiah," he declared. "I never have an officer cadet who moves like you do, with the spirit of the bayonet. You truly have the spirit of the bayonet. Now when you thrust the tip of your bayonet, it's just a little to the right, a little too much. Now, I want you to come at me. Do a thrust, vertical butt stroke, and slash. And let's see how we do with that."

I followed his order. As I was coming through with the slash, he caught my rifle and froze it in his enormous hands. I couldn't move it! As he held the rifle, he told me, "Here's what I want you to practice."

He said I should correct my technique by using the tip of the bayonet to guide my stroke, and we went through the drill again. And he said, "OK, that's enough for you today. Return to your post. Thank you for being here."

I respected the Iron Major—we all did—but now I knew that he respected me. Later on, other cadets began jokingly referring to me as "Bayonet Kelly."

SECOND LIEUTENANT KELLY

I passed the fifth board examination, the last major hurdle of my training, and became an officer. That examination alone eliminated about 25 percent of the company. Of the two hundred cadets who had started with me in May, sixty-six finished and were commissioned as second lieutenants. Seven of the twelve African American cadets graduated, a higher percentage than for the entire cadet class.

I had begun to learn an important lesson in the army. Many officers were willing to judge me on my abilities rather than my race. The entire army wasn't like that, but it was changing. I was treated fairly as a soldier. Gradually, I overcame my suspicions that black cadets would be encouraged to wash out of ocs.

On August 16, 1945, I was commissioned Second Lieutenant Samuel Eugene Douglas Kelly in the U.S. Army. It was a wonderful day for me. We newly commissioned army officers, however, didn't spend much time thinking about the ceremony because the war in the Pacific was not yet over. The United States had dropped atomic bombs on Hiroshima and Nagasaki, but the Japanese had not officially surrendered. There was still the possibility of a massive invasion of Japan, even bigger than D-Day. Fort Benning was rapidly turning out hundreds of officers because it was said that the life of an infantry lieutenant in combat was roughly the same as that of a machine gunner, about fifteen minutes.

I didn't think very long about that bit of army wisdom. My dream was to be a rifle company commander, the guts and soul of the infantry. The company commander is on the front lines. He's the one who leads troops who secure the mountains and the hilltops, pour fire down on the enemy, and then close in and kill the enemy. That's what I trained to do; that's what I wanted to do.

My first assignment as an officer was at Fort McClellan, Alabama, on August 26. By this time, we all knew that the war was effectively over. Most of the soldiers and officers were pleased and relieved, but I was ambivalent; I did not know if or when I would get the combat experience I fervently wanted.

I was to be attached to the Infantry Replacement Training Center (IRTC), assisting in training troops to be infantrymen. I was assigned to a training company as a platoon leader, which would have been my combat assignment as a basic infantry officer. That was my military occupation specialty (MOS), 1542, a rifle platoon leader.

A SEGREGATED ARMY

The Japanese officially surrendered on September 2, 1945. I was glad that the war, with all its death and destruction, was finally over, and I understood the combat soldiers around the world who just wanted to come home. But I had gone through extensive, rigorous training, and, quite frankly, I wanted to see combat.

I knew that after my graduation from Officer Candidate School, I would return to the army's segregated daily working environment, which included separate officers' clubs in the South (we called them "Uncle Tom's Cabins"), separate sleeping quarters, and separate dining facilities for officers. When officers did eat in the same dining hall on northern bases, black officers and white officers had separate tables. The civilian world was even worse.

I didn't think there was anything about me that required my being separated from other people. I could do things as well as, if not better than, white people. I hated segregation. I hated it in the military and in civilian life.

I devised my own plan for challenging segregation and proposed it to all the young black officers who would listen. By outperforming white officers, I argued, we would prove our worth. Then there would be no choice but to end segregation. Once you outperform them, beat them at their own game by being the best officer you can be, they could not possibly continue to justify racial segregation. That attitude had already paid off for me. But my African American fellow officers laughed at me, calling me naive.

These black officers from the South, Harlem, and the South Side of Chicago had grown up in a world of segregation, and they didn't think anything could be done about it. For them, segregation was a fact of life. Both in the army and in the civilian world, white men dominated the political, economic, and social structures. We were only eighty years out of slavery, they argued. And given what we were assigned to do—load and unload ships, deliver goods to frontline soldiers—it seemed that slavery continued. Of course they understood that there would always be more support troops than frontline soldiers, but they wondered why most of the black officers and enlisted men were assigned to port companies and quartermaster companies. They asked, "Are we not, in fact, just cheap conscripted labor?"

SEGREGATED AMERICA

Three episodes toward the end of my training at Fort Benning made me, for the first time, disenchanted with the army. The first took place the day I was commissioned at Fort Benning. I went on the standard nine-day pass that every new officer was granted after completing Officer Candidate School. I took a bus from Columbus to Atlanta and had a six- or seven-hour layover in Atlanta before taking the train north to Connecticut.

I checked my bag at the counter and took a taxi to the Atlanta Colored United Service Organization (USO), where I read magazines and wrote some letters. About five hours later, I went to the station and got in line to retrieve my bag. I was about the tenth person in line, and someone behind me nudged me on the shoulder. I looked back and saw a white private first class.

"Look, don't push me," I said.

"You're not supposed to be in this line."

"Young man, you don't talk to me like that. I'm an officer, and you're a PFC. I'm your superior officer."

"That bar doesn't mean anything to me."

And before I knew it, we were in a shoving match. As he came at me, I said, "Don't you push me like that, because if you do, I'm going to hurt you."

By that time, about twenty-five people had gathered, and I beckoned to two white military policemen who were about a hundred feet away. They looked at us, turned away, and left.

"Look," I told him, "I'm going to put you under arrest unless you stop talking to me and using your voice in such an insubordinate manner."

"Your bar doesn't mean anything to me. Who the hell do you think you are? You're in the South, and we don't pay Negroes any attention here."

A white major walked up and grabbed me by the arm. "Look, soldier," he said, "you just leave and go over in the corner and let this man get his bag."

He escorted me to the side. At first, there had been about twenty-five people, talking and pointing at me, and as he talked to me, the crowd swelled to about fifty people. The major said to the crowd, "I have this under control." He took me by the arm. I'll never forget that major and what he said to me: "You know, this shouldn't ever have to be this way." To this day, I don't know if he meant the PFC should not have challenged me or I should have been smart enough not to be in the white baggage line. He then escorted me to the train.

When I got to my seat, I sat down and cried like a baby. I felt so low. How could I, wearing the uniform of the U.S. Army, be treated like that, especially when I would be going overseas to fight and possibly die for my country, for every person in that train station?

The second incident occurred soon after I returned to the South. I was stationed at Fort McClellan, and two white officers and I decided to share a taxi into town. We hailed a cab driven by a civilian. The old man stopped the car and said, "You know, we don't allow Negroes and white people to ride a cab together."

I was furious. I cussed the guy out. One of the white officers said, "Look, Kelly, you take the cab. We two will handle this." They left, and I took the cab and went on to the station.

I learned to avoid incidents like this by staying on post as much as possible. That practice began soon after I arrived at Fort Benning. In fact, my tactical officer, during my first interview before I even started OCS training, advised me that it would probably be a good idea if I stayed on post.

Of course, I had to leave the confines of the military base sometime. If an officer or cadet had a car, for instance, I would hitch a ride into nearby Columbus, always into the predominantly black area. Once in town, I'd take a bus to my destination, but I just didn't go to town very much because it represented the world of the Jim Crow South.

The third incident occurred in November 1945, after I received my orders to Japan, my first overseas assignment. I had come up to Richmond to spend some time with my mother, who had traveled down from Connecticut to meet me. At the end of our brief visit, I took Mom to the Richmond train station for the trip back to Greenwich. I was in my uniform and had my bag. She had her bag, and there must have been seventy-five black folk at the station, trying to get aboard a Jim Crow coach. I said, "Mom, we can't wait for this."

"Well, son, you know the South," was her response, as if to calm my growing anger over another example of the indignity of racial segregation.

"Well, you come on with me."

We found the conductor, and I told him, "Sir, I'm on military orders."

I showed him my orders and told him what my assignment was. "I have to be in New York to make that assignment, and my connection is within the next two hours."

He said, "Oh, a lieutenant?"

"Yes, sir."

"All right, look, wait a minute."

He backed everybody off and escorted my mother and me into that Jim Crow coach. Not the "white" coach but the "colored" coach just behind where firemen were chucking coal into the engines. The Jim Crow coach was always toward the front of the train. Again, I felt very low. I appreciated the conductor's help in accommodating my mother and me, but his escorting me to the colored car brought back the stark reality of segregation in the United States.

I never quietly accepted Jim Crow treatment. I always had that sense of needing to fight back. I had grown up in racially integrated Connecticut. I had attended schools with some of the brightest and wealthiest white students in the nation. I was a soldier in the army of the United States and had earned a coveted officer's commission, competing successfully against many white cadets who had washed out. As a soldier, I was trained to fight, trained to defend the country and myself and to inflict harm on its enemies. How could I be expected to meekly submit to the indignity of segregation imposed by people who, in my mind, had neither the intelligence nor the courage to wear the uniform of a U.S. Army lieutenant? I didn't feel I should ever have to back down from them.

As we boarded the train, I saw all the black faces, many belonging to soldiers and others to mothers, wives, and civilian girlfriends of soldiers, all in their own way silently sacrificing something of themselves for a nation at war.

Yet some of these black people, including enlisted men, would not be allowed on this train even though they had purchased their tickets, because there just wasn't enough room in the colored cars. They would probably have to wait another day or two before they could travel to their destinations. If they were military men under orders, they were in danger of violating those orders because of segregation. If they had only a few days of leave, their time would be cut short by the segregation laws of Virginia and other southern states. There were, after all, a limited number of colored seats on this train. Yet we all could see that the white coaches were half empty.

Soon afterward, I received orders for my first assignment. I was headed to Camp Stoneman, California, and then on to Japan to become part of the U.S. Army occupying Japan. It would be the first time I had set foot outside the United States. Given my experiences in the South, I looked forward to an assignment in another country.

CHAPTER 4

In Occupied Japan

Camp Stoneman was located near the city of Fairfield-Suisun, California. We processed out of Fairfield Army Air Base nearby and boarded a ship holding twelve thousand soldiers for the twenty-two-day voyage to Yokohama, Japan.

While on board, we learned we were to be part of the 610th Port Company, 492nd Port Battalion. The black officers and enlisted men were still quartered aboard ship in a segregated area. As the ship sailed across the Pacific, I kept my men occupied with drills and other activities.

When we disembarked at Yokohama, we were immediately assigned to new units. I signed up for the unit that would work on the island of Hokkaido. I traveled for three days, and by the time we got to Hokkaido, the unit had been brought back to Yokohama. We turned around and went back to the U.S. military base at Yokohama.

YOKOHAMA

Yokohama, nineteen miles from Tokyo, was at that time the major port for receiving U.S. military supplies entering occupied Japan. Our job was to get these supplies from the ships to infantry forces stationed throughout the country.

The war was over; the Japanese government had accepted the unconditional surrender terms dictated by General Douglas MacArthur on September 2, 1945, but we remained uncertain how the Japanese people would respond. There was still the possibility tha

t Japanese army units or civilians might resist U.S. occupation. As it turned out, the Japanese were surprisingly cooperative. We never had an incident, which amazed me considering the fierce resistance they had put up from 1942 right up to September 1945. Japan was, after all, being occupied for the first time in its history. Here I was, a nineteen-year-old second lieutenant, taking it all in.

The port at Yokohama was in hideous condition. You could drive from Yokohama into Tokyo and see nothing but destruction. You could see the impact of the firebombings; every building, almost every tree and bush was burned black. Very few structures other than those with reinforced concrete were left standing, but the Japanese didn't have that much concrete to begin with. The central area of Yokohama had only a few Western-style concrete buildings that survived the devastation.

Some gorgeous homes up on the western bluff overlooking the city somehow had survived the bombings. Those homes were now occupied by senior U.S. Army officers. There was also a beautiful officers' club, which we called "The Bankers' Club." Other attractive buildings were occupied by senior brass. Most of the junior officers and the noncoms and enlisted men, however, were in tents on the shore.

Nine or ten of the Yokohama piers were used for unloading vast quantities of military supplies and materials arriving daily on Liberty ships. As property officer, I had responsibility for these piers. I "owned" them, so to speak. I had to reconcile the original inventory with the ship manifests, because the army had entered into a period of postwar accountability. During the war, all effort was focused on winning the conflict. To ensure that victory, the army and the civilian sector that supported it did everything possible to make sure supplies and equipment arrived where they were needed. Accounting for individual items took a backseat to making sure enough supplies were available. An infantry unit's success, not to mention the lives of soldiers, depended on getting equipment and supplies to the front lines as quickly as possible.

Now that the war was over, the army still wanted the supplies to get to their assigned destination, so it adopted an elaborate inventory system to keep track of materials that would not have been a priority during the actual fighting. My job was to monitor this vast amount of material. I had to survey the items, locate them by serial number, and follow them as they moved through the port toward their eventual destination.

There must have been seventy-five eight-foot-high forklifts on the piers at Yokohama. There were also smaller, stout forklifts for short, heavier loads. I had responsibility for approximately one hundred of the stout forklifts, along with forty trucks, and four hundred skids. We dropped the skids on the pier and then GIs went in with forklifts to move them into the warehouses. From there, we dispatched the equipment to other places for storage throughout Japan.

My company had about two hundred men, and I shared command with another lieutenant. There were five holds in a typical Liberty ship, and the men were divided into five sections, one for each hold, responsible for unloading and distributing material, checking manifests, and inventorying equipment. It was quite an operation.

On average, our company worked twelve hours and had twelve hours off. Our men could unload a Liberty ship in seven to nine days. We had more than three hundred ships off Yokohama in Tokyo Bay with all kinds of equipment, so there was a huge backlog. The army had expected to launch the main land attack on Yokohama and Tokyo, and all those ships were there in anticipation of the invasion. The Japanese had surrendered, so we didn't have to invade, and now all the material-handling equipment, weapons, and ammunition had to be stored. Of course, the equipment was used to support the various infantry divisions such as the First Cavalry and several others situated all over Japan. Those divisions had originally been assigned as the invasion force. Now they were part of the occupation force.

In 1946, I married Eunice Lyon, an African American Red Cross worker and assistant director of the Golden Dragon Service Club in Yokohama. She was a very attractive lady with a degree from Howard University. My marriage to her helped me somewhat in the eyes of the higher brass, but I was drawn to her because of her beauty and maturity, and because there were few college-educated black women in Japan. Yet we had huge differences. She was Catholic and I was Protestant, and she did not want to have dark-skinned children. She expected me to rise in rank quickly and saw herself as an officer's wife with all of the prerogatives associated with that status. The strain of dealing with these differences would eventually take its toll on our marriage.

A BLACK AND WHITE ARMY IN JAPAN

On November 30, 1946, one year after I arrived in Japan, I was promoted to first lieutenant and also reassigned to the gear and maintenance section of the Eleventh Transportation Major Port. I found a motorcycle, discarded by the Japanese, which I used as my personal transportation. The motorcycle, I reasoned, helped me perform my job by allowing me to move efficiently across various areas of the huge Yokohama port complex and monitor the equipment.

Morale among soldiers was low, particularly for African American troops. The army quartered them in tents, while white troops were quartered in concrete buildings. There was also a significant difference between the food and supplies available to white and black troops. White soldiers had ice cream months before it was available for black soldiers. The excuse was that the combat troops who came in deserved to get the good stuff first. I had to deal with the bitterness and lowered morale caused by such blatantly unequal treatment.

Then there was the matter of equipment, especially the heavy winter uniforms and coats. Many times, we had equipment or clothing passed down from white troops. The treatment of black troops was, I thought, abominable. Most black officers shared the low morale of the enlisted men. The idea was that we had get out of this "so-and-so" outfit because there's was "nothing in it for us" or that "'The Man' just wants to use us as cheap labor battalions."

Most of these battalions were led by white company commanders who also had low morale. If an officer had a grade of captain or above, ninety-nine times out of one hundred, he was white. Rarely in 1945 did you see an African American at a captain's rank. The joke among the junior black officers and probably the enlisted men as well was that once you got to be a first lieutenant, that was as far as you were going to go, so why should you work any harder? If you did encounter a black officer at a captain's rank or higher, you immediately knew he was a physician or a chaplain.

The root of this low morale was segregation. I grant you that there were other considerations. All troops, white and black, were disturbed that the war had been over for months but they were still on active duty far away from home. The army steadily processed troops out and sent them home, but for those left behind, the wait seemed forever. When black soldiers looked around and saw that the only people in camp were black men in the battalions of quartermaster and transportation corps troops, those assigned to load or unload ships, we questioned whether the army had much respect for its African American personnel.

The military by and large accepted the lowly status of black soldiers and officers. That was the policy. Black officers were treated a certain way. We couldn't go to certain places. We ate at our own tables at the mess. Social events at the black officers' clubs were more infrequent and limited compared to those in the white officers' clubs.

Segregation was even more obvious for enlisted men, especially off base in the taverns and bars with exotic dancers where troops could drink Japanese beer. These facilities remained staunchly segregated and inferior. Black troops didn't go into white areas, and white troops didn't go into black areas.

The clubs were not Japanese owned or managed even though the employees were Japanese. Most were operated by U.S. civilians. Buildings in various command areas were actually owned by the U.S. military and run by the post command. There were a few small Japanese-owned pubs, but generally they followed the policy of racial segregation that was standard in the larger establishments. The Japanese adhered to this pattern of racial segregation, but they hadn't initiated it. Segregation was dictated by the U.S. Army.

By 1947, there were some small steps toward integration. Unlike in the United States, the segregated officers' facilities in Japan opened up to both blacks and whites. By early 1947, a black officer could go to almost any officers' club without restriction.

In that year, I was assigned as property officer to a gear and maintenance office. I later learned that the assignment was part of an experiment intended to allow senior military officers to observe the performance of black officers in an integrated situation. I was one of three black officers given this type of assignment. Captain Milford Stanley was the highest-ranking officer who took part in this experiment. Another junior officer, a Lieutenant Jones, was assigned to the general staff office. As I recall, it all worked out reasonably well.

MOMMA DOTTIE

I had an affinity for Japanese people and made friends even during those dark days after the end of World War II. Initially, all the stevedore work was performed by U.S. servicemen. When Japanese men appeared in our military area to work as stevedores in 1947, I was the officer responsible for integrating them into the army's work assignments.

The secretary who kept my records was called "Momma Dottie," perhaps because she was like a mother or grandmother to all of us in that office. She was older, and she occasionally invited junior officers to picnics at her house in the beach town of Kamakura. I met some of Mamma Dottie's relatives on these visits. I grew to know her family and a few other Japanese people very well, including the men who, in 1946, were barbers for the GIs. I felt comfortable moving about Japan. Wherever I went, I always attracted Japanese friends, because I treated the people with respect.

Momma Dottie supervised a small staff of Japanese civilian clerical workers. By 1947, there were also hundreds of civilian Japanese dockworkers who supplemented the GI workforce on the waterfront. By this point, the GIs primarily supervised the unloading of cargo, while most of the backbreaking work was done by Japanese men and women.

One Japanese man drove a huge forklift for my unit. He operated it with such skill and precision that I offered him a cup of tea to get to know him better. He accepted. He was a very gracious fellow. Unlike most Americans working with Japanese laborers, I called him by name and got to know him well. I learned, to my surprise, that he had been a soldier in the Japanese Imperial Army. I asked him what his assignment had been, and he responded that he had flown airplanes. I laughed at that, thinking how ironic it was that only two years earlier, he would have been in a position to try to kill me and as many other American GIs as possible. He had transferred his pilot's skills to forklifts.

SEX AND RACE: AMERICAN GIs IN OCCUPIED JAPAN

American GIs were not allowed to date Japanese women, not in 1945. If you were caught touching a Japanese woman, a delinquency report went to your commander. He would administer whatever punishment Article 15 mandated.

Sadly, we had some instances of rape. As one of the additional duties assigned to all officers, I was charged with defending a nice-looking, young white soldier who was accused of raping a Japanese woman. It was my first experience with a military court-martial and, in fact, my first experience with any type of criminal justice system. All I knew about the law or the military justice system was what I had learned in basic training and in Officer Candidate School. However, my assignment was to defend this soldier, and I gave it my best. The soldier was acquitted because we were able to prove that the incident hadn't happened the way the young woman said it had.

There were several "joro-houses," or houses of prostitution, around our base. They had sprung up by the dozens all over Japan for the sole purpose of providing pleasure for American soldiers. The U.S. military command determined which joro-houses would be for black and which for white troops merely by putting them in the area where troops of a particular race were stationed.

I never knew how the Japanese felt about this segregation. On the one hand, since they saw us as all part of a single occupying force, I am sure they were initially puzzled by it. On the other hand, it probably did not take long for them to pick up on the army's distinctions between black and white troops.

CHANGING TIMES

After a few months, we reduced the backlog of ships waiting to be unloaded in Yokohama Harbor. We worked twelve-hour shifts and then ten hours and finally eight hours. Eventually, we got to the point that we had weekends off as well. By early 1946, things were so routine that I started playing golf. I hadn't played golf since entering the army in 1944. In the spring of 1946, I began playing at the Hodogaya Golf and Country Club on the edge of Yokohama. This facility was turned into an officers' club, and I started playing after the club was opened to white and black officers.

Other officers' clubs, including "The Bankers Club" and the Sangukuhara Club, were integrated by 1946. We learned to fraternize, and I don't recall any racial incidents between black and white officers. We didn't realize it at the time, but we were building an important new legacy of racial integration in Japan, far from the continental United States.

Integration extended to officers' quarters as well. Senior officers always appropriated the confiscated homes of former imperial officials or wealthy Japanese citizens high on the bluffs overlooking the city. By 1946, however, the army began building housing: single homes, duplexes or fourplexes, assigned according to rank. Lieutenants lived in fourplexes, captains got duplexes, and anyone with a rank of major or above was entitled to a single home. These accommodations were raffled off to those remaining in the occupation forces.

By 1946, much of the army that had poured into Japan right after the surrender had been demobilized and sent back to the States. Those who were left, officers and enlisted men, were regular army. They were the ones who had seen combat in World War II and chose to remain in the smaller peacetime military. There were also soldiers like me who had not yet seen combat but had not completed their terms of enlistment. As time passed, the soldiers who joined us were postwar volunteers or more likely draftees who had never experienced combat. The army was changing rapidly.

By the middle of 1946, we had fairly good barracks, including some well-constructed buildings that had survived the war. My unit, the 610th Port Company, part of the 492nd Port Battalion, was housed in war-damaged three-story concrete buildings that the army had rehabilitated. The buildings were sturdy and easy to keep clean. Japanese construction workers provided the labor, supervised by the Army Corps of Engineers.

That was pretty typical of the entire occupation. The Japanese provided the labor for everything we did. We had Japanese servers in the mess halls, Japanese barbers, and Japanese who provided massages or operated public baths.

By 1947, life for the typical U.S. soldier in occupied Japan was very good. Pay went further in Japan and East Asia than it would in the States. Married officers could bring their wives and children and were usually assigned two or three servants whom the officers paid about ten dollars per month.

We also traveled around the country. I visited Nagoya in the south and Sapporo in the north and went to Beppu, the Miami of Japan. I loved it, particularly the weather and the hot springs. I touched all the major islands from Hokkaido in the north to Kyushu and Okinawa in the south. I visited Tokyo on many official and unofficial occasions.

Soldiers from my unit participated in parades for General MacArthur in 1947 and 1948. On a few occasions, I went to Tokyo to see a Japanese opera. Whatever the size of the town, there was always a theater. It was amazing. Even though the performances were in Japanese, I could somehow understand. I saw Madame Butterfly twice in a gorgeous Japanese-owned theater in Tokyo.

Japanese people treated me with kindness and great respect wherever I went. I believe the same respect was also extended to other black enlisted men and officers. Most of the black officers had Japanese girlfriends. Many black enlisted men and several officers married Japanese women and brought them home to the States. Even though these marriages were permitted, the black officers who married Japanese women didn't fare as well as those who were not interracially married. They had a difficult time advancing in rank. There is no doubt in my mind that they were treated very differently from black officers with African American wives.

REMAKING JAPAN

The U.S. Army was not simply occupying Japan. We were preparing the Japanese for the transition from their imperial past to a democratic future. That meant that we promoted democracy among the Japanese while steadily turning over various political and military functions to Japanese officials so that they would have complete independence from us. For example, in 1946, Japanese civilian authorities could not try an American soldier for murder in their courts. By 1948, that policy had ended.

I was impressed by how the Japanese people responded to U.S. racial divisions. Some of them learned about the nature of racial discrimination from white GIs. Many could not understand why racial discrimination existed in the United States, because occupation forces reminded them every day that the United States was a democracy. Sometimes they talked with me late into the night about what they understood as contradictions between American ideals and actual practice. These contradictions would continue to puzzle some of my Japanese friends, who would later express their feelings to me when I returned to Japan in the

1950s. Even then, a decade after the U.S. Army had abandoned its official policy of segregation, they still talked about the racial discrimination they had noticed on the part of white soldiers and officers against their black counterparts.

By late 1947, I was receiving more varied assignments. Some—in the transportation corps, for example—reflected the old segregated army. Others, however, such as my assignment in a security guard detail, hinted at the coming end of segregation. The security guard company was similar to the military police. I liked that assignment, with its unique helmets, distinctive uniforms, and weapons. I liked the drilling and thought the job suited me to perfection. I was embracing the army way of life.

CHAPTER 5

Integrating the Army

I almost didn't have the chance to see an integrated U.S. Army. The year the army integrated, 1948, was also a year of personal and professional crisis. I left the service in April, taking a six-month unplanned break from the military. At the time, I thought the separation was permanent.

It all began with my court-martial in November 1947. That fall, during my assignment as first lieutenant in the port security platoon, I was in charge of the vehicles for the two hundred troops who guarded the materials, equipment, and supplies that came off the Liberty ships. The docks had all kinds of food, including canned pineapple, canned pears, and other items that GIs could sell on the black market for a small fortune. My job was to prevent such illegal activity.

LIEUTENANT FOSTER

On November 5, I was leaving the port company orderly room when Lieutenant John Foster, the officer of the day, told a sergeant that he was taking a jeep but did not want the Japanese driver. I knew Foster, although not well, and I told him, "You're not supposed to be driving that vehicle, Lieutenant Foster. I'll provide you a driver."

It was standard operating procedure (SOP) that a driver would operate the vehicle for the officer of the day. I reminded Lieutenant Foster that the standard operating procedure was written by me and approved by the company commander.

He became indignant and said, "I don't give a damn who wrote the SOP. Battalion has said nothing about it."

I repeated that he must take a driver and it was my duty to see that the SOP governing our vehicles was strictly adhered to.

During the course of the conversation, with Foster sitting behind the wheel of the jeep, I leaned in on the passenger side. When I did, Foster shoved in the clutch, yanked the gearshift into first, and said, "I don't care."

I reached over with my left hand and tried to tap the shift back into neutral. "Just one moment," I told him, "I will get you a driver."

As I said that, Foster took off, and the jeep hit my shoulder and knocked me to the ground.

I was damned angry and told the executive officer what had happened. Before he could say anything, I declared, "We're going to get our vehicle back."

"Well, take it easy, now, Sam," he cautioned me.

But I was not about to listen to anybody at that moment. I jumped into another jeep and went after Foster. I finally spotted him talking to a couple of sergeants.

"Foster," I said, "don't try to duck me. You must take a driver with the jeep." I then grabbed the right lapel of his battle jacket and said, "You damn near killed me back there! Get out of the jeep."

He got out of the jeep and grabbed my collar. I dropped my hands and said, "Take your hands off me."

When he refused, I grabbed his shoulder with my right hand. Foster was the officer of the day, which meant he had his standard army issue .45 caliber semiautomatic pistol. He drew the pistol and pointed it in my face.

"You are under arrest," I said.

"Get back, Kelly," he said. I didn't realize how close I was standing to him.

He repeated his command. "Get back. I am the officer of the day, and I'm in charge."

I looked directly at the .45, still more angry than frightened, and said, "I need your vehicle. Either you give it to me or you take it over to get a driver."

His response was quick. "Get back."

This time, he cocked his pistol, placing a round in the chamber, and pointed it at my chest.

I said in the calmest voice I could muster, "Lower the pistol and then we can talk. Lower the pistol. Put the pistol down. What, are you crazy? Lower the pistol before it goes off. Lower the pistol!"

I didn't realize how many times I had said "lower the pistol," but it must have worked. Shaking, he lowered the pistol away from my chest and down past my stomach. As he did, it went off. The bullet shot through the fleshy part of my inner thigh. It didn't knock me down, but it sure staggered me.

Although I could feel the blood running down my leg, I lunged at him, grabbing the pistol. I then punched him in the jaw and knocked him down. I immediately pulled the .45 from his right hand and told Sergeant Knox, "Here, sergeant, keep this pistol. I've got to go to the dispensary."

Foster looked up at me, his eyes glazed, and said, "You are under arrest."

So I had struck the only blow of the entire encounter—after Foster shot me.

Lieutenant John Foster had seemed like an odd guy long before this incident. He had an attitude, and I didn't think he was completely stable. He was prone to getting into arguments, and when he debated, he argued his side so vociferously that he shook. This was not just my sense of him. Most officers I knew thought of him in the same way.

COURT-MARTIAL

When I got to the dispensary, the medical officer patched me up, and I was ready to return to duty. In my mind, it wasn't a big deal. My superiors didn't agree. My company commander said, "I'm on order to put you under arrest in quarters. This is an Article 32 investigation."

I knew what that meant. You can't go anywhere unless cleared by a senior officer, and you are also required to cooperate in the investigation. Under Article 32, I had to make a sworn statement about the incident and be confined to quarters.

The investigation was conducted by a black major named Walker who had just arrived from Washington, D.C. An Article 32 investigation is similar to a grand jury; it determines whether military law has been broken and whether there is cause for court-martial.

At the hearing, Major Walker asked if I thought the shooting by Foster was intentional.

"No, it wasn't intentional. When I told him to put the pistol down, he lowered it at my command. He lowered the pistol, and he was shaking, and he was nervous; it went off accidentally."

I knew the senior brass would not like my testimony because they wanted to get rid of Foster. I frankly think they wanted to get rid of both of us.

I told the major my story and said that I had no problem with Foster, other than that he had disobeyed an order and that he was required to have a driver for the jeep. I later learned that Foster had said essentially the same thing. Then the major returned to me.

"Did you threaten him?"

"No, I did not threaten him. I did not put my hands on him before the pistol was discharged. I wanted the vehicle, or I wanted him to go over with me to get a driver."

I told Major Walker that Lieutenant Foster had been shaking and that the pistol had gone off accidentally.

"Are you sure of that?"

"Yes, I am," I answered.

"How do you know?"

"Well, I am an expert in small arms."

The major responded, "He hasn't talked to you?"

"No, he has not. Why would you ask?"

"He didn't say to you, 'Well, I'll write it down as you say it'? You don't like Lieutenant Foster, do you, Kelly?"

"Well, that's true, sir. Lieutenant Foster is not a friend of mine, but I honestly can say that when I told him, 'Put the pistol down,' he put the pistol in the middle of my chest and lowered the pistol down the middle of my body to my navel and my crotch and then the thing went off. I don't think he wanted to shoot me in the forehead or the belly or anywhere."

Major Walker completed his investigation and concluded that there was enough evidence to court-martial both Foster and me. I was the first to go to trial.

The proceeding took place in Yokohama, led by Lieutenant Colonel Fred Atkinson, a West Pointer. Atkinson, a severe-looking man, was president of the General Court, which tried officers, where punishment could range up to life imprisonment.

The counsel, who was pushing me hard, asked, "Well, didn't you threaten Lieutenant Foster?"

"No, I didn't threaten him."

"Well, he hated you, didn't he?"

I knew what was going on. The counsel was trying to build a case of animosity between us. "Captain, it's not a hate case. It was an accident."

Then he accused me of being out of control. "Well, he was in fear of his life, wasn't he?"

"No, he wasn't," I responded.

"Well, then you were assaulting him."

"I never laid a hand on him until after I was shot and never threatened him."

"But your language was such that he was assaulted."

I told the court-martial board about the pistol.

"What language did you use to get him to put the pistol down?" they asked.

"I was direct," I responded. "It was my duty to tell Foster to put the pistol down." I explained to the court that regardless of Foster's assignment as officer of the day, he wasn't going to arrest me. I wouldn't have allowed that. I'd wanted him to return the vehicle and get a driver.

"So when he put the pistol down, didn't he tell you he was going to shoot you?"

"No, he didn't."

That's how the interrogation went. Ultimately, the only things they said that I did wrong were being too forceful in my language when instructing Foster to put the pistol down and striking him after I was shot.

The court decided it had to have a conviction. I thought that was racist. I still do. The court convicted me based on the language I had used to tell him to put the pistol down. They said I had assaulted Lieutenant Foster, convicted me, and fined me three hundred dollars.

The assault conviction was based on the summary statement that had been read at the beginning of the trial—I remember it to this day. "An officer never does by force that which he has the authority to do by word of mouth."

I always thought that I *had* used word of mouth, but the court convicted me anyway.

The army then court-martialed Lieutenant John Foster after completing its Article 32 investigation. He later told me that he had said the same thing in court that I had. Just before his trial, his defense counsel had asked if I would testify for him. I'd said, "Sure, I'd be glad to." Both Foster and his counsel had been surprised at that. It didn't matter, however, as he was convicted as well. They fined Foster more than double the amount they had fined me. Then we both went back to active duty. Strangely, after that incident, Foster and I actually became friends. I think we both felt railroaded by the military justice system.

My court-martial took place in November–December 1947. I returned to duty and went to parties during the holiday. My life appeared to return to normal. I was happy soldiering again. By January 1948, we were hearing rumors about too many officers on active duty. The rumors became reality in March when the Reduction in Force (RIF) program was implemented. I was discharged from the U.S. Army in April 1948 and was one of the first officers sent back to the States.

The decision as to who got "RIFfed" was administrative; it happened with the stroke of a pen. I was a reserve officer, so I was more likely to be RIFfed out of the service, but I also had no doubt that the court-martial had moved me up on the RIF list. Foster and I were in the same room on the ship that transported us back to the States, and we decided to make the best of the situation. We stayed on the West Coast and partied and had fun. We saw some old friends of mine in Oakland and hung around there a couple of weeks, then went back to our respective homes.

I was still furious. I had not yet decided to make the army a career, but neither did I anticipate being a civilian again, at least not like this. I returned to Greenwich to try to start over.

CIVILIAN LIFE, 1948

The next six months were miserable. First, there was the complete collapse of my marriage to Eunice. We'd gotten married for the wrong reasons, which I realized during the court-martial, which was not the cause of the breakup but certainly did not help the situation. She thought I was a twenty-one-year-old hothead and offered me no support. By the time the court-martial was over, we were separated, and she moved back to the American Red Cross facility in Yokohama.

Eunice and I got back together briefly in Connecticut that summer, when she stayed with me at my mom and dad's house in Greenwich. But we just couldn't make the marriage work. By October 1948, we were permanently separated. We had, as the saying goes, irreconcilable differences. The divorce became final in 1950.

My job situation in Connecticut was not good. I was able to return to work at Northern Warren Cutex Corporation in Stamford, but I didn't go back as a foreman. I didn't make much money, so I began looking for a better job. I found one at Condé Nast Publishing. I remember dressing up in a nice suit and tie for what turned out to be a very fine interview, and I was offered a job. The interviewer told me to report back in three days. Anticipating a professional position, I came back in a suit but was assigned to the publishing house's night shift, assembling pages for magazines and placing the magazines into bins. It was monotonous work. So I said, "I'd like to do something different." They then put me at the end of the conveyor line where I shipped and sent out magazines for subscribers. While others stamped address labels on magazines and wrapped them in bulk brown paper, I packed one-hundred-pound bags of magazines onto a truck. This was only slightly better than assembling magazines, but I needed the work.

I kept both jobs for a few weeks until my supervisor at Northern Warren heard I was working for another company. I was called in and asked if I had another job.

"Yes," I said, "I can't make enough money here to support myself like I want."

My supervisor responded, "Well, you can't work two jobs."

"Well, where does it say that?" I declared, getting a little testy. "It's my right to work where I want to work! And my job performance has always been superior."

Northern Warren fired me.

A DIPLOMA

There was one bright spot in this rather dismal six months: I received my diploma from Stamford High School. I had always been self-conscious about being a high school dropout. Between my trips to Washington,

D.C., I contacted my favorite high school teacher, Louisa Harvey Bohn, and we arranged to meet for lunch. She was dismayed to learn that I had not yet received my high school diploma. After lunch, we went to see Cecil Rhoades, my old high school chemistry teacher, who was now the principal of Stamford High. I had not done well in his class, and I felt a bit like a lamb bound for slaughter.

I was expecting the worst, but the two of them quickly agreed that I could test for the credits I lacked so that I could receive my diploma. They awarded me partial equivalency credit for my military training and then presented me with written examinations in courses including mathematics, science, and social studies. Mr. Rhoades offered me the comfortable executive chair behind his broad, leather-trimmed wooden desk. I sat there for more than four hours, answering all the questions to the best of my ability. After I completed the exams, I asked, "When will I know the results?" My two champions said they would correct the examinations on the spot if I had time to wait for the results.

Later that afternoon, they informed me I had passed with flying colors, and I left Stamford High School with the diploma I would have received in 1944 had I not dropped out. I was elated; the anxiety and embarrassment I had felt because I did not have a high school diploma disappeared on that day.

I never gave up on the army. I decided to use some of my contacts to try to get back into the service, and eventually I succeeded. I made a few trips to Washington, D.C. On one of those trips, I saw Colonel Campbell C. Johnson, a distant relative of Eunice's who was connected through the informal network of black officers and former officers. I got a recommendation from him to return to active duty. This network of officers also included Colonel James Evans, a military assistant to the assistant secretary of defense. Later, Colonel Evans was named vice president of West Virginia State College, where I taught between 1958 and 1962. Colonel Evans wrote a letter on my behalf, stating, "I believe the Army would be justified in recalling Lieutenant Samuel E. Kelly back to active duty based on the facts surrounding his case of discharge."

I received my orders to return to active duty on October 1, 1948, within thirty days of his letter.

My decision to return to the U.S. Army had much to do with the situation I encountered when I returned to civilian life. I had been an officer with significant responsibilities. I had led men, yet I was able to find only menial jobs as a civilian. Even with all the problems I had encountered in the army, it was still the best opportunity for me to succeed. I knew I could do better there than in the civilian world.

I believe that view was shared by thousands of black officers and enlisted men in 1948. The army was segregated, but so was the world outside. There were few opportunities even for gifted, talented former black officers in the civilian world. The prospects for former enlisted men were even more dismal. Black men in the service faced the prospects of a military life that was far from perfect, but we also knew that the civilian world was generally far worse in terms of opportunities for advancement.

FORT LAWTON

When I rejoined the army, I was determined to make my way back to the infantry. My intentions notwithstanding, the army had other plans for me, and I was sent to Fort Lawton, Washington, and reassigned to a transportation corps. The infantry, I later heard, was overstaffed with officers. Just as in Japan, I was an officer who supervised the loading and unloading of ships. I was also reunited with the president of my court-martial, Lieutenant Colonel Fred Atkinson, now the executive officer at Fort Lawton. Although things were not working out as well as I had hoped, at least I was back in uniform.

Fort Lawton is on the tip of the Magnolia peninsula, which extends into Puget Sound. It is an urban military base, surrounded on three sides by the city of Seattle. I recall traveling to Seattle for the first time and arriving on a sunny October day. I took the taxi from the train station through the section of the city called Magnolia Bluff. From there, I looked out over Puget Sound. The combination of land, sky, and water was beautiful. I said then that if I had the chance, Seattle would be my home.

My initial Fort Lawton orders assigned me to supervising black soldiers who loaded and unloaded ships. But because the army was still testing integration, I was temporarily reassigned to Lieutenant Chester

(Chet) Edwards from Ohio, the post's athletic director. Lieutenant Edwards and I got to be good friends. We even double-dated.

Among other duties, Chet coached the post's basketball team. I said I would love to follow him into this assignment of running the sports program when he was reassigned. With his recommendation, I was pulled up to post headquarters as the athletic director, the person who develops sports programs for the enlisted men. After World War II, the U.S Army placed a heavy emphasis on athleticism and physical competition. Depending on the post, there were major command teams in football, baseball, and volleyball. We played football against Fort Lewis, south of Tacoma, Washington. The Fort Lewis players shellacked us, because their base had about ten times as many men in the pool of athletes from which to draw. We also played a regular schedule against U.S. Navy teams throughout the Puget Sound region.

The heart of the program, however, was the intramural competition, which involved both women and men. Every company-size unit sponsored a team for basketball and softball. We had a team for golf, for football, and for baseball. Our intramural softball program had forty-five teams. They were broken out into leagues, with each team competing for trophies. I supervised a staff of about seven or eight people, including enlisted men, assigned exclusively to maintaining the athletic fields.

This was a fun time for me. Some teams had college athletes who were officers or sergeants with experience in multiple sports. Some players were semipro athletes who were in the army temporarily.

By far my most powerful memory of Fort Lawton was witnessing the integration of the U.S. Army. I recall the day with great clarity. It was October 15, 1948, only fifteen days after I returned to active duty. President Harry S. Truman issued Executive Order 9981 integrating the U.S. military in July 1948. That order was to become effective at Fort Lawton on October 15.

When the order came down, I was athletic director as well as a staff officer. I was familiar with the troops, especially the black soldiers, and thus was assigned to facilitate this order, to literally command these troops as they moved to their new integrated quarters.

Officers' call came on October 15 as normal. Colonel Ruxford Willoughby was the commanding officer, and Colonel Fred Atkinson was his executive officer. All officers were summoned to the post's smaller theater, which held about 150 people. After being called to attention, Colonel Willoughby spoke first. Willoughby was a Southerner, with deep red skin and creases from too much sun. He had been a cavalryman and was a well-respected old "horse soldier," as we called him. After he was introduced, the colonel said briskly, "Ladies and gentlemen, the president of the United States, the commander in chief, has published an order to integrate all forces of the United States Army." With that announcement, a few of the white officers went, "Ohh!" as if exhaling loudly. Then the room was eerily quiet.

Colonel Willoughby continued, using his own language rather than the words of the executive order: "I'm telling you that we are going to integrate within the next twenty-four hours. If any sonofabitch violates this order, I'll put him in the stockade within thirty minutes and try him by court-martial within seventy-two hours. That's all, gentlemen."

With that, another officer called out, "Ten-hut!" Colonel Willoughby stomped off the stage and out of the theater without speaking to anyone.

I walked out of the theater and down the hill to an area of ancient tarpaper shacks in the hollow of the post. During World War II, Italian prisoners of war were held in this area. I didn't know much about it at the time, but I would later learn that a number of black troops had been tried and convicted of rioting at Fort Lawton in 1944 following clashes with those prisoners. Twenty-eight soldiers were convicted of rioting, and two soldiers, Corporal Luther Larkin and Private William G. Jones, were given manslaughter convictions in the death of Italian POW Guglielmo Olivotto.

The Fort Lawton trial was second only to the Port Chicago mutiny trial in terms of the number of black servicemen accused of unlawful behavior in World War II. Now, ironically, black soldiers were living in the old POW quarters, and it looked as if no work had been done since then to improve the housing. There was a separate sergeants' club in the area as well. The latrine buildings were out in the middle of the street, making for a cold walk outside in winter when soldiers had to relieve themselves.

Nothing could have symbolized racial segregation more than the concentration of black enlisted personnel in the post's shacks while white troops occupied buff-colored, two-tier barracks on the bluff. I marched a platoon of fifty black soldiers up the hill toward the barracks on the bluff. I did not know what to expect, but when the enlisted men arrived at their newly assigned barracks, they fell out and were greeted by white troops. Guys shook hands with one another as the black soldiers took up their new quarters. There was not a single fight, not one disagreement. You would have thought it was a party. It turned out there was plenty of room for these black soldiers in the formerly all-white barracks.

There were a few negative incidents in the days and weeks after integration. As the post's athletic director, I managed a program that was already integrated, but there was still an occasional problem. Once, I had about four buses loaded to take soldiers to Fort Lewis, where we were scheduled to play an interpost football game. One bus was to carry white women soldiers and about twelve black men. Sergeant Bonano, a Filipino American sergeant, wouldn't let the black troops on the bus. Knowing that we needed to leave soon and not realizing Sergeant Bonano's action, I said to the soldiers milling around outside, "Come on, men, get to!"

One of them responded, "Well, look, sir, the sergeant here says no."

I confronted the sergeant, "Bonano, what's the problem here?"

He hesitated and then said, "Well, sir."

Before he could answer me fully, I said, "Oh, I see what the problem is." And with that, I opened the bus and said, "Men, get the hell on this bus." Then I turned to Bonano and said, "Don't ever do that again."

Attempting to justify his actions, Bonano said, "Sir, there's a policy of not mixing colored troops with white women."

"That's not the policy as I see it," I fired back.

By this time, all the soldiers were on the bus, and I waved the driver to leave with his passengers, white women and black men together.

There were also some white officers who saw me only as a "nigger." They didn't say that, but in 1948, one major suggested as much in my efficiency report at Fort Lawton, Washington. He noted that I was "intimidating" officers by looking them in the eye and speaking directly. When I confronted him about his report, he said, "Well, Kelly, sometimes you are kind of uppity."

Choosing my words carefully and showing proper respect, but not fawning, I responded, "You mean uppity like an 'uppity Negro,' sir?"

"Well, no, but you march straight, you're not like the other 'Nigras.' You march straight; you march like you're taking command. Sometimes when I talk to you, I begin to think you're the major and I'm the lieutenant."

"Sir, if you have a problem with that," I responded, "then you must have a horrible feeling of inferiority!"

With that, the major laughed and said, "Sam, that's the most honest thing that's been said about me." Then he reversed his tone. "You know, you got a lot of nerve, as a lieutenant, telling your superior officer exactly what you feel."

"Sir, I'm just trying to be what you think an officer should be. You give me an order, I'm going to perform to the best of my ability. If I have to shoot up some folks in combat, I'll do that. But I'm not going to betray you in terms of your rank."

When the Korean War began in the summer of 1950, I was reassigned from Fort Lawton to Far Eastern Command (FECOM). I didn't go directly to the combat theater, however, but returned to infantry school for advanced training. The course was designed for those with the rank of captain and above, so, as a first lieutenant, I was fortunate to get in. Although I would eventually get to Korea, the route was through Georgia, where I took company officers' advanced training at Fort Benning.

JOYCE

My life changed dramatically in 1950, not simply because of my orders to Korea. On November 5, I married Joyce Estella Lyle. We had met at a fashion and talent show at a community center in Seattle. She was not part of the program, but she wore a stunning blue gown and fuchsia gloves. She was beautiful. I began chatting with her and asked for her phone number, which she handily provided.

Joyce Estella Lyle was born in Fort Collins, Colorado, in 1926. She moved to Seattle with her parents, William and Mattie Lyle, in 1942 and graduated from Broadway High School in 1944. Both parents were trustees of the First African Methodist Episcopal Church, the oldest black church in the city. Her uncle, Rev. L. R. Hayes, was the pastor of the church from 1939 to 1945. Joyce's father, whom I eventually called "Pop" Lyle, managed the stockroom at the National Bank of Commerce at the corner of Second and Cherry. He also was responsible for transferring the daily deposits to the vault.

Both Mom and Pop Lyle were very conservative religious people. Pop Lyle, a dyed-in-the-wool Republican, was a child of the Depression. He didn't believe a person should buy anything on credit except a car and a home. Everything else should be purchased with cash.

Joyce and I began dating in late 1948 and continued to see each other for the next two years. When the Korean War broke out in the summer of 1950, we were on a picnic with some Asian and black friends at Lincoln Park in Seattle. I turned off our radio because they were announcing that all military personnel were to report to their posts and bases as soon as possible. There was no question that I would soon see combat, but I wanted to savor what I knew would be fewer and fewer precious moments with Joyce and her friends in Seattle.

Joyce was a comparative literature major in her senior year at the University of Washington, and she worked part-time in Suzzallo Library on the campus. She convinced me to enter college for the first time in my life. I enrolled as a part-time student at the University of Washington, taking a night course in economics. I still remember how white the campus appeared in 1949. Out of the twelve thousand students enrolled on campus, there were no more than a dozen African Americans. However, I was not as conscious of the racial disparity at the university in 1949 as I would be two decades later. What was important was my love for Joyce. Our lives seemed perfect.

But perfection is fleeting. Joyce and I had dated for almost two years. My divorce from Eunice was not yet final, and someone who knew that wrote Joyce a poison-pen letter. Her parents were quite upset when they learned about my marital status. They immediately concluded that it wasn't a good idea for me to continue to see their only daughter.

I visited their home to plead my case.

"I'm sorry I did not explain my marital situation, but I will treat your daughter with respect, and with my honor and my dignity. The greatest thing a man can give a woman is his manhood, his honor, and his dignity."

Mr. and Mrs. Lyle ignored my pleas. Joyce was their princess; they were not about to see her life ruined by someone they believed unworthy of her love and their respect.

Joyce and I stopped dating for about five weeks. Then she telephoned me at the base. "I'd like to chat with you, Sammy, at Fort Lawton."

"I thought we were not supposed to see each other," I responded, with much disappointment and a tinge of anger.

"Let's talk about that. Can I see you?"

Soon, both my disappointment and my anger disappeared.

We met at the officers' club to talk but didn't seem to resolve anything. I decided it was best to drive Joyce back to town. I dropped her off about a block and a half from her home because her parents would have been livid if they had seen the two of us together. As she left my car, I reached out to her, confessing, "I don't know what to say. I'd like to see you, but your family feels that I'm just not good enough for you."

Strangely, she said, "Oh, I don't think so. Let me talk to them."

So I was invited to dinner the next Sunday. When the opportunity presented itself, I ended the small talk and repeated the words of my earlier conversation. "I've always said there were three things a man could offer a young lady—his manhood, his honor, and his dignity." I hoped these words, which I had heard so often as a boy from my minister father, might have the desired impact. When they didn't, I added my own, "I'll always honor Joyce. I love her. Yes, I am facing a divorce, but that will come soon, any day now." Then I added, "I have orders to go to Korea."

This time, perhaps realizing the potential danger ahead and my willingness to face it, Joyce's parents relented and allowed me to date her once again. Six months later, we were married in a formal military ceremony, on November 5, 1950, at the chapel at Fort Benning. We began our marriage in typical military fashion. Joyce stayed with me for four months during my Georgia training, and after I graduated, we drove across the country to Seattle, where she lived with her parents, while I returned to Fort Lawton to ship out for Korea.

JOYCE ESTELLA LYLE AND SAM KELLY, AFTER THEIR MARRIAGE AT FORT BENNING IN NOVEMBER 1950. COURTESY OF THE KELLY FAMILY.

CHAPTER 6

Korea

The Korean War was a turning point in my military career, the opportunity to finally prove myself. I had always felt a gnawing pain in my belly about not being treated fairly because of the court-martial and had determined then, as a Spartan would say, "to come back with my shield—or on it."

I really meant that. I always wanted to be with my troops. I wanted to fight and, if necessary, to die leading my men. If I go down, I said to myself, I'll take a lot of people with me, and somebody will know about it. I shared that feeling with only one other person, Lieutenant Julius Becton, who had attended Officer Candidate School with me in 1945. He told me he felt exactly like I did.

Becton was assigned to the Second Indian Head Division, which arrived in Korea before I did. I saw him once briefly, when I was on my way to the front and he was returning. He had just finished his combat tour. His last words to me as we passed each other were "Kelly, keep your head down; it's rough up there."

I will never forget those words; coming from him, they meant a great deal to me. By the time our paths crossed again, Julius Becton had won two Silver Stars, two Bronze Stars, and the Distinguished Service Cross.

When my orders to go to Korea via Fort Benning first arrived, I was not happy. I petitioned to go to the front as early as possible. The U.S. Army had been knocked back by a very aggressive North Korean Army, from just below the 38th parallel all the way to Pusan in the southwestern corner of the peninsula. Our troops were outmanned and outgunned and took a mauling from Chinese soldiers who came across the border. As a trained infantry officer, I felt my place was with our beleaguered soldiers.

The Chinese first entered the war in December 1950 and caused quite a bit of disruption through the early months of 1951. We were always outnumbered at least seven to one in Korea, but we always had air superiority and generally had indirect fire and artillery superiority. So many times when we fought the Chinese, they had more people than rifles. With that numerical superiority, they had the capability of mounting sustained and continued offensive operations at the small-unit level. What they lacked in military equipment, they more than offset with their bravery and ferocity on the field of battle.

When the Eighth U.S. Army, at that time commanded by General Walton Harris Walker, was pushed back to the Pusan perimeter, it was the worst period of the war for U.S. troops. It took months for our troops to break out of that small area. General Walker was a pudgy little tanker, an armor officer who told his men, "Die in your foxholes. Die in your foxholes." That grim message was not appreciated by the soldiers. I recall the negative comments I received when I joined the regiment and talked to my men about that message. When Walker was killed in a jeep accident, General Matthew Ridgway took over. The new commanding general was a dynamic personality who infused aggression into the Eighth Army. He said, "Gentlemen, I want to see your plans for attack, not defense." Our basic philosophy changed 180 degrees.

In late 1950, U.S. military forces broke through the Pusan perimeter, and Ridgway took the army to the Naktong River line, just fifty miles south of Seoul. The Twenty-fourth Division helped reestablish a defensible military line all the way across Korea.

All of this happened as I was still on my way to Tokyo, where I was processed for combat. In April 1951, with my combat gear and new rifle, I flew to Pusan to join the Nineteenth Infantry Regiment of the Twenty-fourth Division, which was spread out along the Naktong River. We were headed for the division rear. In a combat theater, the fighting regiments, the battalions and companies, were on the front lines. Regiments at the rear were generally support troops, such as the quartermaster corps, and reinforcements waiting to be sent to the front lines. The rear was never more than five miles from the fighting.

WITH THE NINETEENTH INFANTRY REGIMENT

The Nineteenth Infantry Regiment was legendary in military annals. During the Civil War, the regiment had fought so fiercely against Confederate forces in the Battle of Chickamauga in northern Georgia that, at the end of the day, a second lieutenant was in command of fewer than two hundred troops. A regiment usually has one thousand troops and is commanded by a colonel.

Six other newly assigned lieutenants, all of them white, reported with me to the regimental rear. Colonel G. S. Garland went down the line, asking where we were from and also asking the question that determined each officer's assignment: "Well, what kind of job do you want?"

One officer said he was a motor officer. Another said he was good at post exchange activities, "in the rear!" The colonel responded with an emotionless "OK." The third lieutenant said he was good at signal work, and two officers wanted to be assigned to the commissary. Colonel Garland made some notes as he interviewed each junior officer. Finally, he turned to me. I didn't hesitate. "Sir, I understand there's a lot of employment for rifle platoon leaders. That's my MOS. I'd like to apply."

The colonel looked at me and smiled. "Are you sure?"

"Yes, sir," I said. "I'd like to have a rifle platoon."

"Well, young fella, I think I can accommodate you."

I was the only officer volunteering to go to the front. Later, I learned that Colonel Garland shared our exchange with my battalion commander and added, "Watch for this black officer named Kelly. I think he shows something."

I was the only African American officer in the Twenty-fourth Division, which included sixteen thousand troops. Moreover, since the army had integrated less than three years earlier, I would be among the first African American officers to command both black and white troops in combat.

LEARN FAST OR DIE EARLY

There is no good time to arrive in a combat zone, but I got to Korea during some of the most intense fighting of the war. The North Koreans had been joined by Chinese Communist troops, and our job was to reinforce the garrisons on the Han River line and to push the enemy out of South Korea. The Eighth Army had already begun an all-out counteroffensive when I arrived in April, and I soon became part of it.

I had little time to adjust to life in combat. I reported to I Company and was astonished to learn the next day that I would be given a combat patrol to lead within forty-eight hours. I had never been in combat before, but I did my best to hide that fact from Lieutenant Paul Braim, my new commanding officer, and from my men.

My platoon's assignment was to attack a village near Paegri, to capture spies and bring back enemy soldiers. It was a confusing assignment. I was told to go on reconnaissance, but a reconnaissance patrol, which normally has ten men, should avoid combat. It should, to use the military slang of the time, "snoop, poop, and reconnoiter." But my platoon, if discovered, was to engage the enemy in combat.

After discussing this situation with the battalion intelligence officer, I decided to make my command a traditional reconnaissance unit.

"If it's reconnaissance," I declared, "I'll send back three squads, and I'll take a reinforced squad, and we'll snoop and poop."

"No, Sam, you can't do that," the officer responded. "Battalion command wants you to be combat ready if you're fired on."

I went on that patrol. We were fired on and lost three men. In the middle of this fight, I turned and saw, about eighty feet from where I was standing, a big orange ball of lightning. Dirt flew everywhere. I was lucky, since I was only jarred by the explosion, but I saw a man thrown into the air, still clutching his rifle. For the first time, I saw a combat death.

We regrouped and were about to mount a counterattack on Paegri, but battalion headquarters told us to freeze in our position. We were in the middle of a minefield. We couldn't do much at that point. I directed some artillery fire at the enemy's position. We were given orders to withdraw, and I led my men carefully out of that area. Fortunately, we didn't take any other casualties in that engagement.

I found out a few days after our first engagement that the area we were assigned to patrol had been mined by friendly troops. This really upset me, but I kept my anger to myself. I had vowed to be very composed in Korea, careful about what I did and how I did it, since this was a second chance for me to establish my career in the army.

Nonetheless, the lack of knowledge in the practical application of military science was appalling. At Fort Benning, I had just completed the most advanced training available to officers in the rules of attack, withdrawal, and defense. I understood the most effective use of artillery firepower and airpower; I also understood the advantage U.S. troops had over the North Koreans and Chinese in maneuverability and mobility. My first assignment was an awfully fast lesson in what not to do in combat. The failure of command had cost three U.S. soldiers their lives. The costs could have been far greater.

My subsequent combat operations played out along similar lines. We went on patrol, engaged the enemy briefly, and withdrew. We engaged in these limited-objective attacks over the next eight weeks. I later learned that we were part of a systematic campaign along the entire Eighth Army front over a two-month period to straighten out our combat line. During that time, I participated in probably fifteen or twenty different offensive operations.

I remember one mission very well. We were advancing against a North Korean position and taking intense fire. When my platoon machine gunner was wounded, I ordered my radio operator to take up the .30 caliber machine gun. As we advanced up a ridge, he was shot dead and fell on top of me. Incidents like that helped season me in a short period of time. You learn fast, you learn well, or you die early.

I Company was part of an offensive to seize three heavily wooded hills the army had named Queen, Nan, and William. These hills, held by Chinese troops, were approximately two hundred miles south of Pyong-yang, the capital of North Korea. I Company was assigned to take Objective Queen.

We were supposed to kick off at 6:00 AM but were delayed and initiated the attack at 6:45. I had under my temporary command K Company, an infantry platoon of approximately two hundred men. I was also given responsibility for the weapons platoon of I Company.

As we moved toward the hill, the Chinese put up massive resistance; they stopped us cold. They had Russian-made .30 caliber and .51 caliber machine guns. Each Chinese soldier carried five grenades about four inches in diameter, about the size of a coffee cup. The grenades had a wooden handle. A Chinese soldier could throw these grenades twenty-five yards. That meant they got on very intimate terms with us as we attempted to capture that hill.

Our offensive was stalled for six or seven hours; we gained only about two hundred feet of ground. I went back to consult Lieutenant Braim, the company commander.

"Well, Sam, I don't know what the hell we're gonna do. They got us stopped cold."

"Look, Paul, give me half an hour. Let me see what I can do with the left flank. I believe there's an opening,"

Another second lieutenant and I devised a plan to flank the Chinese on Objective Queen. We found a location where we could put .60 mm mortars not more than one hundred yards behind our men. There were a couple of other points where we could set recoilless rifles. I coordinated the fire of those weapons with our heavy weapons company. We were going to bring direct fire support onto the Chinese positions from various places on and around the battlefield. I coordinated the weapons attack with the company commander and the artillery liaison officers. The artillery barrage would begin with a star cluster, a pyrotechnic that would signal the beginning of our attack. At the same time, I would call in air strikes on the two hills beyond Queen because the enemy there was providing support to the Chinese troops.

At the proper time, I gave the signal for the star cluster. We moved out and, over the next hour, made amazingly swift progress, moving up around the Chinese with an intense amount of artillery support. We caught and killed about three hundred Chinese before they could retreat to the next hill. We took Objective Queen.

There was no time, however, for celebration. Chinese units on Nan and William, which had somehow survived our air strikes, counterattacked. The Chinese hit us with mortars all night long, inflicting numerous casualties, including the young second lieutenant who had helped me plan the attack on Objective Queen and commanded one of the rifle platoons in I Company. We also lost twenty infantrymen. My platoon lost nine of its thirty-two men. We took so many casualties that we consolidated the three original platoons into two effective rifle platoons. I took command of one of the consolidated platoons. Nonetheless, we held Objective Queen. That engagement led to my first valor decoration. I was awarded the Bronze Star for my conduct under fire. The greatest accolade, however, came from my men. After the attack on Objective Queen, my platoon gave me the nickname "Combat Kelly."

The general orders awarding me my first Bronze Star with a V device describes the event in more detail:

First Lt. Samuel E. Kelly distinguished himself by heroic action near Somak Tong, Korea, on 26 June 1951. His company had been assigned the mission of securing Objective Queen . . . he [Kelly] then moved up through the company until he reached a foremost position . . . with utter disregard for the heavy enemy fire concentrated on his position, he fully exposed himself many times to gain better observation of the effect of heavy weapons fire. . . . Lt. Kelly's heroic actions reflect the greatest credit on himself and the United States Infantry.

To this day, I don't know how I survived the engagement. I was under fire from the enemy. I was also alternately up ahead of the combat line directing mortar strikes from our artillery and leading the troops in the consolidated rifle platoon. I was one of the few people who didn't get hit by automatic weapons fire or mortars from the enemy or our own forces. We secured Objective Queen that night and walked up William and Nan the next day without a shot being fired.

I engaged in my share of combat in Korea, but I think the only time I was afraid was when I led my men across the Han River, just weeks after I had arrived in Korea. I was assigned to I Company and commanded First Platoon, about forty-five men. We had just gotten some replacements when the Chinese and North Koreans began chasing us. We were pulling back to adjust our line and had to cross the Han River. That river was tricky. You could cross at some points in two feet of water, and then you'd go downriver another thirty feet and the water would be over your head. We crossed in deep water.

I remember gathering my men and ordering them to hang on to the mess truck because it could float. I hung on because I couldn't swim. I was the only Kelly boy who hadn't learned to swim as a child. I'd go into shallow water as a kid, but I avoided deep water. Now it was all around me. I was scared, but I didn't let my men see it. We drank a lot of muddy water from the Han that day, but I didn't lose any of my platoon. We reformed south of the river and counterattacked, eventually taking back most of the ground we had lost to the enemy.

COMBAT KELLY

We dug in, waiting for the next assignment. It was there that I first learned from my platoon sergeant, Sergeant Tucker, how the troops felt about my leadership. Sergeant Tucker was a white airborne soldier. Weeks later, our conversations about airborne persuaded me that I should eventually add it to my military occupation specialty. The first night on Objective William, however, the sergeant noted that I had involved him and other noncommissioned officers in my plan to take Objective Queen.

"Well, Tucker," I responded, "I bring you in because you have the ability to teach me. You were here in Korea long before I arrived."

"No, no sir, you brought a lot of this with you." Tucker continued, "You're so different from the rest of these officers. The way you plan. All they want to do is run up the hill with rifles and hand grenades and shoot. They think that the only way you can fight a war is just through pushing ground troops and throwing grenades. They don't let the artillery or other mortar fire support directly, like you do, Lieutenant Kelly."

I was really proud of his compliment and pleased that I had the confidence of my men. After that conversation, we had coffee together while we were dug in on Objective William. I began to "mother" my men on Objective William. Joyce sent me some hot chocolate mix, which I prepared for them. The men liked my way of making it. I used the mix, and they contributed the chocolate bars that came in their rations. I'd put the bars and the mix in milk and hot water and make cocoa. Then I would invite them up to my forward observation post, my "hootch" as we called it, which was nothing more than a bunker well covered with timber and with the proper defensive fortifications around it. Four or five men at a time would come to my hootch to share Lieutenant Kelly's cocoa. Eventually, I made cocoa for the entire platoon.

My men and I became very close. We prayed together every day of combat, whether on our knees or just leaning against the wooden beam of a bunker. Sometimes men came to me for confession, often in tears. I'd put my arms around them and say, "Look, we're gonna die together, or we're going to make it together."

I challenged the men to understand what patriotism really meant. We agreed, there in a Korean bunker, that when we got home and retired from the army, we'd fly the American flag from Memorial Day to Veterans Day. I've kept my pledge right to this day. Also, even after my transfer to other units, I continued to say a daily prayer.

Through these simple acts in a combat zone, I developed a bond with my men.

After one of those sessions, Sergeant Tucker had tears in his eyes. I asked, "Tuck, what's the matter?"

"Well, sir," he slowly responded. "Can I say something to you?"

"Sure."

"You're a hell of a goddamn fighter." Then he added, "Nobody expected you as a colored officer to do what you've been doing. The men would follow you down the muzzle of a cannon."

He continued, "There's one thing I want you to know. I've been ordered by a battalion commander's representative to make reports on you while you're under fire and to describe how you react. I told the representative I didn't think it was right. Lieutenant Kelly, I want you to know and I don't give a damn if they know it or not. I think I owe it to you, given what the men think of you."

"Well, Tuck, I really appreciate that. Do you mind me sharing that with the battalion commander?"

He said he didn't.

I didn't show it to Tucker, but I was fuming at that point. I went to Lieutenant Braim, the company commander, and explained what I had learned. He said, "Well, hell, Sam, go ahead down the hill—it's only about one hundred yards from us—and take what time you need."

So I went down to discuss Tucker's confession with Battalion Commander Jesse Cooper. When I arrived, he was meeting with Lieutenant Colonel James Wesley Edwards, a tall, angular, slender North Carolinian. I walked up and waited until their conversation ended. I didn't know that the battalion command was rotating and that Colonel Edwards was to replace Colonel Cooper.

"Sir," I said, "I'd like to have a word with you if I may."

"Why, sure," Colonel Cooper responded. "I'm talking to the new battalion commander. He should hear whatever you want to say."

I should have been intimidated at the prospect of making my charge before two senior officers, but I was so angry I didn't think about the consequences at that moment.

"Well, sir, I understand that I am being spied on, and you're getting reports about my conduct under fire.

"Oh, I can see you've got a snake in your belly, don't you, Sam?"

"I sure do, sir."

"Well, spit it out, young man."

"I don't appreciate worth a damn that a battalion commander has an enlisted man spying on an officer and is getting personal reports as to my conduct under fire. If you had a problem with my conduct, I would think that you would assign an officer of my rank or better to investigate."

Colonel Cooper, who had been looking away from me, turned around. He put his hand on my shoulder and apologized. "You know," he began, "I've gotten reports on you over all of these weeks we've been together. And all I hear is you're just a fightin' sonofabitch. The infantry needs men like you, and I appreciate what you've done for the battalion. I want you to meet Lieutenant Colonel Edwards, the new battalion commander."

I met Colonel Edwards, who also apologized for the spying. Both of them agreed that it shouldn't have happened.

Then Colonel Cooper added what he claimed was his justification for his action. "You know, there's a colored boy over there in the Twenty-fifth Division, Twenty-fourth Regiment, who ran under fire," he began. "I just didn't know what I'd been given, because I hadn't had any Negro officers under my command."

"Well, sir, it would've been nice if you'd given me a chance," I responded.

"Well, that wasn't a chance I wanted to take with my men."

I then asked, "Well, sir, you want me to speak frankly?"

"Yes."

"I think that you don't have to call out a whole race of people and think they're all cowards. I already know there are a couple of white officers down in the battalion area who are counting out supplies or doing something other than what they were trained to do—lead rifle platoons. And they're back there because they're too afraid to go forward, and you've excused them from frontline duty."

Colonel Cooper admitted that was the case, and Colonel Edwards reached out and shook my hand.

Two weeks later, Colonel Edwards called me to his command post and told me he had a job for me. "I need a battalion intelligence officer, an S2. There is also a slot for a commander of K Company. Either of these is a captain's job. You should get your promotion within a matter of a few weeks. I'd like you to take either position," he said.

"Well, sir, where do you need me the most?"

"Sam, I'd like you to take K Company. This company's had a hard time. It's had a high casualty rate. Morale is not the greatest in the world."

"Sir, that's the one I'd like to take."

I was assigned to K Company because the company commander, a captain, had been killed. It was a typical battlefield promotion—an officer dies, and another, often junior, officer quickly fills his place. With this assignment, I had finally achieved one of the goals I'd had since Officer Candidate School, command of a company. I could now put some of my ideas about strategy and tactics into practice. I could also test my own leadership philosophy against the hard reality of command decision making. This is what I had trained to do.

During the next three and a half weeks, I met with the men of K Company individually as well as collectively as platoons and squads. They already knew that I would have artillery support and tactical air support anytime I committed the company to attack. The weapons company would have the armor it needed—the mortars, machine guns, recoilless rifles. Once we attacked, we would light up the ground in front of us with friendly fire and walk up behind it. When we trained, I took the lead in the instruction and maneuvered with them. I taught them the capabilities of the rifle platoon.

However, we didn't have much time for training. We were in reserve for four weeks, and then I was called to battalion headquarters, where Colonel Edwards ordered me to transport K Company about 250 miles south of Pork Chop Hill to save two infantry companies that were pinned down by the North Koreans.

I returned to my troops and gave orders to pack up. Trucks pulled up, and we loaded the entire battalion into a convoy of fifty trucks. I was in the lead vehicle. We rode for seven hours under a clear June sky from the eastern central front to the western central front. The convoy pulled into a large area of dried rice paddies.

I led K Company in the darkness with the Korean guides and got the troops in position. At about four in the morning, I heard someone whispering my name. "Lieutenant Kelly, Lieutenant Kelly!"

I said, "Yeah? I'm here, I'm here."

He came to my tent, holding a candle, and asked, "Lieutenant Kelly. Is he here?"

The soldier was looking directly at me. He obviously did not expect to see a black officer.

I said, "Yes, I'm Lieutenant Kelly."

He asked me again, thinking I had not heard him correctly. "I'm looking for Lieutenant Kelly."

"Soldier, you have found him," I responded in a testy voice.

"Sir, the battalion commander wants me to take you over to his command post. He's got the other commanders over there."

"OK."

I followed him into another dark tent. I could barely make out the figures. Everyone was operating under candlelight. The tent held the operations officer, three other rifle company commanders, and the heavy weapons company commander. The artillery officer was there, along with four or five officers, including the tactical air coordinator.

Colonel Edwards, who had driven all night ahead of us, was in charge. He introduced me to the rest of the men, then grabbed me by the shoulder, and said, "Sam," as he shook hands with me. "I want you to lead K tomorrow morning at 06:00."

"You want me to lead, sir?" I asked in complete surprise.

"Yes, that's right. How's K Company? Are they ready?"

"They're more than ready, Colonel." I'll never forget the deep feeling of pressure, the anxiety that swept through my body. So I swallowed hard and said, "OK, sir, we'll be there."

Colonel Edwards told me where my men would be positioned and what time I was scheduled to cross the line of departure.

I looked at the map, and said, "Sir, I'm gonna lead with two platoons. I will be with the lead platoon."

"The lead platoon?"

"Yes, sir, I have to know the terrain. I've got to know what's happening up front or I won't have the observation necessary to dispatch my other platoons for the best offensive operation."

"OK, but I would normally expect you to be behind, at least in the second platoon."

"No, I can't do it that way. The terrain is too wooded, and I can't command if I don't have the observation."

Colonel Edwards reluctantly agreed.

I returned to K Company, gathered my platoon leaders, and gave them the orders. After sketching the operation on my map and on the ground, I told them what I was going to do. I would lead with my old platoon, the first platoon, with the second platoon on my right. A third rifle platoon would follow in reserve, no more than fifty yards behind us. I told Lieutenant Schauss, who commanded Third Platoon, that I wanted him to be able to move quickly and effectively.

Company K woke at about four thirty and had a breakfast of C rations while I checked the supplies. I ordered the men to carry two bandoliers, one across each shoulder, forming an X on their chests. I checked their waist belts and ammunition pouches; I wanted them to have eight clips of rifle ammunition and two fragmentary grenades hooked to their harnesses on their packs. We were overloaded, and I knew it. I also ordered them to fix bayonets before we crossed the line of departure. We then assembled about forty-five minutes before crossing the line of departure, approximately one hundred yards ahead. We pulled up in an assembly area, and I moved off in my first combat operation as K Company commander.

We crossed the line of departure as scheduled at 06:00, two platoons abreast. One, which I was leading, veered slightly to the right, on its way up the valley with a river about one hundred yards wide to our right flank. Hill 750 was directly to our left front. As we crossed the line of departure, the battalion commander, Colonel Edwards, gave a ceremonial wave.

Moving forward initially, we did pretty well. I spread my troops out so that one round of mortars wouldn't take out four or five soldiers. Then, about seventy-five yards into our advance, we came under a hail of mortar fire and long-range .51 caliber machine-gun fire. We hit the ground. I located the enemy's machine guns, on Hill 750, and called for an air strike. Almost immediately, there was a big boom, and the enemy guns went silent.

I was also able to get 4.2 mortar fire from the chemical mortar platoon. As they fired over our heads, we moved up pretty sharply. We hit the dirt again when we took additional enemy ground fire. I located the guns and called fire on those positions. Then I gave the order to run forward, leading the platoon around to the enemy's right flank as the second platoon followed closely behind. We outflanked the enemy on Hill 750. This was a textbook-perfect maneuver; it looked like a chapter out of the Fort Benning combat manual. My training was paying off.

We occupied Hill 750 and dug in for the night. The next day, it was our turn to provide supporting fire for the left battalion of the regiment. We inflicted some heavy losses, repulsed the enemy, and rescued some of the soldiers of the two trapped infantry companies. The enemy withdrew under a barrage of aircraft fire, which continued to hammer them as they retreated.

All in all, we had a pretty easy time of it. The men felt so good about the day's work that they yelled and hollered. I had one man killed, Lieutenant Schauss, and two wounded. I was sorry for that; the lieutenant was a brave officer. We were also very lucky. In one of our maneuvers, we ran through an unplotted enemy minefield where one or two men were struck by shrapnel. I was later told that it was surprising I hadn't lost a third of my command. That news didn't make me feel very good.

A DESERTER

The company had come through in very good shape, even though I'd been distracted by an incident that happened just before the attack. A young white soldier requested to speak to me.

"What about, soldier?"

"Well, sir, you're the new company commander. I want you to know that I have anxiety reactions, and I'd like not to have to go on this mission."

"What do you mean, anxiety reactions, soldier? We all have those. I haven't attacked anywhere since I've been over here that I didn't have anxiety reactions, but our duty's our duty. And this is what we have to do because we're soldiers."

He cried a bit, and I said, "Look, I'll tell you what I'm going to do. I'm going to assign you to the carrying party. I'll put you under the sergeant who supervises the carriers. It's a big job, and it's an important job. And I want you to know, I want the ammunition. You will take your orders from him, on time, and you stay close to him. If you do that, you should be all right. We'll talk about this anxiety reaction thing after this mission."

He agreed, and I thought that was the end of it.

After the attack began, however, I found out that another corporal had taken his job. The young man had deserted his post. We fought the Koreans that night and got down to perhaps two clips of rifle ammunition, sixteen rounds of M1 rifle ammunition per man. The machine guns were woefully short. We were under attack most of the night and finally got resupplied, but the young soldier had left us in the lurch while we were under attack, and there was no excuse for that.

I didn't see him again until his court-martial in Seoul. I was asked if I was sure that he had deserted, and I told them that I was. The president of the General Court then asked me what I thought of him as a soldier. I responded without hesitation, "I think he should be shot. He left the company at a point when we could have been annihilated because we were short on ammunition and unable to defend ourselves except with bayonets. That's not the way to win a war." The man was convicted of desertion and sentenced to life in prison.

After the battle for Hill 750, I led K Company in a series of limited-objective attacks. One was the "jerkwater" operation through Inchon. General Ridgway's operation called for the Eighth Army to land forces just west of Seoul at Inchon, where it would flank at least three Chinese corps. The plan worked. We had them in a vise and inflicted major casualties on the North Korean and Chinese armies. We felt pretty good about this operation. We were making very good progress, and our casualty rate was quite low.

We finally pulled up just south of the 38th parallel, north and east of Kimpo airfield, and went into a static defensive posture. Our objective

SAM KELLY, LEFT CENTER, WITH A CHINESE PRISONER IN MAY 1951. COURTESY OF THE KELLY FAMILY

SAM KELLY INSPECTING GUN AND AMMUNITION IN A BUNKER POSITION IN KOREA IN 1951. COURTESY OF THE KELLY FAMILY.

LIEUTENANT KELLY OBSERVING THE CHINESE POSITION FROM A DEEP COMMUNICATION TRENCH IN 1952. COURTESY OF THE KELLY FAMILY.

was to secure the best terrain, and I assigned my men to go on combat patrols scouting forward positions. Occasionally, we captured enemy troops for questioning. We also got into some pretty nasty rifle duels with the North Koreans and the Chinese.

I had commanded K Company for three months when a rumor began circulating that the command of M Company, the heavy weapons company of the battalion, was rotating. The commander, Captain Lloyd Patch, was a West Point officer whose father was a lieutenant general and whose uncle was a four-star army commander. My effective utilization of Captain Patch's indirect-fire weapons, mortars, recoilless rifles, and machine-gun platoons had made him look good.

Captain Patch recommended to the battalion commander, Colonel Edwards, that I take command of the battalion's heavy weapons company. Shortly thereafter, I assumed command of M Company, Third Battalion, Nineteenth Infantry Regiment, Twenty-fourth Infantry Division. I conducted operations for the next several months with M Company.

AN INTEGRATED ARMY IN KOREA

By 1952, I had begun to notice more discussions about race relations among the enlisted men. I was one of only two African American officers in the entire division of eighteen thousand soldiers. Lieutenant John McAdams, Twenty-first Infantry Regiment, from Washington, D.C., was the other. Having successfully commanded troops in battle, I was called in to discuss ways to make integration more effective.

The units I commanded were 48 to 55 percent black. When I commanded K Company, two of my four platoon sergeants were black. When I was with I Company, three of the platoon sergeants were black, as were half of the enlisted men. I am not sure if the entire army in Korea was like this, but I don't think I was assigned to these commands because of the disproportionate number of black soldiers in them.

In fact, I noted something entirely different among these African American soldiers. When I came around, they seemed to exhibit a feeling of pride. That pride extended to the noncommissioned officers as well. One of my platoon sergeants, Sergeant Taylor, said, "We heard you were coming. We are awfully proud of you."

The black sergeants who worked for me had a particular loyalty. One of them said to me, "Sir, we got your back covered. Whatever it is that you want done, let me know, 'cause if the other platoons can't do it, I will take my platoon and get it done."

There was competitiveness, as each of the noncoms seemingly wanted to make me look good because I was the only black officer in the regiment. That came through time and time again. I couldn't help but wonder about the veracity of the often repeated description of the all-black Ninety-second Division in World War II as unreliable soldiers. I also thought of the time when Colonel Cooper justified spying on me because another black officer had cut and run. There was a kind of unwritten agreement among the enlisted men, the noncoms, and me that black soldiers in this unit would do nothing to bring shame on the race.

While I was commander of M Company, my relationship with the new regimental commander, Colonel John P. "Poopie" (as we called him in a joking way) Connor, grew quite close. Colonel Connor was a West Point graduate, class of 1942. I remember once when I was checking one of my machine-gun positions and encountered him up the mountainside. After we talked briefly, he asked, "Look, you got a drink of water?"

I gave him my canteen. He took a sip and said, "Oh, my gosh, what's this?"

I had forgotten to tell him that my canteen was always filled with grape Kool-Aid. My wife, Joyce, used to send me packages of Kool-Aid. Since it made the local water, which we had to treat with halazone tablets, taste better, I developed the habit of drinking Kool-Aid. I sold Colonel Connor on the Kool-Aid idea, and he started doing the same thing.

Colonel Connor told me how glad he was that I was with the regiment and doing such a fine job. I did not know at the time that he had already requested that I receive a Bronze Star for continued outstanding service as a troop commander in a regiment. The colonel did other things to make life easier for me in Korea. He told me, "Sam, if there is anything you want when you get back stateside, you give me a call. And we'll do it. I mean anything."

"I want to go airborne, sir."

"Let me know wherever you are," he responded. "I'll get you into airborne school, and when you complete it, I want you to serve with me."

Colonel Connor was a serious, tough commander. He was also a man who worked hard to promote the integration of U.S. forces. I respected him for both of those reasons.

GOING HOME

In the spring of 1952, we received an alert order that the Twenty-fourth Division was going to be replaced in Korea by the Sunburst Fortieth Infantry Division out of California. I don't think anyone in my regiment regretted the order. I had been in a combat zone for an entire year and had established my leadership skills in combat. My regimental commander, Colonel John Connor, said I was the best rifle company commander and the best heavy weapons company commander of the division. I had a great deal of confidence in my own military ability, not because I was some natural leader of men but because of the tremendous

LIEUTENANT KELLY ON R&R IN YOKAHAMA, JAPAN, IN NOVEMBER
1951. COURTESY OF THE KELLY FAMILY.

training I had gotten at Fort Benning. When we left our position, the guns of our heavy weapons company were at that time the farthest north of any U.S. forces in Korea.

Duty, honor, country meant a great deal to me. I felt enormous pride when I came out of combat successfully. My medals proved that I had served my country honorably. In those days, people did not question the president, the commander in chief. We followed his orders and the orders of all officers of superior rank. The widely held view at the time was "My country, right or wrong; if you don't like it, get out." I proudly subscribed to that view.

BROTHERS JAMES KELLY, CAPTAIN SAMUEL E. KELLY, ROBERT KELLY, JOHN KELLY, AND BILL KELLY IN STAMFORD IN 1953. COURTESY OF THE KELLY FAMILY.

From the time I donned the uniform of a U.S. Army soldier in 1944, I had an obligation to my country, to defend it from all enemies, foreign and domestic. There has been enormous ambivalence about the United States military among African Americans. We may have understood racial injustice both in the military and in the civilian world, but we have always been proud of the soldiers and officers who served their country despite that injustice. That pride was evident in the Civil War when nearly 200,000 African Americans fought to preserve the United States; it was evident during the post–Civil War period with the Buffalo Soldiers in the west. That sense of pride was clearly evident in World War II, when 1 million black men and women wore the uniforms of the various services. It was certainly evident in the 1950s when I was a young officer.

I did not die in combat and come home on my shield. That made me all the more determined to fight for racial justice, a struggle that would, at times, be as difficult as anything I had faced in Korea.

CHAPTER 7

A Career Soldier

When I returned to the United States in May 1952, I was assigned to Fort Monmouth, New Jersey, a U.S. Army Signal Corps center. The center needed officers who were experienced in sports programs, and I was made the assistant athletic director. The captaincy that had been promised to me in Korea finally caught up with me in June 1952.

Shortly thereafter, the Signal Corps center arranged to have a parade of eight thousand troops in my honor, and I was awarded a second Bronze Star with a cluster for my service in the Korean War.

BILLY

I was delighted to be back in the States. I was reunited with Joyce, who gave birth to our first child, a son, William Lyle Kelly, on December 18, 1952, at Fort Monmouth. Billy was a tiny baby, just under five pounds, and remained in the hospital for a few extra days. When he came home, he needed to be fed every two hours; we were elated when he was able to take a full ounce of formula. I took the night feeding shift so Joyce could rest. I must have walked him hundreds of miles over the first six months.

A few weeks after Billy's birth, I became the director of athletics for Fort Monmouth. Major General K. B. Laughton, the commander at Fort Monmouth, called me in to discuss racial integration in the army. He was concerned about the morale of the black troops and their interactions with white soldiers on the base. When he asked me what I felt about racial conditions at his post, I told him I thought things were moving ahead nicely for black soldiers, not that there weren't problems. As long as segregation and racism existed in American society, there would be some problems in the army, which, after all, was a reflection of the larger society. But the word was out among white officers that they had to treat

WILLIAM LYLE KELLY IN FORT MONMOUTH IN 1953. COURTESY
OF THE KELLY FAMILY.

black troops fairly. That was a far cry from the pre-1948 days in the segregated army.

Shortly after our conversation, Major General Laughton asked me to
accompany him to the post stockade, where about fifty African American soldiers were incarcerated. We interviewed every one of them, all
night long, until five o'clock the next morning. The commanding general asked each soldier, "What can I do to keep the next man from going
to the stockade?"

About two-thirds of the way through his interview, one black soldier
became outlandishly cruel and crude. I lost it and had to get in his face.
I stood him to attention and told him, "The general doesn't have to be
here asking you this question. He's trying to save other soldiers from
making the same mistakes that you are making. And for that, you should
appreciate him as I do."

After I chastised him, the young man hung his head, and said, "I do,
Captain Kelly, I do."

Following the interviews, Major General Laughton implemented sev-

CAPTAIN KELLY IN FORT MONMOUTH, NEW JERSEY, IN 1952. COURTESY OF
THE KELLY FAMILY.

eral policy changes, including giving some priority in on-post housing
assignments to black officers and noncoms who faced housing discrimination in the New Jersey neighborhoods off post.

GOING AIRBORNE

Overall, I found a good heartbeat developing in the military in terms
of integration. Wherever I was stationed during the 1950s, things were
opening up in a more fair and equitable way, so much so that, after
nearly two years at Fort Monmouth, I called my old friend, Colonel John

"Poopie" Connor, now the chief of staff of the Eleventh Airborne Division at Fort Campbell.

"Sir, I want to go airborne."

"Sam, well, by God, it's about time!"

Within four weeks, I was packed up, on my way to jump school with my orders for the Eleventh Airborne Division, Fort Campbell, Kentucky.

I made my way from Fort Monmouth to Fort Campbell via Charleston, West Virginia, because I had arranged for Joyce and Billy to stay with my brother, Jim, and his family; at that time, Jim was dean at West Virginia State College in Institute.

Before going to Fort Campbell, however, I was required to attend Parachute Infantry and Jumpmaster School at Fort Benning, Georgia, for training. Initial training included running five miles each day, then training on a stationary mock aircraft, executing at least three hundred parachute landing falls (PLFs) a day for five days from a height of six feet. Next, we jumped with static chutes from the thirty-four-foot tower, to perfect aircraft exiting technique. In order to qualify, we had to complete at least twenty-five out of one hundred jumps perfectly. Then we moved to the one-hundred-foot tower, where we were pulled up wearing a regular chute and required to complete twenty perfect jumps. From that tower, we progressed immediately to the C-119 aircraft, completing five jumps from two thousand feet. After passing those challenges, I was awarded my jump wings on February 5, 1954.

Jumpmaster School was the next hurdle, requiring even more intensive physical exertion. A jumpmaster designation qualifies a man to command a mission and direct troops to jump. This training included five jumps with one hundred pounds of equipment attached to our harnesses and three night jumps. After I received my parachute infantry and jumpmaster designations, my family rejoined me at Fort Campbell. VIP quarters had been reserved for us, and we moved into a beautiful three-bedroom home. Colonel John P. Connor told me to take as much time as I needed to settle in, because when I started work I would rarely get time off.

I got my family squared away in a of couple weeks, canceled my leave, and reported for duty. I met Colonel Connor at the division headquarters, where we discussed assignments. He wanted me to go on the division general staff, which was quite a compliment.

I told Colonel Connor I thought I needed more experience. So he took me to the 188th Airborne Infantry Regiment, Colonel Harry Lombard commanding. Colonel Lombard asked me to take a job as assistant operations officer for plans and training, a job normally assigned to a major in a regiment.

Although I appreciated the offer, I told him that since this was my first parachute infantry airborne assignment, I preferred to go to a battalion and asked if he had a heavy weapons company that was open. He and his operations officer, who came with us to Colonel Lombard's office, laughed at my question. Then Colonel Lombard said, "I got the worst goddamn heavy weapons company in the division. I just fired a company commander who's down there now, and came near to court-martialing him."

"Well, sir, I'll take it."

Colonel Lombard looked at me and said, "You're serious?"

"Yes, sir, I am. I'll take it."

So I took command of Delta Company, 188th Airborne Infantry Regiment. A sorrier group of men I've not seen, then or now. We had an awful lot of work to do. I talked to every man individually throughout the first week, interviewing each one of them. "What's wrong with the company? What would you like to do better?"

I interviewed my sergeants and noncommissioned officers. Finally, I interviewed the captain, the outgoing company commander who signed over the property of the command to me. This man was really a first-class jackass.

He was responsible for turning over a property book that accounted for all the guns, equipment, and paraphernalia the company used. It seemed the captain was short some equipment. He had one of the soldiers "accidentally" drop his property book in a bucket of water, making it impossible to determine the inventory of company equipment. I called the regimental commander and told him the first thing I'd like to have done was to remove this captain from my company area.

I had some good men in Delta Company, however, including an

excellent first sergeant and two very good platoon sergeants. I gave all the men the option of transferring out of Delta Company within ninety days. Few took that option. Meanwhile, the company was preparing for an army training test. We had a full plate.

A NEW GENERATION OF BLACK OFFICERS

I also came in contact with a new set of black parachute officers at Fort Campbell. They were good soldiers, very aggressive types, very sharp. Some had come in after President Truman's executive order. We were all very pleased with the integration of the army because now we would have a better opportunity to compete. We realized that things were not perfect. Off post, we still could not enter some of the places that admitted white officers. On post, however, we could go to any of the officers' clubs and do what we wanted to do. We had some very good times at Fort Campbell.

Black men in uniform were quite aware of the growing protest movement across the United States in the 1950s. Like the rest of the nation, we followed the *Brown v. Board of Education* decision and its aftermath. We knew about the Montgomery bus boycott and that young preacher, Martin Luther King, Jr. Almost any time a cluster of black officers gathered, we'd talk about these episodes and the growing civil rights movement. We were especially proud that civilian blacks were showing some backbone and were protesting.

The reverberations from these protests hit the military, and we found that good black officers were being sought by the various services. Those of us who were doing our duty often got breaks that we hadn't ever expected.

I don't think there was a black officer in the U.S. Army who wanted a return to the days of racial segregation. Nonetheless, whenever we were on military posts like Fort Campbell, we sought one another out. Before 1948, that was not a problem. When the army was segregated, we had a black officers' club because we were not allowed to go into the white officers' club. With the desegregation orders of 1948, Fort Benning's main club, the Patton House, was open to all officers. When I was first assigned to Fort McClellan, Alabama, in 1945, we were not able to use the main

officers' club and instead went to a shabby facility on the edge of the
base, a reconverted fire station, which we jokingly called "Uncle Tom's
Cabin." When I returned to Fort McClellan in the 1950s, the Cabin was
gone. I noted that, especially in the South, the army was always far ahead
of the surrounding civilian communities in desegregating facilities.

Somewhat paradoxically, after integration there seemed to be more
camaraderie among black officers. Whether at Fort Benning, Fort
McClellan, Fort Monmouth, or Fort Campbell, we would always find
one another. Often we'd have monthly social get-togethers, with each
officer taking a turn hosting these "NAACP meetings," as we jocularly
referred to them. Although there would be drinking and dancing, we'd
also get down and talk about how we were being treated or what we
thought of the commander. As I look back on it now, I realize that
the amount of information we officers shared at these gatherings was
stunning.

It did not matter what a person's job was. Chemical Corps officers,
Signal Corps officers, infantry officers all passed on their stories and
information. They could tell you how they were treated and how integration was really proceeding in the army. We came to the conclusion
that, despite some initial problems, such as the enlisted man who was
assigned to spy on me in Korea, by the mid-1950s, things were going very
well for African American officers. We felt that opportunities for us were
quite open. There was a collective sense of relief; a black officer could be
a professional and would be treated with respect by those who ranked
both above and below him.

LITTLE ROCK, 1957

The only event I can recall during this period that negatively affected the
morale of black officers and soldiers involved the desegregation crisis at
Central High School in Little Rock, Arkansas, in 1957. The 101st Airborne
Division was alerted to send troops to Little Rock to escort nine black
students who were attempting to integrate the all-white school, but
President Dwight Eisenhower ordered that the division's black troops
be left behind at Fort Campbell, sending instead only white soldiers. As
I look back now, more than half a century later, I understand why he

might have thought that sending in only white troops might reduce the tension and reestablish peace and stability in the city. But I had great problems with the decision then, and it still hurts me now. At the time, I thought it was a horrible thing to do, a slap in the face of all the black soldiers and officers in the 101st Airborne who were doing their jobs and, in the process, proving on a daily basis why integration works. I think their presence among the troops dispatched to Little Rock would have been a powerful signal to the integrationists, the segregationists, and the rest of the world that was watching the crisis and the Eisenhower administration's handling of it.

Ultimately, Central High School did integrate. Yet this exclusion from duty was all the more hurtful because the mission itself had been to further the integration of American society. Black commissioned officers and noncommissioned officers whom I knew during this period wanted one major thing to happen, integration, which they assumed meant being treated like anybody else. We could successfully compete with white officers, we believed, but only if we had a fair chance.

The practical integration of the military came about during the early 1950s before most of the street protests, marches, and demonstrations that would rock the nation a decade later. We African American officers felt we were earning the respect of all the officers and enlisted men in the U.S. Army. Through our performance, we were proving we could excel and that we had a stake in the United States of America.

Of the dozens of black infantry officers with whom I soldiered, I would have to look hard to find two or three "eight balls," which was what we called the few officers who were not outstanding servicemen. We were proud of our skills as professional soldiers and officers; moreover, we all felt a sacred duty to our country. We would defend it and stand by it irrespective of its terrible history of racial injustice and regardless of the maltreatment we had received. The United States of America, we all swore, was our country, right or wrong. We would stick with the land of our birth; it was the only home we knew, and we were willing to defend it until the day we died. "My country, right or wrong," was not a hollow slogan. Yes, there would be negative comments about individual incidents of discrimination or unfair treatment—I recall uttering some myself—but I believe the bulk of the professional officers, noncoms, and enlisted men felt the same way I did.

In 1954, I had the good fortune of taking Delta Company, First Battalion, heavy weapons company, through its training test. Out of roughly twenty heavy weapons companies in the divisions and brigades, we came out on top. I commanded that company for about ten wonderful months until I was pulled up to staff headquarters, where I was designated the plans, training, and operations officer. I was a captain in a major's job. This became a pattern, and for the rest of my career in the army, I would be given an assignment normally handled by someone at least one rank above me.

In 1955, I transferred to the 508th Regimental Combat Team (the "Red Devils") at Fort Campbell. The 508th was slated to go to Japan in the next few months. When I moved over to the 508th, more than half of my heavy weapons company voluntarily transferred with me. I took H Company, the heavy weapons company, and the 508th Airborne Regimental Combat Team through the same training I had given Delta Company. The gunners in one of these competitions transferred to go overseas with me. I signed them up to be a part of my new company, and we scored highest on the training test, just like Delta Company, First Battalion.

The division commander at Fort Campbell, General Wayne Smith, summoned me to division headquarters to celebrate our achievements. He had two pictures of Captain Samuel Kelly, one on the right of his desk and one on the left, taken as I was receiving the two awards as the heavy weapons company commander from him.

BRENDA AND SHARON

Soon after my arrival in Beppu on Kyushu, Japan, the battalion commander, Colonel Edwin H. "Pat" Patterson, asked me to serve as his operations officer. I became the operations officer for Second Battalion, 508th Airborne Regimental Combat Team, and served in that capacity for the next few years.

My second tour in Japan was wonderful. We had a beautiful home off post and two maids. Life was very good for me and my family, which at the time was about to grow, as Joyce was pregnant again. Late in the pregnancy, Joyce was experiencing a little extra pressure, and I took her to the dispensary. I then went on a scheduled parachute drop on the edge of Oita, on Kyushu, one of the southernmost islands of Japan. We were scheduled to drop about five hundred troops in a training session. During the exercise, I received a distress call from Colonel Patterson, my battalion commander, requesting that I report to his headquarters immediately.

"I'm in the drop zone control; I can't leave," I responded. "This is my duty today."

"Well, Captain, get somebody else to supervise the drop. This is important. I'm going to send a helicopter after you."

I transferred my responsibility to a young lieutenant and took the helicopter. The battalion commander met me at the pad and took me to his headquarters. He asked me about an operation I was preparing for in the Mori corridor in northwestern Kyushu. I noticed he was jittery. We stopped by the officers' club for a cup of coffee, which he didn't finish, and then he said, "Let's take a ride, Sam. I want to keep talking about our operation in the Mori corridor. I have questions about how many aircraft we're going to have."

We drove to the top of the hill, made a left turn, and went down the hill. About a quarter mile away, I saw a group of officers and ladies. Sensing that something was afoot, I asked, "What's that down there, Colonel Patterson?"

"I guess some people are meeting down there."

"Heck, they're our battalion wives and officers."

"I'll be goddamned," he said. "You're right!"

I saw Joyce standing in the middle of the group. Everyone was laughing and having a good time, and she was holding a bouquet of flowers.

I said, "Hi, how are you doing?"

"Oh, we're doing fine," she responded.

"What's going on?"

"Well, honey, I have a surprise for you."

"What is it?"

"We're going to have twins."

I was incredibly happy, but they had to get Joyce off the post right away since there was only one incubator on hand. Less than six hours later, Joyce was flown to Fukuoka Army Hospital on the northwestern coast of Kyushu, about 150 miles from our location. I was concerned about not being close to Joyce just when she was about to give birth.

Three days later, a solution presented itself. Captain Jim Martin, the

BRENDA JOYCE AND SHARON YVONNE KELLY IN INSTITUTE, WEST VIRGINIA, IN MARCH 1958.
COURTESY OF THE KELLY FAMILY.

commander of the helicopter company supporting our regimental combat team, who also had a pregnant wife at Fukuoka, said, "Sam, I've got a Bell helicopter available. Do you want to take a chance? We're socked in due to the weather. I warn you, we'll have to skip rope to get there, over the hills and down the meadows, over the rice paddies."

Not caring about the potential danger, I said, "Let's go."

We hedgehopped all the way to Fukuoka, nearly clipping some trees a time or two, but we got there. Captain Martin's wife and baby were already waiting near the entrance to the hospital. I went up to find Joyce. Little did I know that our twins had been born while Captain Martin and I were en route to the hospital. As I sat with Joyce, the hospital nurses brought out two beautiful girls, Brenda Joyce and Sharon Yvonne Kelly, who were born on March 7, 1956. We were now a family of five.

Family life for us in Japan in the mid-1950s was good. My career as a professional soldier was proceeding successfully as well. We went on military operations to places such as Bangkok, Thailand, and our battalion won awards for parading and combat readiness.

To our surprise, after one year, we were ordered to return to Fort Campbell. The army had decided to reactivate the 101st Airborne Division, which had become famous in World War II for the defense of Bastogne, in Belgium, when its commander, General Anthony Clement McAuliffe, responded to a German surrender request with one word: "Nuts."

I had a new assignment as the operations officer with the 506th Battle Group. The commander was a West Pointer, Colonel "Red" Minor. This division had the key role of developing new combat deployment techniques for infantry forces and evaluating the weapons systems that supported them in combat. We were to create a rapid, highly mobile force capable of moving by air over significant distances to areas where combat operations were imminent. We were trained to seize a piece of ground, hold it, and, when necessary, withdraw from it in a matter of minutes.

Although we didn't realize it at the time, we were helping to create the new post–Korean War global army that could be deployed quickly on any continent to meet any situation. This is the army that would fight both Iraq wars nearly half a century later. This was hard, challenging work that forced us to think differently and creatively about strategy and tactics. I loved it.

WEST VIRGINIA STATE COLLEGE

Even as I assumed new responsibilities as the brigade operations officer, I sought to broaden my education. I enrolled in two college courses that met two nights a week at Fort Campbell. It was the first time I had been in classes for college credit since my nights at the University of Washington in 1949. The professor was from Austin Peay State University in Clarksville, Tennessee, which, under its "separate but equal" policy would not grant me credit. Instead, my credits would be issued by Tennessee State University in Nashville, a colored school. The fact that I had successfully competed with the best and the brightest in my high school and up through the various military ranks convinced me that I was well prepared for college work and eventually graduate school. I was now a full-time officer and part-time college student.

I asked to be assigned to West Virginia State College in Institute, West Virginia, just outside of Charleston, for military science duty. I figured being on a college campus would help me get a college diploma. Normally, a college degree was a prerequisite for duty with the Reserve Officer Training Corps (ROTC), but because of my military record, that requirement was waived. In addition, my brother, James Kelly, was personnel dean and chair of the Philosophy Department at West Virginia State College. I also knew West Virginia State's president, William J. L. Wallace. President Wallace was delighted to have me on the college staff, and I stayed at West Virginia State for five pleasant years, from 1957 to 1962, as a military science instructor and commandant of cadets.

My years at West Virginia State were another turning point in my life and career. I encountered wonderful black professors, including Dr. Herman G. Cannady, Dr. Robert L. Clark, Dr. Loratius L. McKenzie, and Dr. Sophia Nelson. However, I can think of no greater thrill in all my life than to have my brother, Jim, teach me philosophy. Students I have taught over my fifty-year career have often told me that they most admired my interest in helping and encouraging them to grow professionally and personally. I didn't develop this characteristic on my own; I merely followed the examples of interest in and love for students that I saw among Jim and other professors at West Virginia State. I noted the pride and satisfaction generated in those professors when they saw their students succeed. After watching them teach, I realized that I had discovered what I intended to do for the rest of my life.

One of the highlights of my stay in West Virginia was getting to ask a question of the future president of the United States, John Fitzgerald Kennedy. Massachusetts senator Kennedy and Minnesota senator Hubert H. Humphrey were battling for the 1960 Democratic presidential nomination, and West Virginia was a crucial state for both candidates. I attended a Kennedy political rally in April 1960. I was one of the few black faces in the crowd, and dressed in my army uniform, I stood out even more. When the time for questions rolled around, I asked candidate Kennedy, who was making his case as a liberal, "If you are a true liberal, why do you spend so much time with the governor of Alabama?"

I remember his response to this day. "Well, Captain, Roy Wilkins says I'm a liberal." Wilkins was the executive secretary of the National Association for the Advancement of Colored People (NAACP).

"That doesn't make it so," I quipped. The crowd of faculty and students laughed at my remark.

About an hour later, Robert Kennedy tracked me down in the crowd, shook hands with me, and asked some casual questions. He then said, "Oh, I see you're airborne."

"I wouldn't be anything else."

We exchanged a few more pleasantries and then parted. I never saw the Kennedys again.

A PROMOTION AND A COLLEGE DEGREE

I received my promotion to major during my first year at West Virginia State. On June 1, 1959, I earned a BA degree from the college, becoming the third Kelly son to obtain a college degree. I also earned a master's degree in history in August 1960 while I was assigned to West Virginia State, driving the fifty-mile, two-hour round-trip three nights a week, including during summer, to Marshall University in Huntington, West Virginia. In 1962, I earned a BS in education at West Virginia State.

Family life was great in Institute, West Virginia. The town of Institute is about eight miles north of Charleston, West Virginia, in the narrow Kanawha River Valley. Almost everyone who lived in Institute, a town of less than a thousand people, was affiliated with the university.

Joyce and I watched over our three children, Brenda Joyce, Sharon Yvonne, and Billy, who by this time had been diagnosed as developmentally delayed. As the kids grew older and occupied less of her time, Joyce was able to return to college at West Virginia State and complete her degree. While in college, Joyce, who was an honor student in Spanish and English, determined that she wanted to teach English and Romance languages in the public school system. She briefly taught in and served as a librarian at Nitro Middle School in Institute.

I also pledged predominantly black Omega Psi Phi fraternity at West

Virginia State. I "crossed over," as we used to say, when I was still an undergraduate, just before I received my BA degree in 1959. I was not the typical pledge, since I was also on the faculty as head of the ROTC. Moreover, I was a thirty-two-year-old captain in the U.S. Army and would soon be a major. I pledged partly because fraternities and sororities seemed an important part of college life for the undergraduates and the faculty. I concluded my tour of duty at West Virginia State College in the summer of 1962, when Billy was nine and the twins were six.

RETURNING TO KOREA

My next destination was Korea, where I was assigned to the Seventh Infantry Division. I volunteered to go to Korea again because I had decided to retire after twenty years instead of staying in for thirty. This pivotal decision was based on Joyce's deteriorating health due to rheumatoid arthritis and Billy's developmental disabilities. At that time, the army did not have programs and services to meet Billy's special needs, but while in West Virginia, I had learned that Billy's needs could be better met in Seattle. So I went back to Korea on a thirteen-month "undesirable tour" in order to ultimately get a stateside assignment back home in Seattle, where I hoped to become a public-school teacher and maybe eventually a principal.

Joyce and I had already decided Seattle would be our permanent home. I don't think there was any other city in the nation that we seriously considered. We made our commitment to the city permanent in 1962 when we built our first home on Thistle Street in the south end of Seattle. In 1963, Joyce was hired as the first black public-school teacher on Mercer Island, a wealthy Seattle suburb. She and I joked that the school board had apparently thought that, with the name Joyce Kelly, she was a young Irish lady. They were surprised when she turned out to be African American.

I went to the Seventh Infantry Division at Camp Casey, in Korea, and was assigned as an S4 (supply and logistics) officer in a brigade of infantry mostly from the South. It was my worst assignment in the army. There was a fair amount of racial prejudice in that brigade. I was assigned as a logistical officer despite the fact that operations was my specialty. Apparently the senior brass had already chosen a fair-haired boy, a young white captain, who was placed in a major's job. They were trying to do nice things for him, groom him for more important leadership posts. Of course that had been done for me a decade earlier, so I knew what was happening.

A personnel crisis developed in special services, and I was asked to help out at the division level as a special services officer because I had worked in that capacity at Fort Lawton and Fort Monmouth. I took the job and quickly got that program under way. Things were going well when Major General Chester Dahlen asked the division's personnel officer, "What the hell is Sam Kelly doing running special services when we need him as one of our line officers?"

General Dahlen was impressed with my combat record and my ability to discuss planning and operations. After I briefed him, he thought that I should be on the general staff and asked me why I was not serving in that capacity. I responded without directly answering his question, "Well, sir, I'll be pleased to serve wherever you put me."

Within thirty days, I was transferred to the deputy chief of staff G-3 office, under my old friend Colonel Lucian Truscott III. Lucian and I were like brothers. After I finished jump school in 1956, he recommended me for the first operations job I held when we were assigned to the same battalion in the Eleventh Airborne Division back at Fort Campbell. We continued our good relationship even after subsequent assignments separated us. When he left to command the General Staff College at Fort Leavenworth, Kansas, Lucian recommended that I take over his job as battalion S-3, plans, training, and operations officer, and I did so.

When Lucian was assigned to Korea, he requested that I be his executive officer for plans, training, and operations for the Seventh Infantry Division. It was a hellish job—fourteen-hour days, six to seven days a week. We were constantly maneuvering and drafting our best plans and testing our best personnel. We installed nuclear capabilities for attack at the tactical level, aware of the uneasy truce that had existed in Korea for a decade. When I had first come to Korea in 1951, there were 325,000 American servicemen stationed there; ten years later, there were still 62,000 U.S. soldiers on that peninsula. We had to be prepared for any contingency because we were the first line of defense in case the North Koreans, the Chinese, or the Soviets attacked. It was a stressful, tense, thankless job.

FIRST BRIGADE PLANS, TRAINING, AND OPERATIONS OFFICER

I returned to Fort Lewis in June 1964 and was assigned to the First Brigade, Fourth Infantry Division. First Brigade was undergoing the same kind of transition to the new brigade concept that I had experienced at Fort Campbell seven years earlier, so I was well prepared for this assignment.

I was the plans, training, and operations officer of the First Brigade, responsible for making sure its five battalions and task forces of approximately five thousand soldiers were combat ready for any assignment anywhere in the world within a twelve-hour period. We were living on the edge, but it was exciting.

Joyce's illness progressed, and I had problems placing Billy in school, so I requested an assignment to Fort Lawton as an operations officer in the corps headquarters. The distance between my home and Fort Lawton was less than half the distance from home to Fort Lewis. There was a colonel's job at Fort Lawton, and I was a major on the lieutenant colonel list. I was promoted to lieutenant colonel on June 17, 1964.

I secured an assignment as an assistant chief of staff, plans and operations officer, for fifty thousand troops in the Tenth Corps, U.S. Army Corps, at Fort Lawton. These were reserve and National Guard units for which the commanding general of Tenth Corps had operational and mobilization responsibility. One of those responsibilities included preparing to suppress urban uprisings. In 1964, race riots raged in Harlem and Rochester, and there were near riots in a number of other cities. In August 1965, the Watts Riot broke out. That conflict lasted five days, took thirty-four lives, and resulted in four thousand arrests. By the last day of the riot, fourteen thousand National Guard troops were patrolling the streets of Los Angeles.

The army's Operation Angry Arm, was an exercise designed to suppress any similar uprisings in the Pacific Northwest. This top secret operation, which used boats and aircraft as well as thousands of troops in a simulated response to urban disturbances in Seattle and other cities, was meant to support and reinforce the police during civil unrest.

I am sure many of the student and civil rights leaders I would come to work with and admire over the next decade would not understand

my role in directing the suppression of urban unrest. I didn't see a con-
tradiction at all. I understood racial discrimination as well as anyone. I
also supported peaceful protests and would later be on the picket line in
support of many of them. I drew the line, however, at violence and the
destruction of property. I also drew the line at public safety. No racial
grievance justified placing innocent lives in danger. Operation Angry
Arm would be my last major military assignment. Late in 1965, I decided
to retire from the U.S. Army.

LEAVING THE ARMY

The decision to leave the organization that had been my life for the past
two decades was not an easy one. I had tested civilian life briefly in 1948
and hadn't liked it. I returned to an army that was undergoing a rapid
transformation for the better. Unprecedented opportunities for leadership and responsibility that had heretofore seemed unavailable in the
civilian sector had opened up for black officers like me. The army of 1965
was not the army I had joined in 1944, and I was grateful for the change.

Opportunities, however, were beginning to emerge in higher education, the area I wanted to pursue. In 1965, I began teaching Western
civilization and U.S. history at Everett Junior College, about thirty miles
north of Seattle. The Seattle NAACP, led by civil rights activist Randolph
Carter, had challenged Everett Junior College because it had no African
American faculty at that time. I am not sure why the NAACP singled out
Everett Junior College; none of the twenty-seven junior or community
colleges in Washington had any African Americans on faculty. Nonetheless, I liked my new part-time job and anticipated the day I could work
full-time for the college.

Personal reasons also influenced my decision to leave the army.
At one time, I had envisioned staying in for thirty years and eventually being promoted to general, a position that was no longer out of the
range of possibility for black officers. My friend and ocs classmate Julius
Becton was on the same path and in 1978 became a three-star lieutenant
general. There was no doubt in my mind that I could have achieved that
rank had I remained in the army.

COLONEL SAM

On January 1, 1966, just twenty-five days shy of my fortieth birthday, I retired from the United States Army. During my twenty-two years of active service, I rose from the rank of private to lieutenant colonel, served as part of the occupying army in Japan, saw combat in Korea, joined and led an elite airborne unit, and crafted plans and operations for upward of fifty thousand soldiers. I had attained what the infantry likes to think of as the apex of success by leading two different combat units success-fully. I had been decorated throughout my military career, earning two Bronze Stars for valor, four commendation medals for efficiency, and more than ten letters of commendation for superior service. This was not a bad career for a Connecticut kid who had dropped out of high school.

It's impossible to be part of an institution as large and complex as the U.S. Army for all those years without being profoundly shaped by its values and ideals. I once said to an interviewer, "The Lord's been good to me, but the army's been better." I learned much from my time in the army. I benefited from the tutelage and support of three different West Pointers who would become generals—my regimental commander in Korea, Colonel John P. Connor; my Airborne Division commander, Colonel Tommy Sherbourne; and Major General Teddy Sanford, also of the Airborne Division. These men are legendary in the annals of air-borne forces. I also had tremendous instruction from officers at Fort Benning and the Command General Staff College at Fort Leavenworth.

I was a good professional officer and enjoyed the prestige that accom-panied officer rank. I loved the uniform—there's no doubt about that, I loved the uniform. I particularly loved that little airborne patch on my cap and jump boots. I even loved staying sharp by changing uniforms two or three times a day in response to duties and assignments.

These were exciting years for me. The Cold War was in its first two decades, and we in the army knew that with changing military and political alliances and the advent of new technology, including nuclear weapons capabilities, old strategies were no longer valid. I learned to think critically, analyze carefully, and present effectively. An operations officer is always briefing, and thus the accuracy and persuasiveness of the

JOYCE KELLY WATCHES MAJ. GEN. C. F. LEONARD, JR., PRESENT THE 2ND OAK LEAF CLUSTER TO THE ARMY COMMENDATION MEDAL TO LT. COL. KELLY AT HIS RETIREMENT CEREMONY AT FORT LAWTON, WASHINGTON, IN DECEMBER 1965. PHOTO BY SP4 JERRY A. NEWHOUSE, SIGNAL PHOTO DIVISION, U.S. ARMY GARRISON, FORT LAWTON, WASHINGTON.

presentation are critical. Lives may literally hang in the balance because of the presentation, since decisions to commit human and material resources rest on its effectiveness. I was taught this by my college professors and the officers at the Command General Staff College at Fort Leavenworth. I learned how to size up men and women and situations. Most important, I learned how to motivate soldiers—how to get them to do things they believed themselves incapable of doing. I would learn that these skills are equally valuable in the situations I would face in schools, colleges, and universities and in the private sphere for the rest of my life. I may have officially retired from the army on January 1, 1966, but I will always be a soldier.

PART III

Educator

"I invented controversy."

CHAPTER 8

Community College Instructor

After earning three degrees while I was in the army, a BA and a BS from West Virginia State College and an MA from Marshall University, I felt confident that I'd be able to get a job when I retired from military service. I thought I'd teach high school history and work my way up to principal, but Joyce introduced me to one of her friends who was a friend of Jeanette Poore, the dean of students at Everett Junior College, north of Seattle. I'd met Jeanette in 1964, along with some of her friends who taught at community colleges. At that time, I also visited Everett Junior College. When I delivered a Veterans Day speech at South Mercer Island Junior High School, where Joyce taught, some of the Everett faculty who were in the audience were impressed. As everyone gathered at our home afterward, one of the teachers said, "We want you to leave the army and come and teach at Everett." The die was cast. By 1965, after twenty-one years in the army, I had begun to think of and prepare for life after the service.

I started teaching part-time at Everett Junior College and found the work to be exhilarating. Every Tuesday and Thursday night, I drove forty miles north from Fort Lawton to Everett, where I taught courses in European and U.S. history. After a year, the college administrators asked if I could teach full-time. I had two years left in my obligation to the army, so I had to negotiate my separation. Fortunately, the commanding general at Fort Lawton, Major General C. F. Leonard, said he would release me "with regret." He understood my personal reasons based on Joyce's health and Billy's special needs. He reminded me that by teaching in the Washington community college system, I was continuing my patriotic duty to the nation.

Dr. Rob Berg, the president of Everett and a reserve lieutenant colonel, helped smooth my transition with his ability to anticipate my feelings as I separated from military service. So when I retired in 1966, I became a full-time instructor at Everett Community College, teaching courses in U.S. history and Western civilization.

Unfortunately, I did not teach my first love, East Asian history. I had taken formal graduate training in that field when I studied with Professor Herschel Heath at Marshall University. I wanted to establish the first course in East Asian history at Everett but was unsuccessful. Nonetheless, I made many good friends. I also had the dubious honor of being the first black professor in the community college system in the state of Washington.

BLACK STUDIES AT SHORELINE COMMUNITY COLLEGE

After three years at Everett, I decided to take a position at Shoreline Community College, which was twenty miles closer to my home. I became friends with Richard (Dick) White, the forty-year-old president of Shoreline. He had a tremendous sensitivity to questions of racial equity at the college. Moreover, he trusted me and I trusted him. We went out together with our wives and played golf at Fort Lewis. Joyce and I invited Dick and his wife Jean to our home on Mercer Island, and he also arranged for Joyce and me to entertain the Shoreline board of trustees. As we became close, we both recognized the need to promote a curriculum that included discussions of people of color and to initiate programs for increasing minority enrollment at Shoreline. Dick asked me to lead this effort, and I agreed to do it.

Running the program led to my first of many encounters with militant black students. My first confrontation came in 1967, when a grim-looking young man came into my office and gave me a black power salute. He had attended Harvard, gotten kicked out, and returned to Seattle and enrolled at Shoreline. He was now a "professional Black Radical." "What's that stuff?" I inquired naively.

Ignoring my question, he said, "You know, you ought to do something to make sure you will stay around here, Mr. Kelly."

"What do you have in mind?"

"Well, you oughta be doing something besides this gig. Can't we get some programs going or something?"

"What do you mean? Teaching's enough. How long do you think it took me to prepare to be a teacher, young man?" I scolded him.

"Yeah, but all the stuff that's going on at the University of Washington and across the nation," he said while waving his arms to indicate that black students, and black people, were in rebellion elsewhere. Then he concluded, "We ain't doing anything out here."

He criticized the name of the Nat Turner Literary Society, the major organization of the handful of black students on campus. The society, formed early in 1967 by Andre Stratman Wooten, the stepson of Seattle attorney and former legislator Charles Stokes, was our liaison with black students at Shoreline. This student objected to the name and purpose of the organization, saying Shoreline's black students had no time to participate in literary societies and engage in mundane debates when African America was about to be convulsed in revolution. When he left my office that day, I was still puzzled as to what he wanted me to do.

Within a week, Dick White approached me and said, "Sam, you know, we have some problems with blacks and whites—should I say 'Negro' or 'colored' or 'black'?"

"You say what you feel comfortable with," I responded. Then I added, "'Black' is fine, 'African American' is fine, but 'colored' isn't fine."

The black and white students on the football team had recently called each other racial names. Then he said, as if providing a solution to that problem, "We should do something around here to bring more minority students to the campus, not just a paltry number. Right now we have only fifteen to twenty black students."

"What do you have in mind, a special program?"

We brainstormed for forty-five minutes in my office. I said, "Dick, I can add some units of African American history to my U.S. history curriculum and see how the students respond. I started that effort at Everett, but I can do more here."

"I wish you would."

Soon after, I started teaching Shoreline's first black history courses.

My efforts at Shoreline Community College exceeded what the University of Washington was doing at the time. I was proud of that. I also recognized that Shoreline could implement such courses virtually overnight—that's one reason I liked the community college system. It seemed there was less bureaucracy; the president decided something should be done, and that was the end of the discussion. As soon as President White declared his commitment to the new courses, I consulted with eight or nine faculty members and administrators, and the courses were added to the curriculum.

THE MINORITY AFFAIRS PROGRAM

Shoreline did not stop with black history courses. President White responded favorably to my request to create an office of minority affairs to recruit primarily black students from Seattle's inner city. The office would also provide academic and social counseling and some financial aid. Eventually, we added a faculty recruitment component to the office. These four components—academic courses, academic and social counseling, financial aid to minority students, and recruitment of faculty and students of color—would later become the divisions of Shoreline's Minority Affairs Program (MAP).

I made my proposal before the board of trustees, which unanimously supported the Minority Affairs Program, which would later become the model for the University of Washington's Office of Minority Affairs (OMA). At about that time, I also had my first contact with University of Washington black student activists such as E. J. Brisker and Larry Gossett just as they were beginning to challenge the university administration to bring more black students to the campus and provide the resources to support them. They carefully monitored Shoreline's new Minority Affairs Program, which combined curricular and institutional reforms to integrate students of color into the campus. There weren't very many models. Few Black Studies programs existed anywhere in the United States in 1967. Those that did usually relied on soft money to recruit inner-city students or support them once they reached campus. More programs emerged in the wake of the assassination of Dr. Martin Luther King, Jr., in April 1968. We knew campuses such as Stanford were considering some version of these programs, but we just dove in head-first at Shoreline, not thinking that we ought to wait until the large, prestigious institutions showed our community college the way.

With the first Black Studies courses in place, I hired a program assistant, Mrs. Clemoris Allen, and turned to recruiting black faculty. It was crucial that we have faculty who were competent to instruct the courses we were developing, but we also wanted to create role models—black instructors whose very presence on campus would, we believed, encourage African American students to raise their occupational and intellectual aspirations while challenging white students to deal with professional black women and men. Although it seems difficult to imagine today, in 1967 there were virtually no black faculty members or administrators in higher education in the state of Washington and few across the nation.

I traveled across Washington and eventually the United States, describing our efforts and asking prospective instructors to come to Shoreline to be part of this new program. Most community colleges don't recruit faculty, especially from outside their communities, but Shoreline was setting up an entirely new program that required something beyond the normal patterns of hiring faculty and staff. I may have been naively optimistic in my recruitment efforts. A few potential instructors in the East showed interest, but eventually I came to realize that our most promising prospects were local people.

While I was at Shoreline, I was also director of education for the First African Methodist Episcopal (AME) Church in Seattle. First AME, founded in 1886, was the oldest black church in the state. Its congregation included a large number of college graduates and some members with advanced degrees. I learned that one of the Sunday school teachers, a Mr. Jordan, was a graduate of Howard University and had an MA in history. When I heard that, I contacted him and asked him to come to Shoreline to teach. Now there were two instructors in African American history. In the three years I worked at Shoreline, the Minority Affairs Program recruited about a dozen black faculty members. In fact, by 1970, when I left the campus, Shoreline Community College had a greater percentage of African Americans on its faculty than any college or university in the state of Washington. I also recruited Chicanos and Native Americans into the faculty. Dr. Ken LaFontaine, a Native American, remained on campus for twenty-nine years. Dr. Andrea Rye, an African American woman who later became a Shoreline vice president and worked there until her retirement, was originally a student on my staff at the college.

One section of Shoreline's Minority Affairs Program was devoted to recruiting students, while another provided them counseling and academic advising. The program even arranged bus transportation to and from the college for students from Seattle's inner-city area. Our office developed special courses for students in English, math, and literature taught by leading instructors on campus and community volunteers. They were liberals, and I use that term in the best sense of the word. I remember especially Amy Mates, a native of Great Britain, who was on the Shoreline faculty and volunteered to teach MAP students.

The Minority Affairs Program also designed courses to compensate for the woeful education that many of our students had received in public schools. Some of the students were sensitive about being in "remedial" courses, even when the courses contributed to their success on campus.

When I arrived at Shoreline in 1967, there were no more than 15 black students on campus out of a total enrollment of approximately 1,000. When I left three years later, there were 125 students out of a total of 3,000. I was personally involved in recruiting most of these students. They came because they wanted an education and the college's scholarships eliminated the greatest handicap for most of them, lack of funds. About 80 percent of the recruits were on some form of scholarship or financial aid.

I visited schools, churches, and even barbershops to tell prospective students about the opportunity to earn an associate of arts degree at Shoreline. I reasoned that if we could get these students to begin to realize that educational opportunities were being created for them, and have them enroll at Shoreline, they would next apply successfully to the University of Washington and other four-year institutions.

Another portion of the program was devoted to curriculum change, developing courses that highlighted the African American experience and recruiting faculty to teach these courses. We had some help in this area. A grant proposal I wrote to the National Committee for Advanced Teacher Education (NCATE) obtained five thousand dollars to train teachers on integrating curriculum and incorporating new curriculum development in the area of Black Studies.

PROFESSOR CHARLES H. WESLEY

I spent much time on the road in 1967 and 1968, seeking information on how to improve our program. I remember my encounter with Professor Charles Harris Wesley, the distinguished historian of African American history who was executive director of the Association for the Study of Negro Life and History and editor of the *Journal of Negro History*, the oldest and most prestigious African American scholarly publication in the nation. I will never forget the day I walked into his office in the association's national headquarters on Fourteenth Street NW in Washington, D.C. The narrow building, essentially a row house converted into an office, was decrepit and poorly lit. Professor Wesley was in what apparently had been the living room of the house, which was now filled with books of every description. There was a desk and a fireplace.

Professor Wesley sat in the middle of this clutter, immaculately clad in a starched white shirt and tie despite the summer heat and humidity. He was already legendary in black history circles, only the fourth African American after W. E. B. DuBois; Carter G. Woodson, founder of the *Journal of Negro History* and creator of Negro History Week, which eventually became Black History Month; and Rayford Logan to receive a PhD in history from Harvard University. He was also a former student of DuBois's and Woodson's. Professor Wesley himself had been president of Wilberforce University and Central State College, both in Ohio.

Despite his hectic schedule, Professor Wesley spent two days discussing black history with me and helping me think through how to craft a program in what is now called African American studies. Shortly after our visit, he shipped to Shoreline three boxes of files and books that became the nucleus of the Black Studies collection at the college. The files included black history publications by various authors and material from Woodson and Logan regarding their advocacy on behalf of Negro History Week.

I also attended lectures on black history and black studies and gathered books for the college library. I recall proudly presenting Shoreline's librarian with copies of Lerone Bennett's highly popular *Before the Mayflower: A History of the Negro People* and Kenneth Stampp's *The Peculiar Institution: Slavery in the Ante-Bellum South*. In the late 1960s, there really weren't many books on black history and the African American experience, but I was determined to bring all the major works that were available to Shoreline.

Two faculty members volunteered to teach the first African American history courses with me. Dr. Kirby Chandler, who was chair of the social science program, was one-third of that team. He knew African

SAM KELLY, KIRBY CHANDLER, AND BILL WAUGH DISCUSSING NEW AFRICAN AMERICAN HISTORY
COURSES AT SHORELINE COMMUNITY COLLEGE IN 1968. COURTESY JACKETT STUDIO, SEATTLE.

history, which provided the rich background for African American history. I think because Kirby was white and very patient and gentle, we
were able to defuse much of the initial suspicion that the courses would
be less-than-rigorous excursions into victimology. Bill Waugh, the other
instructor, was also white. He had a master's degree from the University of Montana and was a passionate lecturer who would take over the
African American history courses after I left the campus in 1970.

The Shoreline administration was especially pleased that these courses
soon became popular among white students. I was elated that students
from Seattle's Central District were coming to Shoreline precisely
because it had a curriculum that included their history and experiences.

BLACK PANTHERS IN THE CLASSROOM

By 1968, I was on good terms with virtually every major group in
Seattle's black community, including the Black Panthers. Aaron and
Elmer Dixon, founders of the Seattle chapter of the Black Panther Party,

were among the University of Washington students I met while at Shoreline. Several were there to take my course in African American history. I explained to the class the myths of history, why these stories were taught, and their impact on African American history. I encouraged them to see black history as providing a context for understanding many contemporary student demands and reminded them of the various levels of discrimination, giving as examples the racist acts I had faced when I was an officer in the army.

I also reminded my students that the U.S. Constitution had not been created with African Americans in mind and had to be modified by the Thirteenth, Fourteenth, and Fifteenth Amendments and that we were not and often still are not treated with the respect due full-fledged citizens. I recalled for them that the federal government did not allow blacks to be treated as citizens, yet that same government had no problem asking us to pay taxes or offer our lives in defense of a nation that would not defend us. I told all of my students that if they became teachers, they had an obligation to share this contradictory and hypocritical history with their students, just as I was sharing it with them.

The Panthers came in after one of my classes and asked, "Can we talk to you, Brother Kelly?" They wanted to sit in on the class. I agreed, and from that point, they were there every day in the front row. I saw the Panthers' free breakfast program firsthand and thought it was very good for the kids. The radical element didn't frighten me, and I didn't neglect them. I recall a number of white professors who worried, "I don't know if they're angry at me or not, and the way they dress and the way they talk . . ."

"You just teach what you teach, and they will respect you," I replied.

One example of that respect came when I asked Larry Gossett to speak in my African American history course. He was not a Panther but a University of Washington student who regularly visited my Shoreline class. Larry was a history major who did well in class and showed great promise. He would be one of the leaders of the 1968 Black Student Union sit-in at the university's administration building, which indirectly led to my coming to that campus as vice president for minority affairs.

During my first year at Shoreline, my brother Jim, who was deputy director of NCATE, helped arrange a grant that enabled the college to host more than one hundred teachers at a national conference on teacher training and development in Black Studies. This was a rare instance of a national conference being held on a community college campus, and it was certainly one of the first events devoted exclusively to the still evolving discipline of Black Studies. Political activists and leading scholars, including Martin Kilson of Harvard University; Kenneth Stampp of the University of California, Berkeley; and the Seattle Urban League's executive director Ed Pratt (who would be assassinated three years later), came to Shoreline for the conference.

E. J. Brisker and Larry Gossett, leaders of the University of Washington's Black Student Union, also attended. Gossett was initially skeptical of me because of my military background. When someone informed him that I was a retired colonel, he turned to me and said, "Colonel? Sam, you're doing this for us? You must have been one of them good colonels. There aren't very many of those in the Man's army."

Given my conservative politics and his radical stance on nearly every social and political issue of the day, it would have been natural if Larry Gossett and I were immediate political enemies. Nothing could have been further from the truth. Larry and most of the other University of Washington Black Student Union leaders knew that I had the best interests of students at heart and that I meant to serve those interests come what may. We shared the goal of getting as many young black women and men into college as possible. That goal united us far more than political questions divided us. Larry would become one of my first staff members in the Office of Minority Affairs at the University of Washington.

Before I left Shoreline in 1970, the college's Black Student Union presented me with a bust of a young black man with his forehead wrinkled and his head tilted to one side. I didn't quite know what to make of it. The union's president said it exemplified my look when I was troubled, and the students reminded me that they appreciated all the challenges I had faced when forming the Minority Affairs Program. They also reminded me that I didn't get along with all of the black students and remembered the student who wanted to "pimp" the administration, as they called it. He had come on campus making all kinds of outrageous demands, assuming the administration would give in to him, intimidating black and white students alike. Eventually, he told me, speaking of the campus, "You're gonna have trouble, Kelly. I'm gonna take this sonofabitch over!" Finally, he confronted me in my office and said, "I like your office. I want one just like it next to yours." I threatened to throw him out of the building and got up and went after him. He didn't expect that from a forty-two-year-old black man and ran out of the building. Two white faculty members saw me going after the student and reported it to President White. The president later told me what they had said: "Sam Kelly stands up for right, irrespective of color."

I continued to teach while I was assistant to the president for minority affairs. Despite Shoreline's size, its Minority Affairs Program had state-wide and some national visibility. We sought to grow the program by building a network of on-campus and off-campus supporters. For example, I arranged for black students at Shoreline to stay in the homes of white faculty members who volunteered to provide housing. I probably placed twenty black inner-city students in suburban homes throughout the Shoreline community. Through these experiences, black students and white teachers began to dissolve the walls of mutual suspicion. We helped both the students and the faculty see each other with fresh eyes.

HELPING SHORELINE'S STUDENTS OF COLOR

The Committee on Minority Affairs at Shoreline provided advice and helped defend the program from its detractors on and off campus. It soon created a fundraising arm, Friends of the Minority Affairs Program. Dalwyn Knight helped enormously on this project, serving as the group's president and raising thousands of dollars for scholarships for MAP students. Dalwyn and her husband Harry were both University of Washington graduates. They were also Christian Scientists who lived in Shoreline and supported the college. Because of that connection, Dalwyn and Harry became dedicated to helping young, needy African American students at Shoreline. Dalwyn raised money among her friends. She also persuaded me to go into the North Seattle community to speak at churches, civic organizations, and business groups, both to explain our program and to raise money for student financial aid.

At Shoreline, Dick White continued to listen as I talked about the needs of minority students. I discussed how we had to continue building a curriculum that reflected their experiences and make the environment at Shoreline welcoming for them, and I also explained that they needed to see people of color among the college staff and faculty. I argued that we needed to take those steps in order to ensure that the inner-city students we recruited would succeed in what was for them an alien environment.

Fortunately, Shoreline was in an excellent financial position because the mid-1960s was a period of rapid economic growth in Washington; the Minority Affairs Program had an ample budget. Since the college was only a decade old, there was little tradition to get in the way of our work. President White authorized me to recruit ten to twelve minority faculty and staff members. I looked particularly for black, red, and brown faculty candidates because these groups had been most underrepresented on college campuses.

Approximately ten faculty and staff members of color were hired at Shoreline Community College, among them, Leroy Fails, from the University of Washington, who became the administrator in charge of financial aid at the college. They proved to be excellent faculty and staff. I also recognized that some whites had both the training in black history and the commitment to building our program that made them role models of a different type, so some of the instructors I hired were white. I felt it was important for black and white students to see white teachers who wanted them to succeed and who appreciated the rich history and culture of black and brown people. These faculty members, black, white, Chicano, Asian, and Native American, helped me build an academic program. In all, we had seven ethnic studies courses by 1970.

As the program grew, I assumed more responsibility for its administration. I was also named assistant chair of social sciences as well as assistant to the president for minority affairs. I often said that I had three jobs but one salary. But working with the staff, faculty, and students at Shoreline was a delight. And I was most proud of being selected by the students as the leading faculty member from among all the instructors at Shoreline.

I also worked off campus with the State Board for Community College Education and with the twenty-seven community colleges across Washington. By 1970, similar programs were beginning to show up at those institutions. Fourteen colleges, mostly west of the Cascade mountains, had assistants to the president for minority affairs. Shoreline's Minority Affairs Program also helped create the Puget Sound Minority Affairs Consortium, which included representatives from all of those colleges and was headed by Dr. Al Smith, Jr.

PURSUING A PHD

While I was teaching at Shoreline, I was accepted into the PhD program at the University of Washington College of Education. I was recruited by Professors Bill Schill and Henry (Hank) Reitan, whom I eventually came to call "my good Norwegian brother." Professor Reitan came to hear me speak at the University of Washington before one hundred social science teachers from across the state on the need for courses on people of color. I remember the title of my talk, "Black Demands and a Responsible Response."

Professor Reitan came up and shook my hand afterward and said, "Mr. Kelly, I'd like to talk with you. I'm a professor in the College of Education at the University of Washington. I want to chat with you about our program."

I replied, "About your program? You mean as a student? Well, I don't know what the hell you want to talk to me about. A fellow over there who later became the dean counseled me out of that idea when I wrote him about getting a doctorate in your program."

Professor Reitan responded, "Well, sometimes we make mistakes, Mr. Kelly."

The next morning, Professor Reitan was in my office.

"I don't know why you're here," I said. "I was counseled out of that program. I don't have time to waste. I'm busy here at Shoreline developing a meaningful program that will stay."

"That's all right," he said. "I want you to know, I want you in our program."

"How are you gonna do that?"

"I'll register you in it!"

"What do you mean? I have to complete my application first."

"No, you don't. I'll be back."

He returned to my office the next day along with Bill Schill. I spent three hours with them. Professor Schill brought me the application to the University of Washington's graduate school. My family and I were scheduled to go on vacation in California, but I needed to take the Graduate Record Exam (GRE) and the Miller Analogies Test (MAT) as prerequisites for admission. I took the MAT at the University of Washington, but in the next six months the GRE would be offered only at the University of California, Los Angeles.

"Look," Professor Reitan said, "you could do it down there." So I made out the application for the College of Education, and he enrolled me in a course taught by Bill Schill. I was provisionally accepted and took my first doctoral course at the University of Washington in the fall of 1969.

Taking the GRE at UCLA was one of the worst experiences in my educational life. I left my family at the hotel and drove to the campus, where I joined a line of three hundred people. On the front door of the building was a three-by-five-inch card: "The GRE is canceled at this location. Please go to building such and such." I spent another forty-five minutes, along with hundreds of other people, looking for the new building and arrived for the test thirty or forty-five minutes late. Needless to say, I didn't do very well.

That didn't seem to matter much. Professor Reitan and the other faculty and administrators in the College of Education had decided I should be in their program. They knew about my educational background, my advanced degree from Marshall University, and my excellent grades as an undergraduate at West Virginia State University. They knew my master's degree work was good. Despite my low GRE scores, I was officially admitted to the University of Washington.

Once I began working at the University of Washington in 1970, I had additional motivation. As vice president for minority affairs, I felt I had to complete that degree in order to demonstrate to our students that it could be done. At first, I thought it was enough to say, "Well, I studied at the doctoral level." Eventually, I realized that if I could pursue a doctorate while holding a full-time job, those who were full-time graduate students had no excuse; I think that mattered. I think many students, including those who started out as undergraduates coming through the Educational Opportunity Program, eventually got master's degrees and doctorates because of the example I set. Let me hasten to say that I had help and support during that difficult time. I also had pressure. Thank God for my chief adviser, Professor Hank Reitan, who mentored me through that program. I would not be Dr. Kelly today if it were not for him.

After three years at Shoreline Community College, I was, as they say, "fat and happy." I enjoyed my job and what I had accomplished. I also knew that my work had affected students, the faculty, and the administration and was having an impact on the local community as well as on those across the nation who were interested in Black Studies. That would not have been true if I had pursued my first career objective, high school history instruction.

In 1969, I received a distinguished visitor from the University of Washington, microbiology professor Dr. Charles Evans. He was not there, however, to discuss science. He came to me as the president of the University of Washington Faculty Senate. That afternoon in my office, Dr. Evans initiated a conversation that would change the direction of my life.

CHAPTER 9

Coming to the University of Washington

Dr. Charles Evans had impressive credentials. In addition to being president of the University of Washington Faculty Senate, he had a PhD in microbiology. As senate president, he had taken the first steps toward organizing a program that would serve the needs of minority students. He was director of the Special Education Program (SEP), which he operated with volunteers and a small budget.

I first met Charles because he attended our conference on minority education in 1967. Over the weeks after the conference, I discussed with him my plans and vision for Shoreline's Minority Affairs Program. When he asked me how I got it done, I explained that the students must be on your side; they must have confidence in your commitment to change. Charles told me he had difficulty getting students to be on his side. I was blunt.

"One of the reasons is that you're white, not black! How can you know how a black person feels when he's riding in the back of the bus? How would you be able to identify with that? I'm not knocking you personally, because we need each other. America's a great country, but we need each other to change the nation."

I told him how I felt about the name Special Education Program for students of color. It had a bad connotation, suggesting that those enrolled in the program had some type of deficiency and did not deserve to be at the university. I don't know how Charles Evans felt about my advice, but he did ask me to consult with him on a paid basis, beginning in 1968. I agreed to walk him through the steps we had taken to set up the successful program at Shoreline Community College.

Charles Evans and the University of Washington needed a lot of help. In May 1968, E. J. Brisker, Larry Gossett, and other black students and their supporters had occupied the administration building. They demanded financial resources for recruiting and tutoring non-white students, a Black Studies program, and the recruitment of black faculty and administrators.

I was more familiar than most of the UW faculty with the events unfolding on the campus that spring. I knew E. J. Brisker and Larry Gossett, both of whom had spoken to my class at Shoreline. Soon I had another advantage; I became a member of the Black Student Union.

Although I was forty-two-years-old, had three degrees, had been a colonel in the U.S. Army, and was assistant to the president at Shoreline, my enrollment in a graduate program at the University of Washington, by my reckoning, made me a student. Since the Black Student Union charter said that any student at the University of Washington is eligible for membership, I presented myself at the meetings. The members accepted me. Attending BSU meetings on the UW campus in 1969 and 1970 gave me a vantage point from which to see the politics of the campus, and from what I observed, I wasn't sure I wanted to be involved.

JAMES GOODMAN

But I also had an important friend and contact on the UW faculty, Dr. James Goodman. Jim Goodman, who held a PhD in sociology from the University of Minnesota and taught in the School of Social Work and in the Sociology Department, was one of only a handful of black faculty members on campus in 1969. He also served as the first director of the UW's Black Studies program between 1968 and 1970 and was thus the first black administrator at the university. Jim mentored me and taught me how to think about the climate of the University of Washington. When he asked me if I would ever consider leaving Shoreline for the university, I rejected the idea.

"No," I said. "Frankly, I think some of those black students are crazy." We were joking, of course, but I knew that none of the students and certainly no one in the UW administration seemed to have a plan for dealing with the grievances that had become public in the spring of 1968.

"I'm an old army man," I told Jim. "I couldn't work there."

"Well, Sam, that's what they need," he replied.

Later, I began to warm to the idea. Despite the success of the Minority

Affairs Program at Shoreline, I knew that the idea of Black Studies, the efficacy of Black Studies as a legitimate academic endeavor, was still in doubt. This view was held by many faculty members and administrators at the University of Washington and across the nation.

Jim and I continued to talk. He helped me develop arguments against those who would inevitably question Black Studies and all programs designed to assist blacks and other students of color. I knew about the controversy. Jim was helping me prepare for it while convincing me that I could succeed in the UW environment. I also sensed that the University of Washington would contact me about coming to the campus permanently. I waited.

I didn't have to wait long. Early in April 1970, I got a call from Dr. Charles Evans, asking me to come to campus and meet with UW president Charles Odegaard and members of his cabinet. I accepted the invitation and immediately called Jim to get some idea of what to expect. Because of my work on the general staff, I had been accustomed to dealing with ranking officers; I was not easily awed by men who were important or considered themselves important, but dealing with high-ranking officials at a major university was new territory for me.

Jim and I talked by phone late into the night about what to expect, and what to request, when I visited the UW campus the next day.

"Sam, they're going to offer you something. Some of the UW black students have been talking up you and the Shoreline program." Then he gave me this advice. "Vice president for minority affairs—don't take it for anything less than that. If you do, you won't matter because you won't have a voice at the highest levels of the administration."

I listened carefully to Jim's suggestion. I knew from my experience at Shoreline that administrators for several minority affairs programs had started out being called "assistant to the dean for student services" or "assistant to the president for curriculum development," and the like. My title at Shoreline was Assistant to the President for Minority Affairs. My case was different. I had the ear of President Dick White.

Other campuses followed a similar model. Stanford's program, which I was probably most familiar with at the time, had an assistant to the president for special students. Stanford did some good things at the graduate level, recruiting a few black students, but didn't do anything to substantially change the campus so that black students would be fully integrated into its academic and social life. I knew about the University of Pittsburgh's program mainly because my brother Jim was now the dean of the College of Education there. The school was having some success recruiting black students mainly because of my brother's influence. Although I didn't have any experience with large institutions such as the University of Washington, I did have an idea of what worked. I also knew that in 1970 very few minority affairs and Black Studies programs had been in existence for more than a year. Shoreline's Minority Affairs Program had been around since 1967. We were already ahead of the curve.

One afternoon in early April 1970, I went to the University of Washington administration building and proceeded to the board of regents' meeting room on the third floor. Nine people were in the room: President Charles Odegaard; Robert Waldo, vice president for university relations; George Farwell, vice president for research; Al Ulbrickson, vice president for student affairs; Ernie Conrad, vice president for business and finance; Solomon Katz, provost and vice president for academic affairs; and Dr. John Hogness, executive vice president. I also met Philip Cartwright, dean of the College of Arts and Sciences, and Jim Ryan, assistant vice president for planning and budget.

At that point, the administrators who ran the University of Washington, a campus of thirty-three thousand students and a faculty and staff of twelve thousand, were all white males. The university was the fourth-largest employer in the state after Boeing, the U.S. Navy, and the U.S. Army. It was a major research institution with one of the nation's leading medical schools. I sat at the end of a table to face the men who ran this huge complex and explain to them why I should work at the University of Washington. I felt confident, almost cocky. I believed, given the unrest and tension on campus, which mirrored the troubles on campuses and in streets across the nation, whether it was Vietnam War protests or demands by black students, that they needed me more than I needed them. I was about to find out if this was correct.

I had talked to myself and said a little prayer the night before. When I entered that room, I felt pretty good. I smiled, but not too much. President Odegaard, with his striking gray mane, got up from his chair and shook my hand. He was very formal, but warm and smiling, and said, "Mr. Kelly, have a seat." I introduced myself to each person in the room and began my presentation.

WHO IS SAM KELLY?

I had no notes. I just ticked off everything from memory. I had already decided that I was going to tell them how I would manage minority affairs on the campus. If they didn't like what I said, well, I already had a job I liked, so I began the interview knowing I had absolutely nothing to lose. When I started talking, I asked them to listen and take notes if they wanted and said that I would respond to questions at the end.

"Who is Sam Kelly?" I asked rhetorically. "What does he represent? Would he be able to manage an office of minority affairs and build a program now unknown to us?"

Before I could continue, Dr. Odegaard interrupted and said, "I'd like you to spend the time just discussing who you are."

I talked for about two and a half hours. I told them who I was, where I had been born and raised, and how these experiences had shaped my life. I went through my combat experience in Korea and talked about racism both in and out of the military. I described how I had risen in the ranks from private to second lieutenant in fifteen months.

The vice presidents seemed especially interested in my awards for valor and commendation medals. There were two World War II naval officers, a major, and a lieutenant colonel in the group, but none of them had been in the military for twenty-two years. I took them through the changes in thinking about operations with infantry and airborne troops. I could tell them about training for combat on a battlefield where tactical nuclear weapons were used. I had quite a story to tell, and they seemed interested.

They also had questions about my vision for minority affairs.

My first job in higher education was because of a protest. I had no problem with student demands that opened opportunities for black people and other people of color. I also knew that once people of color got inside the system, they had to use pressure and influence to continue to open up these institutions to those who had been unintentionally or deliberately locked out.

Then I gave the president and vice presidents a history lesson, so to speak. I described the discrimination black folks had faced throughout the history of the United States. I reminded them of how we had been locked out of schools before and after the Civil War and that segregated education was often not much better than no education at all. I discussed the need for African American students to gain an education at the state's flagship campus and the university's responsibility to help them get that education. I added, however, that the needs of other minority students (the term we used then) were similar to those of black students. I think they were surprised and puzzled at that.

When the Minority Affairs Program started at Shoreline, many of the black students and some of the white faculty wanted to make it for black students only, to which I replied, "No, it should include all minority and disadvantaged students. Chicano students, Native American students, and many Asian American students are in a similar situation. They have been locked out as well. So have poor white students." That was not always a popular position, especially among young militant black students. I stood my ground on that principle at Shoreline and later at the University of Washington. Every minority affairs program I've ever directed would include students of color and disadvantaged whites. I believed it was the right thing to do then, and it is the right thing now.

The conversation turned to my plans for the University of Washington, should I accept a position with the school. One of the vice presidents asked, "If you came here, what would you do to improve the situation for black students and other minority students?"

"Well, frankly, I'd want an organization. I know from my military experience, if you're going to fight a war, you ought to have a good outfit!"

That comment generated a few laughs and cut the tension in the room.

"There's nothing here that approximates an effective organization. You have a Special Education Program, but it isn't an organization. You need an organization to recruit, to speak on behalf of, to represent, to advise, in a special way, these highly visible students, including poor white students who come to the university."

Of course I was thinking of the program at Shoreline. I imagined a UW program would have the same type of thrust. I was not naive about the situation at the UW campus. The university was a much larger and more conservative environment. I was really hip to that. I knew it would be much more difficult to deal with senior faculty members who were set in their ways, who had continuously obfuscated the proper story and place of black people in the history of the United States. I would be going up against them. At Shoreline Community College, I didn't have to face a powerful, entrenched faculty, and I knew I had the support of the president and key administrators.

I concluded my response by saying, "My job here would be inarguably more difficult."

Robert Waldo, the vice president for university relations, asked me, "What would you do if you were asked by the black students to confront the university president? What did you do at Shoreline when they asked you to do that?"

I knew this was one of those questions that could make or break my interview.

"Well, you know, Mr. Waldo," I began slowly, "I don't recall the students ever asking me to do that at Shoreline. As I sit in this chair, I don't recall students ever asking me to confront anybody. I am my own man. Even in the army, when I worked within strict regulations and for officers who could break my career, I was always my own man."

"Well, that's good," he replied but then posed his question slightly differently with the university as the focus. "What would you do if you had to confront students who wanted to oppose President Odegaard?"

"Well, if I were in this room, first of all, I would want the president's permission to argue to the point of decision. If the decision went against me, and I could not support the president, I would resign. I would always argue to the point of decision. Before we reached that point, however, I would probably have kicked his shins under the table until they bled."

Months later, Dr. Odegaard and I would laugh about my comments in that interview. He said he had really liked what I said. "Sam, no one else would have had the guts to tell me that."

I was hired that afternoon following the interview. My title would be Vice President for Minority Affairs. Just as Jim Goodman had advised, I would report directly and solely to President Charles Odegaard. I agreed to come to the University of Washington at the beginning of the next academic year, with an official start date of October 1, 1970. During the intervening months, Dr. Odegaard would have access to my services;

thus I was advising the UW president months before I officially began work on October 1.

My mood over the next few months was bittersweet. I knew I was going to make history as the first vice president for minority affairs at the University of Washington and the first person of color in the top ranks of the administration. But I also loved my job at Shoreline and the students I had worked with over the past three years.

JACKSON STATE: MY FIRST UW CRISIS

My first crisis at the University of Washington began before I officially arrived. In April 1970, college campus protests erupted all over the country when President Richard Nixon invaded Cambodia. On May 4, 1970, the protest at Kent State University turned violent when Ohio National Guard troops fired on the students, killing four of them and wounding nine others. The University of Washington was closed on May 8 in memory of the four students who had died at Kent State. In the announcement, the administration referred to "the Kent State murders."

On May 14, 1970, two students, Phillip Lafayette Gibbs and James Earl Green, were killed and twelve were injured when about two hundred students gathered outside a dormitory at Jackson State University, a predominantly black campus in Jackson, Mississippi.

I received a call from President Odegaard saying there was some difficulty on campus. He "wondered if I could be helpful." I asked him what was going on.

"Sam, five hundred students are in the HUB," he replied, referring to the Husky Union Building.

"Have they taken over the building?"

"No, they were meeting, and now they want to meet with the UW president."

"Let me go over there," I responded, "and I will see what's going on."

I hustled over to campus and entered the HUB in the middle of a tense BSU meeting. The second and third floors were packed. I was greeted by Wade Hill, the BSU president. He and many of the other students knew me because I had attended some of their regular meetings. Most of the students in the BSU trusted me. Some did not.

I soon found out why they were all in the HUB. The students thought there should be a similar closure for those who had been murdered at Jackson State. The Jackson State protests had not been connected with the Vietnam War. Instead, the students, responding to a rumor that Charles Evers, brother of slain civil rights activist Medgar Evers, had been assassinated, gathered on Lynch Street, which ran through the campus. They soon faced Jackson city police and Mississippi State troopers, who marched toward the crowd and opened fire. Gibbs and Green were killed in the volley of gunfire from police shotguns.

As far as the UW black students were concerned, the Jackson State victims were no less deserving of a tribute than the Kent State victims. They didn't say exactly what they would do if the administration refused their demand that it close the campus, but everyone recalled the day when about forty black students had taken over the UW administration building almost exactly two years earlier.

"Sam," BSU president Wade Hill began, "the black students want the university closed just like it closed for the Kent State murders. Why can't we have our people respected and pay homage to their deaths?"

"Well, I think you are right," I replied. When I said that, many of them looked at me like I was crazy. "Yeah, I agree with you."

"You agree with us?"

"Why, certainly I do. I think that's pretty logical. If it happened for white students, then it should happen for us. I'm supposed to be coming down here to start programs and develop programs that will support and assist you. I'm supposed to be the first vice president for minority affairs reporting for work in less than six months, and if I cannot arrange this, I will not report here for that job."

I waited for the students to absorb my words. They thought I had come over to tell them they were wrong or to counsel patience. They had not expected this response.

"Let me find out what's going on," I said.

I told them I would meet with President Odegaard to see what the university's response to their demands would be. I took along the BSU president and three other BSU officers, a sister and two burly black guys.

When the five of us reached the ground floor of the administration building, the staff did not recognize me. I'm sure the four black students accompanying me probably raised the tension level.

"I'm Mr. Kelly. These students and I are supposed to meet with the president of the university. I'd like to be escorted up there."

Just then the chief of the campus police, who knew me, walked up. He said, "Oh, certainly."

The chief at first said I would be the only one allowed to meet with the president.

"No," I replied. "These students come with me."

When I stood firm on this, the chief relented, and we were all ushered up to the third floor. We went to the same boardroom where I had been interviewed a few weeks earlier. There sat President Odegaard with all the vice presidents and the deans of the various colleges and schools. There were newspaper reporters in the room as well, altogether about thirty or forty people crammed into what now seemed like a much smaller room.

When I walked in, I was greeted by President Odegaard. Provost Solomon Katz sat to his left, and Executive Vice President John Hogness was seated to his right.

"Mr. President, you asked me to come down and discuss the students' needs and demands with them. The main demand is the same campus closure in memory of the students killed at Jackson State as for those killed at Kent State. I feel their demand is justified; they have a valid point. I recommend to you, as your incoming vice president for minority affairs, that you grant them that memorial closure."

"Well, we can't always close the doors of the university for any reason, no matter how valid," the president shot back, with both of us fully aware that our words were being recorded by the press in the room.

"The deans have programs with needs; we can't do this on a continuing basis."

"I understand that, President Odegaard, but we don't have student murders on a continuing basis."

At that point, John Hogness entered the conversation. "Charles, I agree."

Odegaard then turned to Hogness, totally ignoring what he had said before, and responded, "Of course, I agree with Sam. All right, what are you going to need?"

"Well, I'd like you to walk with us over to the HUB and give the students the news."

"I'd be happy to, Sam."

With that, Dr. Odegaard, the four BSU officers, and I walked the quarter of a mile back to the HUB.

When we got there, the BSU president spoke first, saying, "Sam Kelly's got a word for us."

I told them that we had met with the university president and his cabinet and that he was going to close the campus. The room went crazy.

After bringing President Odegaard to my side, I directed my comments to the audience: "While we're on this issue, I will be coming to you as your first vice president for minority affairs. I'd like to see the same enthusiasm carried forth in the development of other positive university initiatives. We've got a long way to go on this campus, but we can work together as brothers and sisters, faculty, and administration in a cooperative way."

I then asked President Odegaard to speak.

"I support what Sam Kelly has said," he told the students. "I will order this closure. It is the right thing to do."

On Monday, May 18, 1970, the University of Washington was officially closed in remembrance of the two students who had died at Jackson State.

VICE PRESIDENT FOR MINORITY AFFAIRS

I officially began work at the University of Washington on October 1, 1970, as vice president for minority affairs. The Office of Minority Affairs was located in Schmitz Hall, in the northeastern corner of the third floor.

My initial staff included a bright, eager, and energetic young man, Bill Hilliard, who would become my confidante and deputy; he was responsible for recruiting students of color and managing the student services area. Bill had been the go-between for the administration and black students prior to my arrival. He was a UW graduate who was hired in 1966 to help Charles Evans run the Special Education Program.

In addition to a deputy, I also wanted someone to administer the budgets. This was crucial. I already knew of some other young programs across the nation that were ambitious and did a fairly good job on the student services side but got in trouble because they did not or could not manage their budgets. This was a good way for opponents to attack minority studies and minority affairs programs, through the back door, without saying that they didn't like the programs because they thought the students and initiatives the programs represented shouldn't be on campus. I could even see this with the antipoverty programs that were set up in 1965 after the Watts Riots. Many of them were already in trouble with the Nixon administration because they couldn't control their costs or account for every penny. I was determined that would not happen to the Office of Minority Affairs.

President Odegaard and two vice presidents thought that having two assistant vice presidents was extravagant, but that's what I wanted in my office, and I got it. I hired Jim Collins, a retired navy commander who, like Bill Hilliard, had worked in the Special Education Program. Jim administered the budget. He kept an accounting of salaries, supplies, and staff travel costs and monitored the federal grants and state funds that supported students. This was very meticulous, tedious work, but it was necessary if we were to get our students the monies they needed. To the students, Jim was not as visible as Bill Hilliard, but his work was what kept many of them at the University of Washington. I knew the university had central administration budget folks who kept an accounting of our program, but I wanted someone I could trust, someone who would go into the right places in the budget to make sure students moved through the university.

I went outside of the Office of Minority Affairs to recruit supporters. Some members of the UW faculty became tutors to our students. Many of our students, despite having graduated from high school, were deficient in the basic skills needed to successfully complete UW courses. Building on the SEP model (we got rid of the name, however), we created tutorial courses and asked for volunteer UW faculty to teach them.

Faculty stepped forward. Professor Leonie Peternick, a naturalized Russian and a geneticist, tutored students in biology. Dr. Bill Irmsher and Jean Hundley from the English Department and Trevor Chandler from the Political Science Department gave their time. Dr. Millie Russell

THE FIRST OMA ADMINISTRATION: (BACK) SAM MARTINEZ, SAM KELLY, JIM COLLINS, BILL HILLARD; (FRONT) MIKE CASTILIANO, LARRY GOSSETT, EMMETT OLIVER. COURTESY AUDIO-VISUAL SERVICES, UNIVERSITY OF WASHINGTON, PHOTO BY WILLIAM ENG.

from the Health Sciences Department volunteered, as did Thad Spratlen, a professor in the School of Business, and Lois Price Spratlen, who was pursuing her doctorate.

Amy Mates from the English Department had been a high school teacher and Shoreline Community College faculty member. She set up courses to help OMA students develop their writing skills. In the process, she created an innovative program in which students who took her classes went through the entire year without grades and then were assigned grades retroactively based on the progress they had made over the entire year. Amy had fourteen people in her first class.

Her success gave us the idea of creating a large tutorial center for reading and study skills. Far too many of our students did not know how to study, prepare for exams, or discipline themselves for the academic

SAM KELLY MEETING WITH OMA DIVISION DIRECTORS MIKE CASTILIANO, EMMETT OLIVER, SAM MARTINEZ, AND LARRY GOSSETT IN 1971. COURTESY OFFICE OF INFORMATION SERVICES, UNIVERSITY OF WASHINGTON, PHOTO BY JOHN A. MOORE.

rigor of university courses. Critics of the OMA program said that was exactly why they shouldn't be at the University of Washington; I thought otherwise. If one part of the educational system, the public schools, had failed to prepare them adequately to compete, then maybe another part of that system, the university, could make up some of that deficit and at least give them a chance at a college education.

Some of the black students were already thinking the same thing. They supported the idea of a tutorial center, a building on campus dedicated to teaching reading and study skills. The building would also house academic and personal counselors who would help our students, almost all of whom were the first in their families to attend college, learn how to navigate through this large, impersonal institution of thirty-three thousand students. That idea became the OMA Instructional and Tutorial Center.

When I arrived in 1970, there was already an area in the basement of the mechanical engineering building where faculty tutored students. The students and volunteer faculty understandably wanted out of that basement and argued for a larger reading and study skills center. I also knew that with more students of color headed to campus, we needed more faculty volunteers and a larger space.

The students wanted a place to learn, but they also, wisely, I think, wanted a place to display their own cultural pride and heritage. One of them suggested an ethnic cultural center. Lectures, plays, concerts, and other programming reflecting the heritage of the four major groups of color on campus—African Americans, Asian Americans, Chicanos, and Native Americans—would be slated for the cultural center's theater. The students argued that the theater would also be a venue where whites could learn about people of color.

I requested an appropriation for separate buildings to house the Instructional Center and the Ethnic Cultural Center. I convinced the university to construct these buildings in order to support student success, especially since we knew that many of the students we intended to recruit would need help, particularly in mathematics and English. I made the pitch to President Odegaard and got more than $3 million dollars for the buildings.

On March 2, 1972, the Ethnic Cultural Center opened on Brooklyn Avenue near the southwestern edge of the campus. Benjamin McAdoo, one of Seattle's few black architects, designed the center. It became a hub for students of color, a place where they could study, hold social gatherings, admire ethnic art, and engage in recreational activities. It housed a library of eight hundred volumes. The renovated building across the street from the cultural center opened on September 25, 1972. This two-story building housed the OMA Instructional Center on the upper level and a 205-seat performing arts theater. In the first year, students saw Julian Bond, Bobby Seale, and Chief Dan George as well as live theatrical performances, concerts, and films.

I think the university, or at least the central administration, was learning as well. I remember another demonstration led by black students well into my tenure as vice president for minority affairs. One of the vice presidents called me and asked for my advice as to how to handle it.

He also asked if I could "put down" the students who were involved. "Really, that's not my job, to 'put them down,'" I responded. "My job is to encourage intellectual growth. I will speak against anything that looks as though it is subversive or may lead to violence and riots, but I won't tell the students to stop demonstrating. We are here to save these kids, not quash them."

I also tried to anticipate student grievances so that it would not be necessary for them to protest. I met in my office regularly with BSU leaders. I also continued to attend some general BSU meetings.

I met regularly with organizations that represented the other groups as well, including MEChA (for the Chicanos), the Native American Student Association, and the Asian American Student Association. Bill Hilliard reported to each group on the status of the Office of Minority Affairs and the activities of the staff. We also discussed fundraising efforts, named the people who were contributing, and described where the money was going. I briefed them on campus issues and controversies such as problems with the Athletic Department.

I shared information with the students and expected them to share information with me. If there was a meeting being held or a demonstration planned, I wanted to know it firsthand from them as soon as they knew about it; I needed a direct line to the students.

In addition to the specific organizations, I also created a student advisory council made up of representatives from the various student organizations of color. The student council met at 7:15 every Tuesday morning in the Office of Minority Affairs. I purposely scheduled these meetings on Tuesday. Since the president's cabinet meeting took place on every Wednesday, I knew exactly what students were thinking when I met with President Odegaard and his cabinet. I spent a great deal of time soliciting student opinions.

FIRST PRESIDENT'S CABINET BRIEFING

Charles Odegaard was my boss, but he also became one of my closest friends. I owe much of my success at the University of Washington to his friendship and support. Initially, however, we got off to a rocky start.

CHARLES ODEGAARD. COURTESY OF THE
MUSEUM OF HISTORY AND INDUSTRY.

I had moved into Schmitz Hall in October 1970, and for the next three
weeks and weekends, I worked around the clock with Bill Hilliard and
Jim Collins preparing for my first presentation to President Odegaard
and his cabinet. We focused on my initial budget request of $250,000 for
the Office of Minority Affairs in addition to the money that had already
been allocated to the Special Education Program, which I planned to
subsume in the new organization. I received a date from Dr. Odegaard
for the briefing and got ready for it. I planned to open and do most of
the briefing, but Bill and Jim were going to join me and discuss their sections of the proposed budget. I had done numerous briefings as a staff
officer in the U.S. Army and as director of the Minority Affairs Program
at Shoreline. Nonetheless, I considered this the most important briefing
of my career.

On arriving at Dr. Odegaard's office, I approached his executive assistant, who said, "Would you have a seat, Mr. Kelly?"

She went in to tell Dr. Odegaard that I was there. I expected her to show
Bill, Jim, and me into the boardroom where the cabinet meetings took
place. Instead, she came back out and said, "The president would like to
see you."

I was somewhat surprised, so I stepped in his office. Dr. Odegaard stood up as I walked in. He was red-faced and angry. Before I could say a word, he blurted out, "Mr. Kelly, if I wanted you to bring your staff members," speaking through his teeth, "I would have told you. I wanted you to brief the cabinet."

"Well, Mr. President, I thought we would do a very thorough job, and it wouldn't be that long. However, I am prepared to handle it myself."

My words did not calm him down. President Odegaard was enraged. I had never seen him like that before, nor did I see him so angry again on any day after.

"Well, if you need more time, Mr. Kelly, you can have more time."

"Well, no, President Odegaard. I insist that we do it now because I am prepared, and I will brief you myself, as you suggested."

Again he said, "I think you may need additional time to do this."

At this point, I was getting a bit irritated. "I beg your pardon, but I believe that I am fully prepared to brief you myself, and we have to move on these matters, as you know. You're under great pressure. And the students are looking for me to do something, too, as the first vice president for minority affairs. I do have some requests in terms of the new organization, so I feel very comfortable doing this now."

We stared at each other silently for a moment, and then I said as I turned to leave the room, "Mr. President, I'll see you in the boardroom in ten minutes."

As soon as I got into the hall, I beckoned for Jim and Bill and told them what had happened.

Bill immediately said, "Oh my God, Sam, that's too much for you to do."

"No," I quickly responded, "let me have your notes and just set up the easel in the boardroom."

I gathered their briefing pads and my notes and took all the materials the three of us had planned to use into the room. There must have been about ten people in the room including Provost Solomon Katz, Executive Vice President Hogness, and the other vice presidents. President Odegaard was at the end of the conference table. I turned to him and said, "Well, Mr. President, I'm prepared to brief."

Dr. Odegaard did not respond to my statement. Instead, he said to his cabinet. "Mr. Kelly had his team here. I want to give him more time to prepare, but he prefers not to do that, and he would like to proceed at this time, so let's let him take a crack at it."

I was amazed that Dr. Odegaard was still angry; however, I had no choice but to move forward with the briefing. "Thank you," I said.

As I stood there, and before I said the next word, I couldn't help but think of Dr. Odegaard in terms of the negative experiences I had had in the military in the South, particularly in Georgia and Alabama, with some really racist people, including a few U.S. Army officers who were my superiors. I was not impressed with how Dr. Odegaard had received me, and I wondered if I had gotten myself into something for which I was not prepared. I recalled how these men operated and continued to watch Dr. Odegaard as he settled uncomfortably into his seat at the end of the table.

Looking directly at Dr. Odegaard as if he were the only other person in the room, I told him, "Mr. President, I'm prepared. In an hour and thirty minutes, I will be finished, and I prefer not to be interrupted. I'll ask for questions when I'm finished, and I will cover the entire briefing and questions in that period of time."

He repeated his earlier offer, now in a clearly patronizing tone, "Well, you know, Mr. Kelly, we can cancel this."

"No. No, thank you, Dr. Odegaard. I am ready to begin."

I started my briefing by discussing the difficulties that lay ahead. I told the men assembled around the table that I could build a program to meet the needs of minority students and economically disadvantaged white students at a major university. To this day, I remember many of the words I used.

"I feel like I'm . . . caught between a rock and a hard place because this has never been done. In my study of the history of higher education in the United States and especially in the American West, I found no program that does what I have designed for us at the University of Washington."

I told the cabinet that my military training, steeped in organization and problem solving on the general staff, and my experience at Shoreline Community College in constructing one of the first minority affairs programs in the nation pretty well ensured the success of the UW program. I then interjected into my presentation the research I was doing for my doctorate. That research, I told them, was a model for a successful Office of Minority Affairs. I told the cabinet that my dissertation research provided a road map that I would generally follow. By this point, I was undoubtedly sounding arrogant. I continued, "I fought for this country in World War II and Korea, as did some of you in this room. Just as we achieved victory in what some thought were impossible circumstances, I think we can achieve success here in the face of doubters. Much more can be done at a major university to create an environment where minority students and poor white students can succeed if we, as leaders, accept the responsibility for assuring success."

THE OFFICE OF MINORITY AFFAIRS
AND THE UNIVERSITY OF WASHINGTON

"My plan designs a program that will recruit these students to the University of Washington and provide them with a sufficient support system to ensure their success," I continued. "I have no doubt this can be done, and, with your support, I am prepared to start that program today."

"There is a price for this type of program," I added, without slowing my pace. "So right at the beginning of my term as vice president, I am requesting $250,000 on top of the funds now available for the SEP."

Next, I presented a diagram of the Office of Minority Affairs. I requested permanent funding for two assistant vice presidents, Bill Hilliard and Jim Collins, and explained their roles. I described the various programs that would be created for Native Americans, blacks, Chicanos, and Asian Americans and also described the program for poor white students, which, as I would find out later, was an almost unique feature among programs like this across the United States. I also detailed how our program, led by a vice president for minority affairs, was different from other programs across the nation. Our structure would command respect from other UW administrators and would also serve as an inspiration to students of color, who would see someone who looked like them in a senior administrative position.

I even added that I thought my completing the doctorate in the College of Education that I had started two years earlier would also help, as I would then be a peer educationally to the other vice presidents and to the senior faculty when I advocated for programs that served students of color. I believed then, as I do now, that we were in a position to build a truly unparalleled program that would serve as a model for major universities across the nation.

"I wish to reiterate a few things that I hope you remember. I really want you to think about what I'm saying here, because I do have some experience in race relations and in designing a program to help minority students. I also have a fair amount of life experience that I bring to this plan.

"I've been black all my life and understand racism and discrimination. I felt them when I was a young officer in the U.S. Army. I have been called all kinds of racist names. We had the kind of people who would do that at Shoreline Community College. We have them on this university campus. Those are the obvious racists. They can be easily identified and isolated.

"We also have other people on this campus who would never want to be called racist and who will never use racist language. Nonetheless, they don't want to see this program succeed and will stand in the way even if they say otherwise in public. We had them at Shoreline, and we have them at the University of Washington.

"During the past three years, I have visited at least twenty-five universities and colleges throughout our country, including Harvard, Yale, the University of Massachusetts, UC Berkeley, Stanford, and the University of Pittsburgh. I have seen the programs they designed to alleviate the problems of ethnic minorities. Some of these programs are housed in the back of rickety buildings or in one classroom with a whole bunch of people jammed into it. I never saw one program that had the physical facilities necessary to make the program succeed.

"I don't want OMA to have an office that's down behind the football field near the equipment shed on lower campus. I want OMA in a location on campus that reflects the university's commitment to the success of its programs. I congratulate you on locating my office and SEP in Schmitz Hall. I really want to see the best of the university's facilities at our disposal.

"I would hasten to say that a preponderance of people, including senior faculty, will be against OMA, against the program I am trying to build. Most senior faculty have never had an original idea in terms of the integration of their campuses. If so, we would not need programs like OMA today.

"As I said in my interview a few months ago, I will report only to President Odegaard, and the decisions I make can be challenged only by the president and the board of regents. The moment the president and I disagree on fundamental policy issues regarding OMA, I am prepared to offer my resignation immediately and leave the campus to play golf, teach black and East Asian history at Shoreline, and be very, very happy."

I concluded my ninety-minute briefing with the following words: "Again, we're starting between a rock and a hard place. We are, through this program, in a small way attempting to atone for centuries of slavery and racial discrimination, for Western imperialism. We are making a modest down payment on a debt we owe to millions of people. The Office of Minority Affairs is not Sam Kelly's program; it's our program, gentlemen. It is the program of the University of Washington. There is only one boss of the program. He is the university president, the man to whom I will report as a vice president."

The men in the room applauded. President Odegaard spoke briefly and was very complimentary. At that point, I felt very good.

I then opened the floor for questions. Approximately forty questions followed, starting with a few from President Odegaard and the dean of the College of Arts and Sciences, Dr. Philip Cartwright. The questions and answers went on for another hour. This was a spirited exchange that flew by like it was less than thirty minutes for me.

CONFRONTING THE PRESIDENT

As the administrators left the boardroom, I approached President Odegaard. "Dr. Odegaard, may I chat with you just for a moment in your office?"

"Oh, why certainly, Mr. Kelly, certainly."

I gathered up my briefing materials, put them on the table, and followed him to his office.

Inside, he stopped and turned to face me. I walked up to him until I was about six inches from his nose and said, "President Odegaard, I am a man. I resent how you treated me when I came into your office. I am not a thing. Nobody, no man speaks to me through his teeth like I was a dog or like I was a 'nigger' without me doing something about it. I can assure you that if you ever treat me like that again, you will wind up on your back."

We looked at each other. President Odegaard put his right hand on my left shoulder and said, "Sam, I apologize. I apologize. You've done a good job. We'll be together for many of these meetings, and I appreciate your comment. That will never happen again."

And I said, "Thank you, Mr. President. I appreciate that." We shook hands, and I felt very good.

After that episode, I never again exchanged an angry word with Charles Odegaard. He became my friend and my most consistent supporter while I was at the University of Washington. Whatever our initial difficulties, I came to recognize President Odegaard as a man of vision and integrity.

CHAPTER 10

Building the Office of Minority Affairs

In making the move to the University of Washington, I believed I was following my destiny. When Paul Robeson had directed me to do something "for the race" so many years before, I had taken it to heart. The black students at the university needed leadership and direction. They were young, inexperienced, and without adult leadership. Many were the first members of their families to attend college. Their primary goal was to get an education and to make a place for themselves on the huge, complex campus. Clearly, not many of them knew how to craft a program, nor was it their responsibility. Nonetheless, they were frustrated. Few black faculty members had stepped forward to help, and the thirty-three thousand white students on campus seemed indifferent at best and often hostile. I believed I could help by giving these students a voice on the inside.

So I left Shoreline Community College to pursue Robeson's call. I felt good about that. Those of us who could were required to help lift up the race, which in my mind meant helping impoverished black students gain a university education so that they could provide a better life for themselves and their families. Then maybe they would do the same for others.

By 1970, the United States had seen a decade of demonstrations and protests. The nation's cities, including Seattle, had erupted in violence and rioting in 1967 and 1968. I didn't believe that was the way to make progress, but I knew older, successful African Americans like me couldn't just sit around and complain about what the young blacks were doing. We had to provide an alternative.

At Shoreline, I had met many of the students who had led the University of Washington protests, and they had influenced my thinking about the UW job. I also had great support from the brilliant Jim Goodman, a young assistant professor who had recently received his PhD in sociology from the University of Minnesota. He was also a Morehouse man, a graduate of the college that produced Martin Luther King, Jr., Benjamin Mays, and many other great black leaders. He was articulate and wise beyond his age, and the students loved him. He had a good grasp of the needs of the black community, and often we would get together over a little scotch to discuss the problems and needs of black students at the university late into the night.

It was unusual for me to be named a vice president at the university. Most of the programs across the country had at best a director of minority affairs or an assistant to the president for minority affairs. I visited at least twenty-five colleges to learn about their organizations, and in no case did I find a vice president with line/staff authority and a separate budget who was reporting directly to the university president. Just about all of the early minority affairs programs ran on soft money from the Department of Education. When I asked, "What is your university doing? What is your school's commitment to your program out of its regular budget dollars?" I learned that no one had a program funded out of the state budget.

The problem of racial discrimination in higher education had deep roots and was pervasive. It did not take a genius to figure out that if a program was going to be meaningful and create lasting change, it couldn't stay at the federal trough, dependent on the whims of bureaucrats in Washington, D.C. The Department of Education expected educational institutions to assume the funding of fledgling programs after two years of federal support, and as a result, by the mid-1970s, many of those programs were dead or dying. Expecting a program to succeed when the director had neither line/staff authority nor a permanent budget was at best unrealistic and at worst a cynical setup for failure.

At the time, the University of Washington didn't have a clue about how to address these problems. When I accepted the UW position, I negotiated the same arrangement I had at Shoreline, in which the president was my boss and the only person I reported to. Years later, UW president Charles Odegaard told me, "Sam, I never thought of making you a vice president, but you were right. The only way you could have had the clout to do the things that were necessary on this campus was to have direct access to me as the president. Your position also instantly revealed to my own staff and my cabinet how important the issue of diversity was to my administration."

THE OMA STUDENTS

As I saw it, the Office of Minority Affairs had various responsibilities. The first was to recruit students of color to the University of Washington. My office would seek out economically disadvantaged students, including those who historically had not been welcome at the University of Washington. The university's inflexible academic requirements for admission, I believed, excluded many capable students who only needed a chance to show their abilities. It was time to change the university's admission apparatus so that it could address the needs of the thousands of students who were denied access to the state's flagship public university.

Almost everyone on and off campus understood that the office would serve students of color—African Americans, Asian Americans, including Pacific Islanders, Chicanos, and Native Americans—but I included disadvantaged white students as well. In the focus on impoverished people of color, few realized that in 1970, 95 percent of the more than 200,000 people in the state who did not have more than an eighth-grade education were white.

My arguing for disadvantaged whites was a new twist, and I met with some resistance from both students of color and the administration. I stood my ground on that issue, and I'm happy I did. Historically, poor white students did not have the financial resources to enter the University of Washington and in most instances did not have family members who had attended institutions of higher learning to guide them. I presented their case to President Odegaard: "There's not much difference between a poor white student who has an empty belly and no means to improve himself, and a black student in the same condition." When I described the group of students who came under the OMA program as "economically disadvantaged," by and large I was talking about white students.

My commitment to these white students was soon tested. There was an Asian division counselor who I believed discriminated against the white students in the program. He often made them wait at the end of the line and signaled through his attitude and behavior that he didn't feel they should take part in the program. When I found that out, I fired him and created the economically disadvantaged division of the Office of Minority Affairs so that our commitment to these students would be public and unequivocal. I called Dr. Odegaard to tell him what I had done, and he supported my actions.

CONSTRUCTING A PROGRAM

I organized my office with two assistant vice presidents, Jim Collins for administration and Bill Hilliard for student services. I then created four ethnic student divisions—black, Chicano, Native American, and Asian —and added a division for economically disadvantaged white students; each division had a director and office assistants. Some of these positions were filled by students. Larry Gossett, for example, was the first director of the black student division, and he hired John Gilmore, Lamar Mills, and Margaret Brown for his staff. A number of students served as recruiters and counselors, one for every fifty students the Office of Minority Affairs recruited. I required them to attend their respective student organization meetings each week and be involved in the community activities of their student target groups. They also were required to produce a plan for recruiting students.

I asked the university to provide transportation to the Yakima Valley to recruit Chicano students, to reservations across the state to seek Native Americans, and across Seattle and western Washington to recruit black, white, and Asian American students. We contemplated a national recruitment plan but decided to concentrate our resources in the state and region.

With the OMA recruiting structure in place, we hit the road, crisscrossing the state to identify potential students. The student recruiters were to seek out anyone in our target populations—people of color and the economically disadvantaged—who wanted to attend the University of Washington. They visited homes and community centers, churches, and pool halls. They visited places where recruiters would have thought it unlikely to find young people interested in going to college, especially the places kids of color frequented. They went there to tell the University of Washington's story.

We put recruiting packages in the hands of potential students and gave brochures to students, their parents, and teachers. We sold the advantages of attending the University of Washington in communities that were as close as the Central District, a predominantly black community four miles from the campus, and as far away as the Colville Indian Reservation in the northeastern corner of the state. We sent recruiters to all of Washington's more than forty reservations, and I often went myself to meet with tribal leaders. OMA recruiters spent a great deal of time in the Yakima Valley because of the large concentration of Chicano students there. We contacted the principals of schools asking for time to make presentations, although many were reluctant to let us in. It was the era of black power student protests, and many of the OMA recruiters showed up with big Afros, wearing dashikis and the black power fist as a medallion.

Once people got to know us, they respected our professionalism. Much of that came from my military background and my years of experience as a staff officer. OMA recruiters arrived on time, looked sharp, and articulated their presentations in clear, decisive voices. My top staffers, Bill Hilliard and Bill Baker, who in 1972 replaced Jim Collins, also brought that demeanor to the office. We were models of professional behavior, and our staff quickly learned I would not tolerate anything less. When I had arrived in 1970, some staffers said that they worked half-time or three-quarter time, determining their own hours. I ended that foolishness. I said to the non-student staffers, "If you can't work full-time, eight to five, you need to look for another job." I had not been happy with the attitude I saw in the office during my first days on campus.

I don't completely fault those who worked under these conditions. The University of Washington had not made a significant financial commitment to the Special Education Program. There was no full-time administrator in charge of efforts to help students of color, certainly no one who reported to a senior administrator or who set goals and standards for the program and its employees. The six people in that office "did their own thing," as they used to say then. There were one or two staffers, such as Bill Hilliard, and some volunteers who were committed to changing the way students of color were perceived and treated at the university, but the office was chaotic. That had to end, and I ended it.

We changed the name of the Special Education Program to the Educational Opportunity Program (EOP), which would provide academic tutorial services, personal counseling, and financial support. Our recruitment programs would fall under the Educational Opportunity Program's umbrella as well. This program was actually a group of programs under the auspices of the Office of Minority Affairs designed to recruit students of color and disadvantaged white students and to ensure their academic success. We began hiring graduate students as tutors, many of whom would work in the Instructional Center for several years.

After about a year, our recruitment efforts began to pay off. In 1970, there were fewer than 900 black students in the Special Education Program. By 1974, we had 1,478 students in the Educational Opportunity Program. We weren't just bringing in bodies. We worked hard to make sure these at-risk students remained at the university and graduated. Year after year, 85 percent of the EOP students remained in good academic standing, compared to 95 percent of all UW students. By 1972, we graduated more black students than all twenty-seven community colleges across the state combined. In 1973, we graduated more minority students than all the rest of the two-year and four-year institutions in the state of Washington.

We also took some risks. One was the creation of the Resident Release Project, which began in 1972. Bill Hilliard came to me with the idea of prisoner education and took me to visit a halfway house in Seattle. I was inspired by his ideas and those of Gordy Graham, an ex-felon and author of *In the Land of the Blind, the One-Eyed Man Is King*. In 1970, people of color made up 4.6 percent of the state population but 29 percent of the prison population. We believed that providing access to college would be one of the most effective means of ensuring that some of the men and women who were incarcerated would become contributing members of society when they were released. President Odegaard agreed and took the courageous step of supporting my plan when it went before the board of regents.

The Residence Release Project, initially administered by Bill Hilliard and later managed by Dr. Karen Morrell, was essentially an early release education program for offenders. The UW project had 80 men and women from four state prisons, two federal prisons, and the King County Jail during its eight-year existence. From 1972 through 1980, 316 men and 49 women came through our program—222 whites, 101 blacks, 16 Chicanos, 16 Native Americans, and 10 Asian Americans. Of these participants, 79 percent completed the program and 80 percent of that group never returned to prison. Academically, there were a number of successes; 141 men and women stayed at the university after they completed the program. Twenty-three received a bachelor's degree or higher and one received a PhD. Nonetheless, the federally funded program ended following the election of Ronald Reagan.

The Office of Minority Affairs also assumed responsibility for the Upward Bound Program, a federally funded national program designed to encourage high school students to spend a summer on a university campus in order to be prepared for university work. The program began in 1965 with English professor Roger Sale as its first director. By the time I arrived, Ralph Hayes, a popular Garfield High School history teacher, was administering the program.

We brought fifty to sixty students from Seattle and as far away as eastern Washington to the UW campus, where most of them were exposed to a college environment for the first time. William H. Stinson was one of the Upward Bound success stories. He was one of the first African Americans to earn a bachelor's degree in geological science (1974) and for some time worked for the U.S. Geological Survey, where he helped craft regulations regarding the Outer Continental Shelf Oil and Gas leasing program. Later, Stinson worked as a geologist for North Pacific Oil and Gas in Houston.

As the OMA program grew, so did my support among African American students, who were the majority of students of color on campus. By 1971, there were 1,100 black students on campus, 300 Chicano students, and 170 Native Americans out of a total enrollment of 33,478. During my first year as vice president for minority affairs, I had the support of the vast majority of these students. But there were some who didn't trust me because of my military background, some who distrusted anybody who wore a suit and tie every day, and some who felt I wasn't militant enough. My job compromised me in their eyes. I think there was also some "I am blacker than you" political posturing going on as well. Most black students didn't buy into that garbage. Some of them knew what I had done at Shoreline, and many more knew or remembered my stand at the meeting in the HUB in May 1970. They had seen a black man who could easily have been part of the establishment take a stand with them.

Most of our efforts were directed toward undergraduates, but the Office of Minority Affairs had a graduate component as well. Herman McKinney, who held a joint position as assistant to the vice president for minority affairs and associate dean of the Graduate School, led our efforts to recruit graduate students of color. I personally recruited about fifteen students who would pursue doctoral degrees in the College of Education. These graduates hold significant professional positions all across the country today. Dr. James Bennett, one of my former students, is now a vice president at Bellevue College. Before he relocated to California, Dr. Leonard Jackson held positions at North Seattle Community College and Lake Washington Technical College.

LOBBYING FOR SUCCESS

During the program's third year, we created an EOP alumni association to keep in touch with the women and men who had come to the University of Washington through the program and gone on to graduate. Two alumni leaders, Larry Matsuda and Vivian Kelley, led the effort to establish a small ceremony to pay tribute to our graduates; the ceremony has grown into the annual Multicultural Alumni Partnership "Bridging the Gap" Breakfast. One of the awards presented at the breakfast is the Dr. Samuel E. Kelly Award, which goes to an alumnus who has made the greatest continuing contribution to diversity at the University of Washington or in the state.

Each year at the breakfast, the total number of students who have come through the various OMA graduate and undergraduate recruitment programs is announced. More than twenty-four thousand OMA students graduated from the university between 1970 and 2007. OMA alumni include Kimberley Bell, chief of staff at Virginia Mason Hospital in Seattle; Ron Chew, former director of the Wing Luke Asian Museum; Larry Gossett, a King County councilman, one of the first staffers I hired to help with the program; Eugene Green, a Seattle attorney; Roberto Maestas, founder of El Centro de la Raza; federal judge Ricardo Martinez; Rodney Moore, the former BSU president who became president of the National Bar Association; and former Seattle mayor Norm Rice and Constance Rice, his wife, who has held many administrative positions in education and the private sector. OMA graduates are in the schools, the community colleges, and city government. They are proof that the program continues to make an impact on the state and the nation.

We also had some success garnering federal funds, thanks to the intervention of U.S. Senator Warren Magnuson. While I knew we could not depend solely on federal funding, I was not about to forgo the opportunity to acquire some federal dollars to advance our efforts on campus. Getting the senator's support for our office began with UW president Odegaard's suggestion in 1971 that I make a trip to Washington, D.C.

Before I could meet the state's senior senator, I was first introduced to Featherstone Reed, his aide. We quickly got to be friends. "Feather" showed me how to present information to elected officials and introduced me to Senator Magnuson. When I laid out our plans for the Office of Minority Affairs and our budget needs, the senator listened and then obtained the funding we needed. I never allowed the program to depend on federal dollars, but Senator Magnuson gave our budget crucial financial support during my early years on campus.

I didn't have as much success with the Washington State Legislature, even though I had friends there, including State Senator George Fleming, who represented the Thirty-seventh District, which included most of Seattle's African American population. Through Senator Fleming, I was able to testify before the Senate Budget Committee and the House Ways and Means Committee, but the legislature didn't allocate any new funding for our program. I do remember one year when the program was budgeted for $130,000, and I wanted more. The legislature ordered another $100,000 but told President Odegaard to get it from somewhere else in the university's budget. I thought Dr. Odegaard would be upset. Instead, he said, "Well, Sam, you gave me what I wanted," and allocated the additional dollars. Apparently, he felt our office should have the larger allocation but wanted to try convincing the legislature to provide the funding. He was shrewd when it came to the politics of the state legislature.

Even though governors could not allocate money to our program, I cultivated them as well. Governor Daniel J. Evans was a vocal supporter

DANIEL J. EVANS. COURTESY OF UNIVERSITY
OF WASHINGTON LIBRARIES, SPECIAL COLLEC-
TIONS, UW 17710.

of our program and agreed to appear on its behalf whenever I asked him to. Anytime he asked me to appear as a campaign supporter, I was there as well. I was closer to Governor Evans than to any other politician of that era, but I counted both Republicans and Democrats as my friends.

There was no Republican or Democratic political stance in the Educational Opportunity Program. That money had no color. There was and still is so much poverty, so much need in our country, that I didn't feel we should fight over who had the best political platform. Whether speaking before Democratic or Republican audiences, my message was the same. I reminded people of the sacrifices black soldiers had made for this country, fighting for rights they did not have. I thought of my own situation, my pride in my country as a soldier willing to die for it even as I personally faced blatant racial discrimination from both soldiers and civilians. This was my history, and it was largely the history of black people in the United States. History can be a powerful weapon. I was loaded with it and used it with Democrats and Republicans and in fact with anyone who could help our students.

BILL GATES, SR., MARY GATES, AND DALWYN KNIGHT AT THE FIRST
FRIENDS OF EOP PHONE-A-THON. COURTESY OFFICE OF INFORMA-
TION SERVICES, UNIVERSITY OF WASHINGTON, PHOTO BY JOHN A.
MOORE.

FRIENDS OF THE EDUCATIONAL OPPORTUNITY PROGRAM

Private fundraising was never far from my mind, and one reason for
the success of the Office of Minority Affairs was our ability to tap into
private donations. Most programs like ours never developed private
funding sources or looked at that possibility until the 1980s, during the
presidency of Ronald Reagan, when state and federal support for these
kinds of initiatives evaporated. We got on that bandwagon early. In fact,
I had first begun private fundraising efforts on behalf of black students
while I was still at Shoreline Community College.

Dalwyn Knight had helped create Friends of the Minority Affairs Pro-
gram at Shoreline. When I arrived at the University of Washington, I asked
Dalwyn to do the same thing for the UW's new Educational Opportunity
Program. In 1973, she and her friend, Mary Gates, who served on the UW
Board of Regents from 1975 to 1993 and in 1985 became the first woman

to chair the board, raised money for the program by organizing the first fundraising phone-a-thon at the University of Washington. There were others from across Seattle who helped, including Toby Burton, Mark Cooper, future Washington Governor Booth Gardner, Vivian Kelley, Sharon Maeda, Benjamin McAdoo, Ray Merriwether, Eliot C. Read, and Ruth Yoneyama Woo.

Between 1973 and 1975, Friends of the Office of Minority Affairs raised $409,000 in scholarships. Contributions came from individual and corporate supporters. SAFECO, the Seattle-based insurance firm, gave more than $20,000 during this period. The program received $6,000 from the Seattle chapter of the National Council of Negro Women and $5,000 from the Links. John H. Hauberg, president of Pacific Denkmann, a tree farm and land management company, contributed $4,500.

Dalwyn Knight and Mary Gates began to approach their friends, who also donated to the program. About seven or eight of these friends were members of Republican Women for Nixon during the 1968 presidential campaign. They scheduled me to make presentations in various homes. Eventually, Dr. Odegaard joined me, and we made a joint pitch for the Educational Opportunity Program. Our talks were called "An Evening with Charles and Sam."

It got to be quite a routine. Twenty to thirty potential donors would gather at a supporter's home, where we had cocktails and then dinner. Afterward, Charles and I talked one-on-one with individuals. Next, we made our pitch to the assembled group. Charles began, describing the challenges the university faced as it evolved into a more diverse institution. Then he turned to me, and I explained the fears and frustrations the students faced in their classes and dormitories. I answered the question that someone invariably asked: "What do they want?" Finally, I asked for support for the Educational Opportunity Program.

COACH JIM OWENS

The program got money from some surprising places, including the newly authorized eleventh football game. In 1971, the Pac-10 increased the number of regular season football games for its member schools from ten to eleven. It was a time of a high racial tension on campus due to the

ongoing conflict between the Black Athletes Alumni Association, led by
Carver Gayton and Joe Jones, and the UW Athletic Department. The
controversy had begun in October 1969, when Coach Jim Owens heard
of a possible boycott of football games by black athletes and demanded
that each player sign an oath pledging loyalty to him. Greg Alex, Ralph
Bayard, Harvey Blanks, and Lamar Mills refused to sign the oath and
were suspended. The rest of the black players then boycotted the UW-
UCLA game on December 14, 1969, which the Huskies lost, 57–14.

The Black Athletes Alumni Association and most of the boycotting
players claimed the suspensions were racially motivated. They accused
Coach Owens of "stacking" the black players, that is, having them all
compete only for certain positions on the team. They also leveled a more
serious charge: that the suspensions really came from Owens's displea-
sure at the black athletes dating white coeds.

The turmoil continued after I arrived on campus. Although Alex,
Bayard, and Mills were reinstated, Blanks remained suspended from the
team. Four other black players—Charles Evans, Ira Hammond, Calvin
Jones, and Mark Wheeler—resigned at the end of the 1970–71 season, and
for the first time, Coach Owens's job was on the line. The Black Students
Union supported the athletes, as did many of the African American
faculty and several black community organizations such as the Black Panther Party. Some blacks and most whites supported Jim Owens's decision
to run the team as he saw fit.

In November 1970, Jim Lambright, one of Owens's assistant coaches,
who had coached at Shoreline when I was there, arranged for me to meet
Coach Owens when he was scheduled to be on Mercer Island to make
a presentation to the Rotarians. Lambright seemed to think we could
establish a dialogue if we had a chance to meet together privately. "Sam,
you and the coach think much alike," he said. "You're aggressive, and
you think about helping the students. You two should get together after
his presentation." Owens arrived at my home around nine in the evening, after his Rotary talk, and we spent several hours discussing the
racial problems plaguing the football team.

A number of people accused Coach Owens of being a racist, but I don't
think he was any more racist or prejudiced than anybody else I've dealt
with most of my life. That's where I disagreed with the Black Athletes

Alumni Association. Later, members of the association wondered, "Why is Sam Kelly working with that racist so-and-so?"

My response to that statement was "I'd work with the devil if it meant that I'd have an opportunity to persuade him to do something constructive for the students, irrespective of color."

Jim Owens and I agreed that I would talk with his coaches. We also agreed that the two of us would meet once a month for dinner. We called ourselves the "Poker Club" and met regularly at my home on Mercer Island or Owens's home on Lake Washington, along with selected people from the Office of Minority Affairs and his coaching staff. We also included a few community people.

I publicly opposed the Black Athletes Alumni Association boycott, not because of my meetings with Owens but because I thought the organization was making a tactical blunder. If you want to change someone's attitude and behavior, you don't isolate him and refuse to talk to him. Instead, you intensify the intellectual dialogue. The more difficult the situation, the more you talk.

Although a number of people on the campus and in the community opposed my meeting with Owens, I thought we were making progress in our discussions, and I said so, which contradicted the statements of the Black Athletes Alumni Association. The association called for a boycott of both the Office of Minority Affairs and the UW Athletic Department. The association branded me and Don K. Smith, the black associate athletic director who was hired in January 1971, "enemies of the people." But they were on the outside, and I was on the inside.

BLOOD MONEY

Jim Owens and I resolved some of the festering problems in the athletics program. He decided to bring back Harvey Blanks, the running back who remained suspended into 1971. Blanks was allowed to play practice games during the preseason and was eventually fully reinstated. Coach Owens also made the decision to donate all the proceeds from the eleventh football game, about a quarter of a million dollars, to the Educational Opportunity Program.

Both Coach Owens and I knew this decision would be controversial.

I carried the proposal to the Black Student Union during its regular meeting. About 250 black students and some black faculty and staff members had gathered in a meeting room in the HUB. Bill Hilliard and I entered the room after the meeting had started, and the donation was already the hot topic. Ed Jones, a UW lecturer who occasionally taught African American history, had the floor. I first met Ed Jones when we were both young army officers in Japan in 1947. We had not hit it off well. I'd had the sense that he placed his own interests above those of his men. Nothing that passed between us at that meeting would make me change my mind about Jones. He said he opposed the Educational Opportunity Program taking what he called "blood money," which was meant to end the boycott and avoid addressing the racism of the UW athletic program.

A young woman, a student and BSU member, spoke next, repeating the charge and urging the program to refuse money from Owens or anyone else associated with the athletic program.

At that point, Wade Hill, the BSU president, said, "Well, Sam's here. I'm sure he would have something to say."

I walked to the front of the room and began my speech: "I have much to say about Jim Owens's proposal. I know the requests that come across my desk every day for putting money into your pockets to pay your tuition and bills. My only concern is where I can get the money to keep you in school so that you can get your degrees. What you do with your degree—if you want to learn to make atomic bombs—that's your business. But my mission as vice president for minority affairs is about getting you the money you need. It is not about the mess you folks are talking about today."

At that point, Ed Jones said, "I don't believe and I don't trust what you are saying because this is blood money."

"Now listen, let me tell you about that." I was livid at that point.

"People who are yelling the loudest about blood money, et cetera, et cetera, aren't putting a damn thing into the program. Bill Hilliard, Sam Kelly, and every member of my staff contributes money, their own money that they are making working at the university, into the EOP program to get students through school."

Jones fired back, "Well, I do other things!"

As soon as the students heard that, they laughed like crazy.

I jumped on his statement. "Now that's what I'm talking about. Other things like what?" I directed my next comments to the students: "Look, you need to understand that as long as I am here as the vice president for minority affairs, I'm going to take every damn dollar I can get from anybody, including Jim Owens and his momma. I know what the staff and I are doing to support you. We need financial help, and the day I find out I can't get that help, I'm leaving you and going back to Shoreline Community College and play golf and have some fun and finish my doctorate. Then I will go somewhere else."

One BSU student responded to my rant, saying, "Sam, why are you always talking about leaving us?"

Before I could answer, another said, "I like the way you said that, Sam. I support you."

Another said, "Yeah, we want the money."

With that, the BSU voted to accept the eleventh game proceeds.

I called Jim Owens later that night. "We had a little tussle about this, Jim," I said, not revealing how close the BSU had come to publicly rejecting his offer, "but they enthusiastically accepted your support. It is vital to our program. I would appreciate you talking to your friends about what we've accomplished, the progress we are making." Then I added, "Jim, I want this to continue, not only the money you have pledged but our dialogue." I was thinking about Harvey Blanks and the other athletes. Jim and I continued to meet for lunch and dinner, and I reported to the faculty senate on our efforts.

Getting support from Friends of the Educational Opportunity Program and from people like Coach Owens was very gratifying to me. In the early and mid-1970s, about 25 percent of the annual EOP budget came from these donations. I used to meet for lunch with a multimillionaire, whose name I can't divulge, once a year, every year, at a downtown Seattle restaurant when I was vice president for minority affairs. Each year, he would write out a check for $1,000 to $2,000 to support the program. I don't think the students of color who were on campus then ever knew the amount of support they received indirectly through wealthy, conservative people, often Republicans, who gave generously to our program.

CARVER GAYTON AND SAM KELLY DISCUSSING THE RACIAL CLIMATE AT THE
UW ON KIRO-TV IN 1974. COURTESY OF THE KELLY FAMILY.

CHANGING THE UNIVERSITY

My primary responsibility as vice president for minority affairs was to develop a program that would seek out students of color and disadvantaged white students and assist them in getting an education at the University of Washington. But I also felt that my position included the responsibility to play another crucial role as the major adviser to the university president and the board of regents on issues of racial equality and justice. My job required that I train and orient my colleagues on the issues and problems our campus faced as we brought these students in and met their needs. Nothing like this had ever happened before. Not only were there far more students of color, but middle-class white students, faculty members, and administrators had to face their own concerns about dealing with a new and, for some of them, disruptive and undeserving element on campus. I was vice president in 1971, for example, when Marco DeFunis, Jr., filed a reverse discrimination lawsuit against the university's law school in *DeFunis v. Odegaard*. DeFunis, a white student, argued that he had been bypassed for admission in favor of minority students with lower academic records and test scores. The U.S. Supreme Court found the case to be moot in 1974 because DeFunis had been provisionally admitted while the case was pending and was slated to graduate within a few months. Many people, however, continued to challenge the presence of both our students and the programs that supported them on the University of Washington campus.

My job was to bring the campus along in terms of meeting the needs and requirements of highly visible students of color and to identify those faculty members, students, and administrators who were potential allies in that effort. I believed that if we could create the right atmosphere, the right environment, we could develop a program that would attract students of color and disadvantaged white students and increase their graduation rates. I wanted 15 percent of the total university student body to be composed of minority students from groups that historically had been denied admission to the University of Washington. That goal was dismissed in the early 1970s as impossible to achieve, yet today, these students represent 33 percent of the university's total enrollment of forty-three thousand students.

The one area that left me frustrated was faculty diversity. When a regent asked me in 1974 what I thought was the greatest impediment to equal opportunity on the campus, I said without hesitation that it was the reluctance of the faculty to recruit and retain minority members. Throughout my years at the University of Washington, progress in this area was glacial, and the excuses given were as numerous as the failures to hire and grant tenure. Some departments claimed they had no money to recruit, and others said that minority scholars weren't the right "fit," that is, their view of the world was often different from that of the tenured faculty. Black faculty members who were considered good teachers sometimes failed to turn out publications; those who published were often pronounced failures at teaching.

Worse still, many departments said there weren't enough minority graduate students training to become the next generation of faculty. Yet by the time I stepped down as vice president for minority affairs, the university boasted record resources to support graduate study even as it lamented the declining number of students of color in graduate school.

There was a deeper problem. Many faculty members, even those who considered themselves progressive, were staunch defenders of old and, in my view, outmoded academic traditions. They would go to great lengths to preserve their status and insulate themselves from change. By virtue of their training, they were often zealous about laying bare the faults of the rest of society—which is quite all right by me—but they were also adept at creating refined and highly polished illusions about themselves as enlightened.

I applaud demands for academic rigor and scholarly research, particularly when they are objectively aimed at solving human problems and improving the quality of life for all the world's citizens. I abhor them when they merely preserve the status quo or perpetuate a conservative mode of thought aimed at allowing into the faculty only those who mirror its current members.

FIGHTING FOR THE OFFICE OF MINORITY AFFAIRS

Some may believe that nothing is more difficult than being shot at each day in the combat zone. I don't necessarily disagree with that, but the University of Washington proved to be a different type of combat zone. Every day, I had to avoid blowing my top and keep from calling somebody a racist SOB. I had to sit in meetings and listen to some antagonist or racist spout off while I struggled to maintain the self-discipline and intellectual capability to continue the discourse. I often felt I was in a hostile environment, and I worried about losing my temper, which I often did—behind closed doors.

I remember a 1974 airport meeting with two hundred businesspeople in Spokane arranged by Bob Waldo, the vice president for university relations. After I briefed them on our work at the University of Washington, one of the businessmen said: "I have an objection to this program, Dr. Kelly. It's for black students only, and that is racist. There's no way I will ever put money into a program like that since all you have are black students down there."

I waited until he finished and then responded, but not very diplomatically. "Now, you have just heard a comment from one of the most ignorant persons I have listened to in some time. Since the day I arrived at the university, our program has always had a component for poor white students. I have continued that component and increased the numbers of white students there because, philosophically, I believe a program like this should be for all students. A poor white man is just as hungry as a poor black man. He needs help; he needs an education. I think the black man needs more help because of his history and his high visibility. You can always identify a poor black man, as opposed to a poor white man, because of his color. But even wrapped in this skin color that I am, I believe it's just as important to educate poor white kids who have not had an opportunity for higher education as it is to educate poor black kids."

That man turned all shades of red, and the Equal Opportunity Program received several new contributions from people in the audience.

It was not just off-campus people who were misinformed and had misgivings about the program. There were strongholds of faculty opposition to it and its students. The conservative minds in those departments saw no reason for my office and programs like those run by the Office of Minority Affairs to exist.

One faculty leader, Pierre van den Berghe, publicly challenged me and the OMA program less than one year after I arrived on campus. Van den Berghe, a white sociologist born in the Belgian Congo, taught courses on Africa. I am sure he felt that he was liberal on race. Soon, however, I was getting complaints from black students in his course, Sociology 362: Race Relations. Some of them accused him of perpetuating stereotypes about primitive Africans. I don't know how true that was, but I do know that in June 1971, some of the students got into an argument with him in his office over the grades he had given them. He briefly left his office, and apparently two of them did something pretty stupid—they changed the grades in van den Berghe's grade book while he was gone.

Van den Berghe discovered what they had done and demanded that they be expelled. He met with me about the incident, and I said that although some disciplinary action was in order, I didn't want the students kicked out of school. He then wrote an article in the *Daily*, the campus newspaper, arguing that the administration should eliminate the Office of Minority Affairs. Why should we have special programs, he asked, for students who don't deserve to be at the university? Why should the entire campus support an Ethnic Cultural Center that serves only students of color? Why should there be a Black Student Union?

Van den Berghe's attack went far beyond what two students had foolishly done and became a general assault on students of color and the programs that served them. Since his chief target was the Office of Minority Affairs, I felt obligated to respond to him. Every day for a couple of weeks, the students would grab the *Daily* to read his latest assertion and my response. I also reported on these newspaper exchanges at the BSU meetings. Looking back, I don't think this dialogue changed the minds of supporters or critics of the Office of Minority Affairs, but the black students especially were really proud that someone had the courage to publicly defend them and the program that supported them. They knew Sam Kelly would fight for them.

By 1975, the Vietnam War was over, and so was the era of black radical protest. The campus had quieted down considerably over those five years. With the changing mood across the campus and the country, some faculty members who had supported the Educational Opportunity Program began to pull back, with fewer of them volunteering to help mentor our students. I did not quite realize it at the time, but my most effective days as vice president for minority affairs were already over.

CHAPTER 11

Final Years at the University of Washington

My training and background in the U.S. Army helped me enormously in dealing with the issues I faced as vice president for minority affairs. Having gone into combat in Korea as a young rifle platoon leader and led men into battle, I had a keen sense of how to treat and care for soldiers under my command. This leadership sense had made me bold and aggressive, and at the University of Washington I was not intimidated in confrontations with students, staff, or administrators. I know the students—who, after all, were almost the same age as those soldiers—sensed that I would stand my ground and say my piece. One student said, "Sam Kelly—he ain't 'fraid of nobody. I think he still cuts!" That was true; nothing anyone could say or do frightened me.

Let me hasten to add that the success of the Office of Minority Affairs came not just from my leadership but from a remarkably dedicated staff who supported me and worked without reservation on behalf of the students. Together, Bill Hilliard and I went through more battles at the University of Washington than I had faced in Korea. I must also give credit to people in the OMA office such as Bill Baker, Cathy Bryant, Sandra Fujita, Larry Gossett, Sharon Maeda, Larry Matsuda, and Gertrude Peoples, all of whom helped me accomplish so much during my six-year tenure as vice president for minority affairs.

I was particularly successful with the central administration and the board of regents. Some people resented that success, thinking, "That Sam Kelly can get anything he wants." I did nothing to dissuade them from believing that. I had direct access to some of the regents, among them, Jim Ellis, Dr. Robert L. Flennaugh, Mary Gates, and George V. Powell, during most of my years with the Office of Minority Affairs. If I had a particular concern, I was not averse to calling one or two of the regents I was close to and letting them know, "I really want your support, and here's what we're trying to do." I briefed the entire board of regents at least once a year and hosted an annual dinner for them at my home. UW vice presidents came for dinner, and I sat in the president's box for football games together with the president's cabinet and the regents. I attended official dinners and teas, as President Odegaard sought to expose me to an assortment of influential people. He also arranged for me to meet leading elected officials, many of whom I eventually came to know on a first-name basis. He went out of his way to indicate my importance to his administration and to him personally. I was moving in powerful company.

I didn't have any serious difficulty with the president's cabinet or with individual vice presidents that could not be hashed out before our cabinet meetings. Although some were surprised that Dr. Odegaard had brought me in as a vice president, they quickly figured out that I was in contact with him on a variety of issues and that, every Wednesday morning at the cabinet meeting, I would be voicing my opinion on what needed to be done to help integrate students of color into the University of Washington.

STUDENT ORGANIZATIONS

I dealt with all the ethnic student groups and attended meetings of the Native American Students Organization, the Asian American Student Coalition, and MEChA. I had the trust of the Native American, Asian American, and black students, but I could never quite reach the Chicano students.

The student organization most supportive of my work at the University of Washington was the Black Student Union. Early on, I won the trust of the BSU student members and every BSU president, beginning with the first one, Wade Hill. From the day they first saw me mediate an agreement between them and President Odegaard over closing the university to memorialize the students killed at Jackson State on May 14, 1970, they knew they could trust me. They saw that my position on many major issues was the same as theirs. The Black Student Union and I did not always agree, but we always tried to find common ground. The students said, "This is a man we can trust. You'd better not say anything negative about Sam Kelly." I have no doubt that their support, and the realization on campus that I had their support, went a long way toward my success in my job.

I attended meetings of the Chicano students and had interactions with them, but it seemed to me that they and their leadership blew hot and cold toward me. Sometimes they seemed to support my initiatives, but often they did not. Unlike the black students, who could turn to a growing number of black faculty and staff members for advice, the Chicano students didn't have many professors or administrators they could call upon for guidance and support.

I believe a number of national issues generated distrust between black and brown students and no doubt influenced the tension between the Chicanos and my office. When I visited friends in California, they reported on the conflict between blacks and browns over control of anti-poverty programs. The Chicanos said the blacks gobbled up all the anti-poverty money and never considered the Hispanics who were equally impoverished. The blacks took the position that since most Chicanos had not participated in the civil rights movement, they had not sacrificed and so should not be rewarded. The Chicanos in California and elsewhere began to attack black leadership in the antipoverty programs, and soon that attitude expanded into a general political rivalry between black and brown communities in places like Denver, Houston, and Los Angeles. I believe what happened on the UW campus at least in part reflected that national rivalry.

All of this came to a head when the Chicano students demanded to meet with President Odegaard about the Office of Minority Affairs. I attended the meeting and for the first time found myself the target of student protests. The leader of the Chicano students said the Office of Minority Affairs was ignoring their concerns. They said the office should be broken up into an Office of Brown Affairs and an Office of Black Affairs, with each office headed by a vice president. President Odegaard stood his ground and said, "I have money for one vice president who will represent all minority groups. This is a major appointment; most universities across the country, I am informed, have not created such a position."

THE PADELFORD HALL INCIDENT

The tensions died down for a while but never really went away. On May 13, 1974, nearly a hundred Chicano students, led by El Centro de la Raza director Roberto Maestas, initiated a daylong protest that helped end my term as vice president for minority affairs. The protesters—including some blacks, Asians, Native Americans, and whites—were angry that Political Science Department chair Richard Flathman had overruled his faculty's vote to hire Carlos Muñoz, Jr., a professor at the University of California, Irvine—and chair of the first Chicano Studies Department in the nation, at California State College, Los Angeles, established in 1968— as an associate professor in his department. They demanded that College of Arts and Sciences Dean George Beckman overturn the decision, hire Muñoz, and fire Flathman. When Beckman refused, some of the more reckless students smashed mirrors and threw files on the floor. Dean Beckman was held captive in his office, and some of his personal effects were ripped up and trashed. Students destroyed typewriters, ripped clocks off the wall, and stole office equipment. When a final accounting was made, there was more than ten thousand dollars in damage.

I went to Dean Beckman's office to talk to Maestas and the other students. I didn't make much progress and was about to leave when some of the students shouted, "Let's hold Sam Kelly." I looked at the student who was attempting to block the door and said, "Fella, you better get out of the way. You won't hold me."

At that point, Maestas said, "No, no, no, that's Sam Kelly. Let him go." They released me, and I went to see John Hogness, who had succeeded Charles Odegaard as UW president in 1973.

"Sam, they've been up there for some time," he said. "Something ought to be done about this activity."

"Well, John, certainly, I think as soon as the dean moves on the Muñoz position, there will be some reconciliation. We are going to have these types of incidents, and I hate to say that, but, John, you could do more to help out here, I hope."

President Hogness angrily responded, "I'm doing all I can."

"Well, I'm going back over there right now, but I wanted to report directly to you what's happened. I'm going to see if they will let Dean Beckman out of there."

I returned to Padelford Hall, where the situation had deteriorated. One student began taunting Dean Beckman, which made him jumpy. I tried to calm him and then turned my attention to the students and warned them to let the dean go. I don't know if what I said made a difference, but they released him later that afternoon.

What I do know is that soon afterward I was blamed for the entire incident. I was already on record as saying the decision by department chair Flathman was a sham: For once, the *Daily*, in a May 14, 1974, article, quoted my exact words: "Because of the political machinations in the department, they seem to be prepared to circumvent the original faculty vote to arrive at the negative results which they originally wanted. Even in the face of a majority vote, it appears a minority will not be hired."

Regardless of how the faculty felt about the Muñoz vote, many said I had overstepped my authority by commenting on a faculty decision. Two English professors even claimed the student takeover had happened because I was building a program with "reckless abandon." The local newspapers repeated the charge and insinuated that I had orchestrated the Padelford Hall takeover. When a campus reporter repeated the charge in an interview with me, I said, "Well, you don't know me very well. With my military background, if I had planned an incident, I have the capability of establishing a plan that would have Padelford Hall sliding down the hill into the adjoining parking lot." Some members of the faculty interpreted my comments as a threat. I couldn't win.

The Padelford Hall takeover divided my staff and indirectly led to my controversial firing of Juan Sanchez, the director of OMA's Chicano division, a year later. I had sent Sanchez to Padelford with specific instructions to do all he could to keep tempers down and discourage violence. Later in the protest, a photograph showed Sanchez with his feet on Beckman's desk. When that photo was made public, a number of people called for his immediate firing.

I initially had defended Sanchez because I was uncertain about his role in the demonstration. In staff meetings, however, he belittled the trashing of Dean Beckman's office. I reminded him and my entire staff that while I supported peaceful protests and was willing to participate in them myself, I would not support or defend students or staff who participated in actions that intimidated people, threatened bloodshed, and destroyed property.

I also had other issues with Sanchez. Almost from the time he was hired in January 1974, he had been insubordinate and disrespectful. He once walked out of an ROTC presentation I had arranged for students. Given his active role in the Padelford takeover and other issues, I fired him. At around the same time, Dean Beckman fired Gary Padilla, the director of Chicano Studies, and Rosa Morales, the secretary in that office, for their role in the Padelford Hall incident.

As far as most people on campus and in the community were concerned, all the firings were in retaliation for the Padelford Hall incident, and I was now acting on behalf of the central administration, which made my actions even more egregious. This led to more attacks on me, and students picketed my office. At one point, the Chicanos boycotted my office, marching in the street under my third floor window in Schmitz Hall and demanding that I resign. At the same time, twenty-nine Chicano faculty and staff members resigned in protest over the firings of Sanchez, Padilla, and Morales. The Chicano students and their supporters, including some BSU members and radical white faculty and staff members, attacked me as a "sellout." Five members of my own staff, all in the Chicano division, addressed me in the *Daily*: "You have chosen the White man's game for yourself and therefore you deserve something less than respect. The day you forgot your Blackness, you forgot your brothers which include all of us regardless of color."

Members of the Seattle Chicano community said that my action could be interpreted as a "black-brown" conflict and condemned the Native Americans and Asians on campus for not supporting them.

Jesse Wineberry, the black president of the Associated Students of the University of Washington (ASUW) and other ASUW student executives also condemned my actions as contributing to the animosity of minority students toward the university. Even Larry Gossett, who was working for the Central Area Motivation Program, a leading Seattle antipoverty agency, publicly opposed me on the Sanchez firing. At the same time, most of the UW faculty and many in the community criticized me for having staff people who engaged in violent protests. The condemnations extended to other campuses, including Western Washington University and Evergreen State College.

Still, I was heartened by the support I received during that difficult time. Some faculty members, such as James K. Morishima in Asian American Studies and Thad Spratlen in the School of Business, came to my defense, along with my old friend, Bill Hilliard, who was serving as executive secretary of the City of Seattle Human Rights Commission. I also received dozens of letters from community people and organizations praising my actions and supporting me. Isabella Tweedy wrote one of the most poignant on May 9, 1975: "Although my heart is with the Chicanos . . . I do not doubt you. I have found tears in my eyes, reading some of the bitter statements being made, but I do understand whence comes 'bitterness' and I am aware you do, too. You are a good man. A brave one."

Not surprisingly the issue allowed some people to settle old scores. Some of my community "supporters" included whites who were opposed to affirmative action. They were delighted that, in their view, I had reined in the Chicanos. Some local black activists also applauded my actions but for different reasons. In their view, the Chicanos and other groups who reaped the fruits of black protest were undeserving and had to be stopped.

By the end of May, it had become clear that my effectiveness on campus was diminished. The Chicano students continued their protests, and the black students, most of whom were too young to have been on campus when I arrived in 1970, increasingly supported the Chicanos.

The Padelford Hall incident and the firing of Juan Sanchez were the immediate catalysts for my departure from the Office of Minority Affairs, but as I look back now, I think the critical moment came when Charles Odegaard retired in 1973. The presidents who succeeded Odegaard did not have the same philosophical commitment to campus change that Odegaard had demonstrated when I first came to the university. Since Charles and I wanted the same thing, we formed the perfect team for achieving that change. When it became clear that I no longer had the same level of support, I concluded that my usefulness as vice president of minority affairs was at an end.

STEPPING DOWN

On September 26, 1975, I announced my resignation, to be effective July 1, 1976. Although I was frustrated by recent events, I could look back proudly and say that under my tenure the Office of Minority Affairs had grown to more than fifty full-time employees and had a biennial budget of $2.3 million. We had developed programs that in 1976 served at least 2,700 students of color and economically disadvantaged white students. We had also helped thousands more graduate from the University of Washington with baccalaureate and advanced degrees.

My resignation announcement generated an outpouring of support and understanding from many people on and off campus. Letters and telegrams came from across Washington. The most moving letter came from former president Charles Odegaard, who praised my efforts to open the university to a wide array of people who had been locked out. He reminded me that while we had agreed on goals, we sometimes had disagreed on implementation but never with a loss of confidence in each other. "I am far from alone," the former president wrote, "in appreciation of you and in being influenced by you. . . . Well done, Vice President Kelly."

When I ended my term as vice president, I continued my faculty appointment with tenure in the College of Education through "retreat rights," meaning that as a former administrator I returned to faculty status. I taught half-time as a member of the College of Education graduate faculty. My offerings included courses in community college administration and the history of higher education.

President John Hogness offered me an appointment as special assistant to the president. I did not know it at the time, but I would remain in that job for six years, half of my total time at the University of Washington. Initially I had one long-term responsibility: I represented the university on the Committee on Urban Public Universities (CUPU). This federally funded national program was created to funnel money to the major universities for the purpose of improving the lives of inner-city residents. The program was intended to bring together university faculty who would devise programs to assist the poor, including a large number of Seattle's African American population. The programs were intended to replace many of the War on Poverty initiatives that were being cut by the Nixon and Ford administrations.

Despite CUPU's laudable goals, the University of Washington never provided its share of the funding. The new president, Dr. William Gerberding, who was installed on July 1, 1979, opposed the program. Although he met with key national representatives of the program when they visited the campus and with campus faculty who supported CUPU, he said the university's lack of resources prevented any major commitment. Ultimately, a financial scandal took CUPU down, and Congress ended the program.

In 1979, Provost Beckman asked me to serve for one year as the interim director of the university's eleven-year-old Black Studies program until a permanent administrator could be found. I agreed on the condition that I would continue to teach half-time in the College of Education. There were only four people, all adjuncts, on the Black Studies faculty: Michael Martin, Dr. Ed Jones, Dr. Wayne Williams, and Artee Young. Dr. Thad Spratlen from the School of Business was the associate program director. We never had the money to hire anyone else. Nonetheless, I saw this as an opportunity to urge that more black faculty and administrators be hired across the campus and to continue my argument that Black Studies should be granted departmental status so that it could tenure its faculty. I was not surprised when I ran into opposition from a number of people on campus, including some in the provost's office.

THE SOUTH AFRICA DIVESTMENT DEBATE

Ironically, the Chicano student protest in 1974, aimed at getting a high-ranking Chicano administrator, brought Hubert Locke, an African American, to the university as associate dean of the College of Arts and Sciences. Locke had come from Detroit, where he had been a minister and civil rights activist. He had also been an administrative assistant to the Detroit police commissioner during the 1967 race riot and wrote *The Detroit Riot of 1967*, one of the major accounts of that civil disorder, out of that experience. He later taught at Wayne State University and the

University of Nebraska at Omaha before becoming an associate dean in the University of Washington's College of Arts and Sciences.

Locke rose quickly at the university; by 1977, he was vice provost for academic affairs. My first encounter with Dr. Locke came during the South African divestment debate, which became a huge controversy at the University of Washington in 1977 and 1978. That debate began with Rev. Leon Sullivan, a Philadelphia minister, who was most famous for founding and developing more than two hundred Opportunities Industrialization Centers (OIC) across the nation, including one in Seattle and one in Portland. At the time, I served on the board of directors of the Seattle OIC. Rev. Sullivan's program trained thousands of inner-city youth for jobs. I admired his work, and we became friends. I first met him in the early 1970s through my brother Jim, who was dean of the College of Education at the University of Pittsburgh.

In September 1977, Rev. Sullivan issued the Sullivan Principles, which called on U.S. corporations to help end the apartheid system of South Africa. U.S. firms exploited cheap black labor in South Africa partly because the apartheid system outlawed black unions and limited black wages to a percentage of those of white workers. Rev. Sullivan wrote the Sullivan Principles and an accompanying pledge, which he hoped U.S. corporations would sign, ensuring better wages and treatment of black workers and thus undermining apartheid. He tried to use U.S. public opinion to pressure corporations to sign the pledge.

A group of University of Washington faculty, students, and staff and Seattle community people had other ideas. They formed the UW Out of South Africa Committee, which called on the university to divest all $4 million of its investments in firms that did business in South Africa. Their argument was that apartheid was wrong, and anyone or any organization cooperating with it in any way simply perpetuated the exploitation of black South African workers. In their view, divestment would force U.S. and other international firms out of South Africa, crippling the economy and thus causing the apartheid system to fall. Even if the regime did not fall immediately, at least the University of Washington would no longer be morally tainted by its investments in exploitation.

I understood their argument, but I didn't agree with it, which put a strain on relationships with old friends such as Wayne R. Williams, who was one of the leading faculty members in the Black Studies program. Wayne was also one of the leaders of the UW Out of South Africa Committee. He had participated in demonstrations and fundraisers sponsored by the committee. Few faculty members on campus were identified more with divestment.

Wayne and the committee wanted my support at the upcoming board of regents open hearing on divestment on April 6, 1978, when the board would take testimony on the issue from across the campus. Eight days later, on April 14, it would decide on divestment. When the committee asked for my support, I responded quickly: "I can't in good conscience support what you're doing here. When someone like Rev. Leon Sullivan tells me his approach will bring the change we want, I have got to hold my ground. He's done so much for black people in the United States. I trust him."

They then turned to Vice Provost Locke, who agreed to support them.

The public forum on divestment was held in Kane Hall. Three of the regents were onstage. President Hogness and his vice presidents were lined up in the front row waiting for their turn to testify. In all, there were about three hundred people in the auditorium, including supporters and opponents of divestment and members of the press.

Locke was one of a number of scheduled speakers. When his turn came, he described how he was approached in his office by the students and recounted how they had asked him to represent them. "And I'm glad to do it. I believe the students have a point." Then he said, "To bring closure to this issue and in support of the students, I recommend that you sign the documents that you have before you."

The pro-divestment students broke out in cheers and applause. I asked one of my staff members, "What are these people cheering about? The document on the table, which Dr. Locke just recommended that they sign, supports the Sullivan Principles."

When it was over, I watched reporters approach President Hogness. "How does it feel to have one of your minority administrators publicly oppose you on divestment?" one asked.

"No minority administrator opposed us today. The document on the table was for a continuation of investment of UW stock in South Africa under the terms of the Sullivan Principles," he replied.

As it turned out, Locke and I were on the same side, but apparently not many of the students realized it at the time; they later determined that they had been misled when Dr. Locke had said he represented their point of view.

BLACK STUDIES AT THE UNIVERSITY OF WASHINGTON

Hubert Locke did oppose me, however, on the creation of a Department of Black Studies. The University of Washington had been offering a smattering of courses on black history and culture since the late 1960s. In 1968, the central administration created a Black Studies program to regularize the course offerings and to develop a small group of faculty, mostly at the instructor level, who would teach the classes. As interim head of Black Studies in 1979–80, I felt it was time for the program to become a standard academic department with its own chair, its own faculty, and the power to award tenure. I had no doubt that unless Black Studies was awarded department status, as had been done at Harvard, the University of Pittsburgh, and Yale, it would eventually fail at the University of Washington.

Confident that I could persuade the faculty and administrators to follow the lead of these prestigious institutions, I addressed the department heads assembled by Dr. Ernest Henley, dean of the College of Arts and Sciences, and made what I thought was a compelling argument for creating a department. Afterward, there was spirited discussion. I don't recall all the questions and comments, but the remarks of Locke, now the highest-ranking black academic administrator on campus, stood out. He became, in my view, an impediment to furthering the cause of Black Studies when said he did not see a pressing need to elevate Black Studies to department status.

"Why should we create a department just because a few other institutions have them?" he asked.

The proposal was defeated. I never again fought that battle, although in 1985 the University of Washington created the Department of Ethnic Studies, which included African American, Asian American, Chicano/a, and Native American Studies.

FAMILY AND COMMUNITY

Throughout all these years of university activities, including considerable traveling and speaking, I always tried to find time for my family. My son, Bill, graduated through a special program from Pacific School in Seattle and began working in the "sheltered workshop" at the Northwest Center for the Retarded. Brenda and Sharon were attending high school and were involved in a myriad of activities. Our Mercer Island home was considered the "Kool-Aid" house and was frequently filled with chattering teenagers. Joyce and I welcomed the crowds.

I was not always there for Billy, Brenda, and Sharon when they were young children. In their first decade, I was an officer in the U.S. Army, which meant I was away from home for weeks or months at a time. When I became an administrator, my schedule was in some ways more demanding, even if I spent every night at home. I did carve out time for family vacations, including a trip to Mexico when the girls were sixteen. They had a ball, even borrowing their mother's dressy clothes to visit a local disco. On Christmas 1973, I gave my twin daughters a 1974 light green Buick Apollo. It was in the middle of the garage, complete with a big red ribbon and bow. The twins were screaming and crying when they saw that car. They later told me that 1973 was their best Christmas ever.

I spent much of my time in the Seattle community, especially the African American community. My ties to that community go back to the years when I was stationed at Fort Lawton in 1948. I remember the first time I went to my longtime church, First African Methodist Episcopal, and met some of the pillars of the small black community. Although I spent a decade away from Seattle in the 1950s, I never thought of myself as anything other than a Seattle resident.

Joyce and I had connections with Seattle. She was a member of the local chapter of Delta Sigma Theta Sorority and later became a member of the Links, a leading national black women's service organization. I joined Omega Psi Phi Fraternity at West Virginia State University in 1959 and became a member of Alpha Omicron, the Seattle chapter of Sigma Pi Phi Boule, in 1970. Its members included virtually every prominent African American man in the community.

JULIAN BOND AND SAM KELLY AT THE NATIONAL CONFERENCE ON RACE AND ETHNICITY IN HIGHER EDUCATION IN 1974. COURTESY OF THE KELLY FAMILY.

SPEAKING MY MIND

By the time I went to the University of Washington, I was known as an "odd duck"—a retired army colonel who dressed in conservative suits, with a conservative military-style haircut, and was a spokesman for militant black students.

In my first year as vice president for minority affairs, I probably made thirty major speeches. From then until my last year at the university, I averaged between fifteen and twenty major presentations a year. I must have given talks at half the black churches in Seattle, Rotary Clubs, and the Chambers of Commerce of Seattle, Spokane, Tacoma, the Tri-Cities (Richland, Kennewick, and Pasco), and other cities across the state.

I was equally comfortable before the all-black congregation at Mt. Zion Baptist or First AME Church as I was before the all-white Rotarians. I used to go down to the Central District to eat barbecue and talk with the customers. I ate at Helen's, my favorite restaurant "down in the 'hood" at Twenty-third and Madison Avenue at least once a month. I ate some of Seattle's best "soul food" in that place. The owner, Helen, knew me, and every time I'd go down there she wanted to prepare my favorite dish, fried catfish.

I also traveled across the nation giving presentations. I spoke at Harvard twice, at the invitation of Professor Martin Kilson, the distinguished professor of political science, and at Stanford University, the University of Massachusetts, the University of Pittsburgh, Wesleyan College, and Yale. I described our program on those campuses and gave the University of Washington national visibility and credibility. Following one presentation at the University of Nebraska, I was offered a university vice presidency. I discussed the opportunity with Dr. Odegaard, who encouraged me to stay at the University of Washington.

I also attended the presentations of leading figures who lectured on campus, including Julian Bond, Harry Edwards, Nikki Giovanni, and Dick Gregory. I generally agreed with what the students invariably called their "rap." But one speaker, Minister Louis Farrakhan, the controversial leader of the Nation of Islam, who was invited by the BSU in 1975, attempted to embarrass me and my staff before an audience at the Ethnic Cultural Center theater.

Minister Farrakhan began his talk by discussing the state of Black America and then zeroed in on the UW campus. He described the "lackeys" and "Uncle Toms" among the black faculty and administrators who were responsible for keeping the peace on campus. He started berating the Office of Minority Affairs, implying that none of the black students were graduating from the university; they were just window dressing in a white institution that wanted to claim to be open-minded and liberal. I am sure Farrakhan made this a standard charge on every college campus he visited, but I was not going to let his statements go unchallenged.

When the question-and-answer session began, I told him that our program had helped 382 minority undergraduate and graduate students earn their degrees in 1974, more than the total number of minority students on campus in 1969. He got ticked off, and as he did, his two bodyguards, the Fruit of Islam, as they called themselves, moved toward me. He then repeated his basic claim, "There ain't more than a couple of students who graduated from this place."

"That's a lie," I fired back. I stood up. John Gilmore, who worked for me in the Office of Minority Affairs, stood up as well. I then said loud enough so that everyone in the theater could hear me, "You know, it makes me sick that you think you've got so much to say because you've got those two gorillas up on the stage looking behind the curtains. Nobody wants to hear from you."

The three hundred students in the audience rolled with laughter. At that, the Fruit of Islam hustled Farrakhan off the stage, and I never saw him again.

DR. SAM

I completed my doctorate in higher education administration while working full-time as vice president for minority affairs. It wasn't easy. I worked on my dissertation over the weekends, at night, and any time I had a few minutes. Of course, the subject of the dissertation was something I knew more about than anyone in the state of Washington—how to organize an office of minority affairs.

Classwork posed a different type of challenge. Fortunately, I had already had two years of graduate courses in education from Marshall University before I enrolled in the UW College of Education. I worked other courses into a tight schedule and passed my comprehensive exams, completed my dissertation "A Model for Emerging Black Studies Programs Viewed in Historical Perspective," and received my doctorate on December 16, 1971. I went from being "Colonel Sam" to "Dr. Sam."

I have no doubt that my doctorate mattered to the black undergraduates. One student said during a BSU meeting, "Oh, you got one of them." The student couldn't even say the name of the degree, but he knew it was impressive. Another student said, "This is awesome—not just a degree, you've got a doctorate."

The degree mattered to the UW faculty as well. After I received the doctorate, there was a sense among more of the members that "he deserves an audience, he deserves to be listened to."

During my years at the University of Washington, the Office of Minority Affairs accomplished something that had not been done at a major university. We recruited and supported highly visible minority students who had previously been underserved by institutions of higher education, and we graduated them in record numbers. Enrollment in the Educational Opportunity Program alone grew from 257 in 1968 to 2,530 in 1975. Overall enrollment of students of color (both in and outside the program) grew to 4,075 in 1975, or 11.5 percent of the total campus student population. We set enrollment goals and held people in the Office of Minority Affairs accountable, which helped ensure our success.

But more than just recruiting students and getting them through the university, we created a culture that said these students could and should succeed in this environment. The astronomical graduation rates reflected the success of our efforts in creating that culture. More than 1,000 students of color received undergraduate and advanced degrees between 1971 and 1975. In 1974, 18 minority students in the law school who had been assisted by our program graduated, and 11 passed the state bar exam on the first try. There had historically been a shameful underrepresentation of people of color as physicians, dentists, and attorneys in Washington. As late as 1972, there were only 24 black attorneys, 2 Chicano attorneys, and no American Indian or Filipino attorneys among the 4,935 in the state. Of the 8,137 physicians, there were only 20 blacks, 5 Chicanos, 1 Filipino, and no Indians. The Office of Minority Affairs was on the road to correcting that underrepresentation.

When I left the University of Washington, I was fifty-six years old and had worked on campus for twelve years. I decided to leave when the state legislature passed an early retirement bill, which allowed state workers to retire if they were fifty-five years of age or older and had at least twelve years of service to the university. The program was designed to encourage early retirement among long-term faculty and administrators in order to ease financial strains on the university.

I took the package and resigned on June 30, 1982. I welcomed the opportunity to move on, but I had no intention of retiring from life. I was still strong mentally and physically, and I had much to offer my next employer. I was ready to begin a third career.

PART IV

Advocate

"I can do almost everything well except retire."

CHAPTER 12

Starting Over

Since my eighteenth birthday, I had spent most of my life with two employers, the U.S. Army and the University of Washington. Now, at fifty-six years of age, I was starting over. I was not ready for "retirement," whatever that meant. Although I loved golf, I could not see myself spending the rest of my days on the links.

My retirement from the University of Washington was not entirely of my choosing. I don't want to disparage anything any UW president has done, but in my view, no one who followed Charles Odegaard into that office, with the possible exception of the current president, Dr. Mark Emmert, has filled the void created by Charles's retirement in 1973. Charles was a brilliant administrator and a fair, open-hearted person. Soon after I was hired, we melded because we shared the same philosophy about making the university more inclusive. He knew when to change direction once he was persuaded that was the correct course, but he did not automatically and easily bend to political pressure.

There were other subtle changes occurring as well. When Charles Odegaard was president, key administrators and faculty knew I had his ear. They understood that Charles supported my goals because these were his goals as well. After Charles left, it was far more difficult to get things done. Instead of resolving an issue in one meeting, it took me two or three meetings and half a dozen phone calls to key administrators to argue my case. Many of those phone calls were not being returned. I no longer got the academic or political support from the central administration that I had experienced when Charles Odegaard led the institution.

I felt awful when I submitted my letter of resignation. I had served the University of Washington for twelve years, six of them as vice president for minority affairs in the central administration. I had been part of the decision-making process for every major university initiative during those years. I have no doubt that I had helped to change the campus climate regarding race. The question was, what to do next?

DONNA

The personal changes in my life were as profound as the professional changes. In 1980, I lost Joyce, my wife of thirty years, who succumbed after a long struggle with breast cancer. Joyce supported me throughout my higher education, the most important years of my army career, and my work in the community college and university systems. She was the "on-duty" parent of our three children when I was away from home and a superb officer's wife. A consummate hostess to the hundreds of people I brought into our home during my various careers, she was a stylish, beautiful woman of whom I was always proud. She completed her own post-secondary education while she was a working wife and mother. Without her in my life, I would not have been able to pursue my career goals and to achieve the success that has been attributed to me.

Following Joyce's death, I married Donna Schaplow, the woman who would be my wife for the remainder of my life. She brought her daughter, Heather, into the family, and in 1985, she and I would have my second son, Samuel Kelly, Jr.

I first heard of Donna Schaplow in 1972, during my early years at the Office of Minority Affairs. The university had a central Personnel Services Department with a Staff Employment Office component responsible for recruiting, evaluating, and referring more than fifty thousand candidates annually for the approximately three thousand nonacademic staff and exempt positions as they became available on campus each year. Members of the OMA staff in positions to interview candidates praised Donna for her work in recruiting women and people of color for positions in the workforce. OMA staffers Bill Hilliard and Mike Castilliano would frequently come to my office to discuss employment issues, and they would say, "Call Donna Schaplow. She can get things done for us." I met Donna in my office sometime in 1972. After that meeting, we did not see each other again for several years.

As part of her work, Donna oversaw the affirmative action employment recruiters for blacks, Asians, Chicanos, Native Americans, and persons with disabilities. Because of her work, the public face of the university changed, as more jobs were opened to people of color and women. Donna was an ally in the fight for diversity on campus. Over time, she became my best friend.

BRENDA, HEATHER, BILL, SHARON, SAM, AND DONNA ON THE FAMILY'S FIRST VACATION
TOGETHER IN OCEAN SHORES, WASHINGTON, IN 1980. COURTESY OF THE KELLY FAMILY.

Although we were nineteen years apart in age and had grown up on the East and West Coasts, respectively, we shared a number of common interests and values, including our commitment to promoting diversity at the university. We also loved the same music, and she allowed me to tell my "war stories" over and over without ever seeming to get tired of them. As I went through the difficult years when Joyce was battling cancer, Donna offered understanding and support. We were married on July 27, 1980, in Lake Tahoe, Nevada, and established our new home in Bothell, a Seattle suburb on the northeast side of Lake Washington.

Our wedding was truly special. Donna's brother, Gary, drove to Lake Tahoe to give his sister away. Our four children drove down also. My nephew James Kelly III and my good friend Ike Kelley, who was our best man, made the trip, too. In all, about thirty family members and friends shared in our celebration.

We became, in the parlance of the 1980s, a blended family. We were also an interracial family. Neither Donna nor I cared much about what the general public felt about our marriage, which happened only thirteen years after the U.S. Supreme Court struck down interracial marriage bans across the country in its *Loving v. Virginia* decision.

We did care about the reaction of our immediate families. My oldest son, Billy, took to Donna right away and she to him. He soon began to call her "Mom," much as I had done when my father married Leah Hockaday. Brenda and Sharon also warmed to Donna. They missed their mother, but they understood that Donna made me happy and completed our family again. Heather was only nine at the time, and she soon became Billy's constant companion.

After the tragic loss of Joyce, we became a stronger family as all of us, including eventually Sammy, faced the future together.

PUBLIC SERVICE

In 1982, I went to work for the state of Washington. Governor John Spellman asked me to sit on the Washington State Board of Tax Appeals, which adjudicates disputed property tax matters. The board consisted of three appointees: the chair, the vice chair, and one additional member, me. We held both formal and informal hearings on property tax cases. At the time, the three members, Eleanor Brand of Seattle, Charles Newschwander of Tacoma (the chair), and I adjudicated every decision, with a two-person majority carrying the day. In 1984, two new members, John D. Jones of Kirkland and Michiko Fujii of Mercer Island, served with me.

The most important case we adjudicated during my time on the board involved the Weyerhaeuser Company, the largest timber and paper corporation in the state. In 1983, Weyerhaeuser made a 6,600-acre land swap with the Washington Department of Natural Resources, partly to help the state consolidate its ownership of land to create the Tiger Mountain State Forest. The King County assessor valued the land as developable property, while Weyerhaeuser claimed it should have been taxed at the much lower forest land rate. The company initially accepted the ruling and paid the higher rate in 1982 and 1983 but then appealed that assessment and requested a tax refund. The board ruled in favor of the King County assessor because we believed Weyerhaeuser should have requested the lower rate when it assumed control of the property.

I enjoyed researching the cases and writing up our findings. Although the work was sometimes tedious, I was fascinated by the legal research and the adjudication process. I appreciated the help of our legal staff, but we were responsible for writing the final decisions.

The only problem with the position was the long commute to

Olympia. I chose not to move my family 76 miles to the state capital and instead commuted (152 miles round-trip) four or five times a week. I had to undergo two painful and complicated back surgeries in 1982 and 1983, the consequence of my airborne soldier days in the 1950s, which made the commute even more difficult, as it exacerbated my back condition. Despite the discomfort of the long drive, I stayed on the board for more than four years.

I also served the state as a member of the Bellevue Community College Board of Trustees, a position to which Governor Dixy Lee Ray had appointed me in 1978. It was a good position for me. I had experience working with students and had been trained in the organization, structure, and mission of community colleges. I had taught classes on the subject at the University of Washington and also brought important African American community credentials.

I saw part of my role on the board as raising issues related to students of color. Many of these students, and the programs that supported them, were relatively new in the community college environment. It is not that board members were hostile to equity or affirmative action programs. Most were businesspeople or politicians who, for the most part, simply were not aware of them until some student "crisis" occurred. Nor were they immediately persuaded of the value of these programs not only to students of color but to the entire state. I felt I could educate fellow board members in those areas.

I was on the Bellevue board of trustees until 1980, when Donna and I married and moved out of the Bellevue district. When I gave my notice, Governor John Spellman appointed me to the board of trustees of Shoreline Community College. I was delighted by the appointment because it reunited me with the campus where I had first become involved in efforts to diversify the student body and because it brought me into a close, but now different working relationship with my friend Dr. Richard White.

SAM KELLY, JR.

One day in the summer of 1983, I played golf with friends in Seattle and, to my delight, broke 80. When I came home and told Donna, she caught me completely off guard when she said, "Well, if you feel good enough to break 80, maybe we should think about having a baby."

"A baby?" I was taken aback. Donna and I had never actually discussed having children; we already had four, and we weren't getting any younger. I told her that I would probably not live long enough to see another child graduate from high school and that if I took him or her on outings, people would think I was the grandfather (which eventually did happen).

When I made that crack, my wife burst into tears at the thought of our not having a baby, so I changed my mind, and we began "trying" to get pregnant. On Memorial Day 1984, a home pregnancy test showed that we had achieved our mission—Donna was expecting.

Because Donna was thirty-nine years old, she was considered a "high-risk" mother, so she underwent amniocentesis to screen for certain age-related birth defects. Regardless of the test results, we had already decided that we would have the baby, since we knew the joy our special son Bill brought to our lives. The test showed the baby was healthy, and we also learned that we were going to have a son.

Then Donna said she wanted me to be present during the baby's birth. My first three children were born in the 1950s, an era when men dropped off their wives at the hospital and then came back after their babies were born. In addition, Billy's birth had been quite difficult, and he weighed less than five pounds at birth; Brenda's and Sharon's birth had been easier, but they were also about five pounds, a good weight for twins but small for a single baby. I didn't feel that I was prepared to actually be present at the birth of my child.

Once again, Donna began to cry, and we signed up for Lamaze classes, which were completely new to me. During the class, we met Celeste Archambaugh and her husband, Earl Fenstermacher. We became great friends and were thrilled when Samuel Eugene Kelly, Jr., and Daniel Earl Fenstermacher were born only sixteen minutes apart on January 21, 1985. I was also pleased that, like me, Sammy was a January baby. In fact, he was born just five days shy of my fifty-ninth birthday.

Samuel Eugene Kelly, Jr., weighed in at slightly more than nine pounds; he was so much bigger than my other babies that I felt comfortable with him right away. Mike Lude, then the UW athletic director, even sent a signed letter of intent to the hospital for Sam Kelly, Jr., to

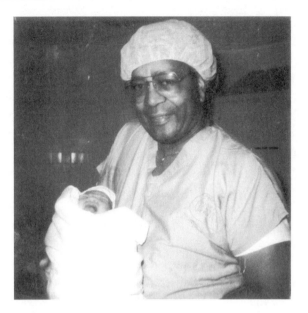

SAM KELLY, SR., HOLDING SAM KELLY, JR., ON JANUARY 21, 1985.
COURTESY OF THE KELLY FAMILY.

play football for the Huskies in 2003. Sammy was born to a white mother and a black father, just as, ninety-nine years earlier, his grandfather, James Handy Kelly, was born to a white father and a black mother.

Sammy grew quickly, but he was also a quiet, peaceful baby. Frisbee, the Keeshond puppy we had gotten for Heather five years before, became the baby's guardian, lying beside him on the floor and guarding his door at naptime. Heather was Sammy's only babysitter until she graduated from high school four years later in 1989. Bill was delighted to have a little brother, until Sammy began toddling around the house and discovered that Bill's room was a treasure trove of model cars and toys. Bill put his own "toddler security plan" into action, promptly removing the drawer pulls and knobs from his bedroom furniture and closet so that Sammy couldn't take his toys without his permission.

Having a son who participated in sports was a new thrill for me. I spent many hours watching or helping coach Sammy's Little League teams. Those were some of the best years of my life.

SAM KELLY'S POLITICS

For most of my life, I considered myself to be politically independent. Still, I was prone to agree with and often found myself in the company of Republicans. Republican Women for Nixon helped me raise the first private funds for minority students at the University of Washington, and many of them became the core of Friends of the Educational Opportunity Program.

I was particularly close to Governor Daniel J. Evans in terms of political ideology and had enormous respect for him, which says a great deal because I rarely hold politicians in high esteem. He supported our programs at the University of Washington when I was vice president for minority affairs—and not just because it was the politically expedient thing to do. In a state like Washington, with so few African Americans, he could have followed the path of so many other politicians and conveniently ignored the issue. He didn't.

Of the governors I worked with, from the 1960s to the 1980s, Dan Evans and John Spellman did the most for me and for the programs I supported. They were on the correct side of the affirmative action debate that was going on across the state and the nation. There was nothing I asked them to do for OMA programs that they did not do. Still, I refused to call myself a Republican, reserving my right to determine my alliances based on a candidate's values.

At one point, I considered running for public office, encouraged by my Mercer Island friends who asked me to enter various political campaigns. Virtually all of them were Republicans. They not only wanted me to run for particular offices but also imagined a political career for me fueled by their political and financial support. I refused all their offers. I thought I could do more for people, and in particular for poor people and people of color, and help bring the races together by remaining a private citizen. I knew my own history of being black and discriminated against, and I had a driving need—some would say, an obsession—to satisfy my desire to move people who were poor and highly visible into the mainstream of the U.S. economy. I could still hear the voices from Harlem, of Paul Robeson, Adam Clayton Powell, Sr., and others who said I must "do something for the race."

SENATOR GEORGE FLEMING, LENNY WILKENS, SAM KELLY, ROBERT WOODARD, JR., AND JAMES R. KELLY III AT THE INGLEMOOR GOLF AND COUNTRY CLUB IN BOTHELL, WASHINGTON, IN 1989. COURTESY OF THE KELLY FAMILY.

I also knew that I was too blunt and outspoken for politics. As I had learned in dealing with the faculty and some of the public at the University of Washington, I did not have the patience to tolerate people who were willfully ignorant on so many important matters, including racial progress. Nor was I capable of being duplicitous. I concluded that I just was not the political type.

I was, however, invited to the White House Rose Garden in 1990. At the time, I worked for Gamma Vision, a Seattle consulting firm, which had sought U.S. government contracts to promote racial and gender diversity among businesses and educational institutions in the region. I got to know Constance Berry Newman, whom President George Herbert Walker Bush had appointed as the first black woman to serve as director of the U.S. Office of Personnel Management. About seventy-five people were invited to her swearing-in ceremony in the Rose Garden. When President Bush shook my hand, I quickly said, "I bring you greetings from Congresswoman Jennifer Dunn from Bellevue, Washington." The president recognized her name and asked me to "extend to her his regards."

PRIVATE SECTOR EMPLOYMENT

By June 1986, the commute to Olympia had become too painful for me to continue, and I resigned from the Washington State Board of Tax Appeals. Soon afterward, I became employed in the private sector for the first time in my professional life. Over the next five years, I had four jobs as a consultant. In three of the positions, I attempted to use my particular knowledge of affirmative action and diversity to help companies and organizations hire and retain people of color. In the firm I helped start, I wanted the public to see that an enterprise controlled by people of color could provide excellent service to the community.

My first consulting job was with North Seattle Chrysler Plymouth, an automobile dealership owned by Bill "Mac" McIntosh, one of a handful of black auto dealers in the nation. By the mid-1980s, however, he wanted to break into fleet sales, in which a dealership contracts to supply automobiles to a local, state, or federal agency. Because of affirmative action, governments wanted to give business to minority dealerships, and Mac asked me to develop a plan for government fleet sales. The plan we crafted became a model for other minority- and women-owned businesses to follow when they sought state contracts. As Mac and I worked together, Donna and Mac's wife, Helen, rapidly became best friends. Our five boys, Bill, Sammy, Brian, Blair, and Blake, became playmates and remain close to this day. Although Mac passed away in 2002, we all had some wonderful laughs reminiscing about him.

We helped open the system to other businesses owned by people of color. We showed African American business owners across the state that a minority concern could get contracts and receive the necessary state certification. We did this at a time when there were only a handful of black- or minority-owned businesses operating in our region. Far more would follow our pioneering efforts and succeed.

In 1988, I became vice president at Myriad Systems and Services, which consulted on environmental testing, affirmative action, and diversity. The job mirrored much of what I had done at the University of Washington, but it ended with the death of the company's president, when the business was dissolved.

My third venture was Madrona Diversified, which I started with a group of local businessmen. Madrona Diversified lasted almost two years, during which we worked on asbestos removal programs and attempted to establish a parking lot near Sea-Tac Airport. We began to encounter more difficulty getting contracts, and eventually I got fed up with the politics necessary to make the company successful. A minority business, irrespective of affirmative action, was always fighting the system and had to run harder to compete effectively. We were black and we were small, which proved to be a disadvantage, despite the "edge" critics claimed minority-owned firms got from affirmative action.

A ROUGH PATCH

When Madrona Diversified dissolved in 1989, I found myself without significant employment for the first time in my life. I longed to return to college administration and perused the *Chronicle of Higher Education* to search for vacant positions. With my experience at community colleges and a major university, I was anxious to continue using my skills to expand educational opportunities for all. I thought I would easily find a major administrative position. I was wrong.

For about eighteen months, I applied for more than a dozen positions, from the presidency of Oxnard College in Ventura, California, to the director of the Department of Parks, Planning, and Resources for King County. I even wrote Governor Spellman to see if he could help obtain an appointment for me in the incoming Bush administration. Unfortunately, I realized that I had encountered a new obstacle, age discrimination. The rejection letters rolled in, frequently citing my "over-qualifications." I was a top finalist for the Seattle Community College chancellorship, but the search committee eventually chose someone else. When I was invited for interviews, the ensuing rejection letters were generally vague but did their job of making it clear that, at age sixty-three, my career in higher education should be over.

I turned again to the private sector and in 1990 accepted a position as vice president of Gamma Vision, a Seattle consulting firm, where I worked for a short time putting together contract proposals. I earned a good salary, but I didn't have the opportunity to do as many presentations as I would have liked. I resigned from Gamma Vision on January 31, 1991.

FAMILY CHANGES

By now, our son, Sam, Jr., was thriving as a kindergartner. Donna had been coordinating a program to teach Japanese students at Edmonds Community College on a part-time basis for two years. Brenda and Sharon were married and living independently, and Bill was working in a sheltered employment center, Custom Industries, not far from our home in Bothell. Heather graduated from high school in 1989 and left for her first year of college at Central Washington University in Ellensburg.

My brother, Bob, with whom I had shared a bed as a boy, relocated to Seattle after Donna and I were married. He was commissioned by the City of Seattle to create the Martin Luther King, Jr., Memorial adjacent to the Seattle Tennis Center. Bob's work is the largest MLK memorial west of the Mississippi and, unfortunately, serves as a final monument to him as well. He drowned in a rogue wave off the island of Kauai in April 1989. I have missed him every day since. Being the last of five brothers is difficult. I miss the stories we told when we got together and the laughter that we always shared.

Four months later, Donna's father died, leaving Irene, his wife of forty-six years, alone in their home in Washougal, eleven miles east of Vancouver, Washington. Each time we made the trip southwest to visit Donna's mother, we found ourselves enjoying the natural beauty and relaxed pace of the area. Soon, on our drives home, Donna and I began discussing the possibility of moving. We sold our home on Norway Hill in Bothell and in April 1991 loaded three moving vans and drove to Vancouver, where we would remain for the next fifteen years.

CHAPTER 13

The Vancouver Years

I began the process of reestablishing my career in education in Vancouver by contacting Paul Aldinger, the chair of the Social Sciences Department at Clark College. We hit it off immediately. Paul needed someone to teach U.S. history, and we agreed that I would begin my employment at the college in spring quarter 1991, only two weeks after our interview.

Returning to the classroom was exciting and exhilarating. After the first couple of quarters, Paul asked me to initiate plans to teach the first African American history course at Clark College. Although I was teaching my first class in more than ten years, I felt as if I had never completely left teaching. Throughout my life, I have yearned to teach and work with young people, and I had often volunteered to teach even when the demands of my job suggested I do otherwise.

If my enthusiasm for teaching had not diminished over a decade, then certainly the students had changed. Although they were bright, the curiosity and activism that had animated campuses in the 1960s and 1970s were mostly gone. Then, students hadn't simply wanted to learn; they had wanted to change things, to confront injustice and eliminate it. That attitude had carried over into the classroom, with students hungry to know about slavery, the Civil War and Reconstruction, and the civil rights movement. The students at Clark College in the 1990s did not exhibit that sense of urgency. The civil rights movement of the 1960s was a historical curiosity to them, almost like the Civil War. They respectfully listened to my stories of discrimination, but for them, much of that was ancient history.

Regardless of the changes in attitudes, I still won teaching awards. My students at Clark twice voted me the best adjunct faculty member of the year. That was gratifying, especially since an earlier generation of students had given me a similar award at Shoreline Community College.

In April 1992, just a few months after I had returned to the classroom,

Donna was hired as the college's director of personnel services. She also served as affirmative action and equal employment opportunity officer until 1997, when she began working half-time so that she could become involved in Sammy's junior high school activities. She remained at Clark College until 2002.

PORTLAND OPPORTUNITIES INDUSTRIALIZATION CENTER

As I was settling into the position at Clark, I received a call from Luther Strong, who had been assistant to the vice president for minority affairs at the University of Washington and assistant vice president for recruitment in UW health sciences. Luther was working for Portland Opportunities Industrialization Center, the local version of the program started by Rev. Leon Sullivan in Philadelphia in 1964. Portland OIC, established in 1967, is part of a network of sixty-six OICs throughout the United States, spread across thirty-eight states and around the world.

I was familiar with Rev. Sullivan's programs, and he and I had been friends for many years. I had served on the board of Seattle OIC for five years, between 1971 and 1976.

Although the major emphasis at OIC was always on vocational training, Rev. Sullivan and other leaders realized that alternative schools were also needed for inner-city students who were unsuccessful in traditional public schools. Some of the students had learning difficulties or poor attendance patterns; others were disruptive and had been removed from regular classrooms. Some needed individual attention, and some were on the verge of dropping out of school altogether.

Luther said Portland OIC needed serious help. Out of courtesy, I responded to his call, but I did not think much of working in that environment since I had absolutely no experience in high school teaching. I told Luther, "No, I can't do this."

"Well, at least come and take a look at the school," he suggested.

Luther told me about the school's director, Rosemary Anderson, who had been at Portland OIC since 1967 and founded the school in 1983 to help her own grandson, who was about to drop out of high school. She had heard about the OIC alternative high schools across the country and decided to establish a similar one in Portland.

Mrs. Anderson called and told me that she wanted to hire me and needed my help in organizing and administering the school and preparing for an upcoming state accreditation review. She said she wanted me in the classroom.

"Well, I don't know about that," I replied, thinking she would realize I was not interested.

She was persistent. I decided I had to tell her in person that I was not interested in the job. As I drove off, I told Donna, "This job's not for me. I'll be back in a short while—I just need to let Mrs. Anderson know that I don't want to be involved in any high school alternative education program."

I drove over the Columbia River into northeast Portland, the predominantly black residential district in the city. The school, located in the Albina neighborhood, Portland's "ghetto," was in a small, dingy building that suffered from lack of maintenance. From all appearances, it was going downhill fast.

As I reached the front door, two young black girls who appeared to be no older than fourteen were bounding out the door. They almost knocked me down. They were calling each other names and cursing, using language I don't think I had ever heard, even in the army. They started fighting as soon as they got outside. I caught the hand of one of them as she was about to land a punch, separated them, and said, "What are you two fighting each other for? You should love each other. You should listen to each other."

The girl who was about to throw the punch asked, "Who the hell are you?"

"Well, I may be your next teacher."

She looked me up and down and said, "Wearing a suit like that and driving that car, you won't be around here long."

"Don't bet on that," I growled.

Mrs. Anderson and her secretary had seen what had happened and were half in tears. "Oh, Dr. Kelly," she exclaimed, "I'm so glad you're here. We need you so."

"What's the matter with these kids?" I asked.

All she said in response was, "Oh, we need you so much."

Mrs. Anderson ushered me into her small office and offered me a cup of coffee. She was still distraught when she asked if I would stay with them for just six months to get the school organized. I agreed to stay for three months, and with that commitment, I began teaching at the Portland OIC Alternative Middle and High School.

I pulled together a curriculum and soon found myself teaching virtually all of the twenty-five students in the school. There were only two other teachers, including one who was responsible for special education, and one counselor. Mrs. Anderson and her secretary completed the staff.

Rosemary Anderson is a remarkable success story, much like the students at her school. A member of the Links and Delta Sigma Theta Sorority, the sorority of my late wife, Joyce, she has worked at the Portland OIC since its founding in 1967. She was the first business skills teacher at the school and served as the school's secretary before a full-time staffer was hired to assume that responsibility. She was married and has several sons and daughters and more than a dozen grandchildren. Her concern about the difficulties one of her grandchildren encountered in a traditional public school generated her interest in alternative education.

She has remained with the school ever since. In fact, she held it together in the early days when the school had a handful of students and no significant funding. She was absolutely dedicated to the students. I admired that quality, and it is one reason I decided to join the school's faculty.

As my one-quarter commitment to the Portland OIC school was about to end, Mrs. Anderson asked me to stay until the end of the 1991–92 academic year. I was prepared to say no until I received a visit from Dr. Ray Lindley, an administrator for the Oregon State Board of Education. He told me, without letting Mrs. Anderson know, that the state was about to pull its funding from the school, but given my credentials, if I stayed, it would continue its support and try to find additional money to hire more faculty. I decided to remain for the rest of the year. I had no idea that I would work at the school, renamed the Rosemary Anderson Middle and High School in 2002, for thirteen years until I retired in June 2004. In my sixth year, I became president and CEO of Portland OIC, replacing Mrs. Anderson, who became chair of the board.

I spent mornings at the alternative school in northeast Portland teaching U.S. history, street law, and contemporary world problems and initiated the first black history course at the school. Then I'd leave around one in the afternoon to drive to Clark College in Vancouver, where I taught U.S. history, history of the Far East, and African American history courses. I was busy, working up to ten hours a day in two states. I did that for nine years and loved it.

SCHOOL PRESIDENT

One of our first innovations at Portland oic was the school graduation. In 1992, I asked the question, "Well, what about graduation?"

Mrs. Anderson responded that we helped the students catch up on missing courses and then sent them back to the traditional high schools that had placed them with us for graduation.

It was clear that we were losing a wonderful opportunity to build a sense of community, belonging, and achievement among our students, the very things they did not get in the traditional schools that had sent them to us. I said to Mrs. Anderson, "Well, if I'm going to be here, we're going to have graduation if I have to walk across the stage and give the students one of my degrees."

The school's first graduation took place in June 1992, when seven of our students met the requirements. We organized a small ceremony in the Portland Cascade Community College theater. That room was supposed to hold about 200 people, but we must have had 250 crowded into that space. Old black women and men, grandmas and grandpas, aunts, uncles, cousins, and tiny brothers and sisters shouted out when the students' names were read and the graduates marched over to get their diplomas. I heard them saying things like, "My child, my child, that's the first child of ours to get a diploma. We are blessed."

It sounded like an old Southern church meeting. There was a lot of shouting and a lot of tears. That's what captured me. I immediately identified with that old Christian scene and with the message that had been instilled in me by my Baptist preacher father, that one's purpose in life was to help and to serve. Through this school, I had found that way. I believe my father would have been as proud of me then as those parents and grandparents were of their kids marching across that stage. At sixty-six, I had found a niche, a new way to be helpful.

I started at the Portland OIC school as a teacher in 1991 and then, in 1992, became the director of education, or in-house principal. The Oregon State Board of Education stuck by its commitment to increase our funding, and we hired four new teachers. The student enrollment also grew, from twenty-five in 1991 to more than two hundred students in 1996. In 1995, the school won a certificate as one of the three best alternative schools in Oregon. By 2003, it had more than four hundred students and nineteen faculty and staff members. That year, forty-two middle and high school students graduated from the Rosemary Anderson Middle and High School.

In the school's April 2003 report to the regional and national OIC offices, it listed its various programs, which included a year-round education program that allowed students to work in the summer on environmental projects, a special program for gang-affected youth, tutorial services, and educational services for young black males who were enrolled in a drug treatment program. We were not judgmental; we didn't ask our students how or why they had gotten into trouble. We thought it was far more important that they got their lives back on track.

FRIENDS OF THE ROSEMARY ANDERSON SCHOOL

Meanwhile, the school needed far more money than Portland OIC or the state of Oregon provided, so I recycled an idea I had first used at Shoreline—private fundraising. At that time, Oregon alternative schools received 80 percent of the funding per pupil that a traditional school would get for teaching and training students. The district retained the other 20 percent to administer the alternative program. Thus, we were always underfunded in comparison to traditional public schools.

When I started at the school, it had only one computer, and Rosemary, the teachers, and I wanted to have at least one computer in every classroom. In 1998, Portland OIC held its first fundraising dinner, a gathering of friends who would form the core of the group that would sponsor future efforts. They were a beautiful set of people, and included Pat and Kathy Carpenter, Larry and Dayna Corwin, Ron and Yon Cusick, Don and Jennifer Ellsworth, Chris Kane, Mark Matthias, Bob and Dawn Nesbitt, Dave and Holly Patton, and Mark Rosenfield. We met some of the supporters through youth baseball, soccer, and football programs that Sammy participated in. They became the Friends of Portland OIC.

Early on, I introduced my new Vancouver friends to Portland OIC school students. Often I invited a group of students to our home, where they discussed their educational experiences over sodas and burgers that Donna prepared. My friends, most of whom were white, listened and learned and, through that experience, were eager to become supporters of the Portland OIC school. They said, "Sam, can we help you? Can we help you do this?"

Bob and Dawn Nesbitt were co-presidents of Friends of Portland OIC. Dawn was a regional manager for Coty Cosmetics and had been with the firm for nearly three decades. The Nesbitts adopted our fundraising campaign and gave generously of their time and resources. In all, about forty residents of Vancouver and Portland worked diligently on fundraising events, including an annual gala, an auction, and a golf tournament. Chris Kane, our mortgage broker, and my old friend Dick Michalek joined the Portland OIC Board of Directors.

I remember our Vancouver neighbors, Jennifer and Don Ellsworth, whom I regard as my younger sister and brother. We actually met them through "elfing." In December 1993, our neighbors secretly put a poem or present on our porch over the Twelve Days of Christmas. They gave simple gifts and funny poetry to show their affection for us. We didn't figure out who our elves were until they revealed themselves on Christmas Eve. We invited them in for eggnog and cookies, and our families became dear friends, sharing potluck dinners and vacations. I believe they became staunch supporters of the school because of our friendship.

All of these fine friends and many others participated in the Portland OIC fundraising activities through the annual golf tournament and auction. The tournament usually occurs around the first or second week of October at Portland's Riverside Golf and Country Club.

My nephew James R. Kelly III (whom I called "Richard"), of Miami, a successful telecommunications entrepreneur and avid golfer, flew in every year to support our fundraising efforts as did my good friend Ike Kelley, from Denver. Local politicians and national celebrities supported the dinner as well. In 2003, for example, Nikki Giovanni, one of the nation's leading black literary figures, spoke at the annual fundraising dinner. Between 1998 and 2005, the dinner and tournament generated about $25,000 annually for the Rosemary Anderson School.

The Portland OIC school also had corporate support. Over a four-year period, it received two major grants of more than $100,000 from Precision Castparts, a supplier for Boeing located in Portland. We also received contributions from Ampere Electric, Beaches Restaurant, Bridgetown Coffee, DaimlerChrysler, Harry's Fresh Foods, Kellee Communications (owned by my nephew James R. Kelly III), McCoy Millworks, Nike, the Portland Trail Blazers, Riverview Community Bank, the Sheraton Portland Airport Hotel, and the Tualatin Valley Shopping Centers.

Our friends gave and persuaded others to give. In the first year, 1998, we raised $25,000. In 2002, we raised $120,000, and in my last year with the school, we collected more than $150,000. Between 1998 and 2004, our fundraising efforts accounted for 25 percent of the total budget at the Portland OIC school. Along the way, the school got its computers and, by 2000, had a fully functioning computer lab complete with thirty computers and a teacher.

Many Portland OIC students completed their programs successfully, received diplomas, and went on to college or good jobs and careers. I estimate that about 25 percent of the graduates attended area community colleges. In fact, the school became a feeder school for Portland Community College's Cascade branch and developed academic partnerships with Portland Community College and Mount Hood Community College.

Local companies also hired Portland OIC graduates. A cooperative program with Bridgetown Coffee trained and hired graduates as baristas for Bridgetown or other coffee chains such as Starbucks. The school operates three kiosks in the city that sell Bridgetown coffee. A portion of the profits from those activities helps support the school.

Much of this progress has continued since I left the school in 2004. My successor, Joe McFerrin II, the grandson of Rosemary Anderson, is now the president and CEO of Portland OIC. He began as a teacher and then became an administrator. In my last years at the school, he was my deputy. Along the way, Joe earned a master's degree in educational administration and enrolled in a PhD program.

The number of teachers at the school fluctuated: When I arrived in 1991, there were two instructors; in 2003, the school reached a high of twenty-two teachers and staff, including my wife, Donna, who had joined me at the school a year earlier as director of business and personnel services. The size of the teaching staff depended partly on the number of students, since Oregon based its funding allocations on enrollment. On occasion, we got a surge of students from the traditional public schools, which increased our funding. Generally speaking, however, we kept a teacher-to-student ratio of one to fifteen.

MEDICAL CRISIS

When we first moved to Vancouver in 1991, we leased a home for two years in the Ellsworth Springs neighborhood of east Vancouver. We decided to stay in the neighborhood and in 1993 built a new home at 1518 SE 104th Court. Five years later, we moved into a larger home at 9512 SE Fourteenth Street.

Then, in anticipation of our eventual joint retirement, Donna and I designed and built our "retirement" home, the last home we would own, or so we believed at the time. We were very pleased with our new one-level home at 1202 SE 116th Court, only minutes from the Columbia River. It had an open floor plan and plenty of space for hosting friends and family. It also had a small putting green in the front yard. Like all of our homes, it also boasted a flagpole from which we flew Old Glory. Half a century after my service in Korea, I continued to honor the pledge I'd made to the men I'd led into battle, that I would always fly the flag between Memorial Day and Veterans Day.

We moved into our new home on December 5, 2003, and were hit with a bombshell only one week later. Donna had taken a day off from Portland OIC to continue unpacking our dozens of boxes. Billy always had Fridays off from his job at Goodwill, so he was helping his mom in the garage. About two in the afternoon, Donna came in to talk with me and clean up from lunch. I was sitting on the edge of the bed, and she asked if I was all right. I said I didn't think so, and she could see right away that I wasn't well; my color was bad, and I was shaking.

Donna knows that I rarely complain about my health and called our family physician, Dr. Nicholas Carulli. After she'd described my symptoms, the doctor told her to get me to the emergency room immediately. Recognizing my weakened state, Donna chose not to drive me. Instead, she called 911. An ambulance arrived in about three minutes, and I was on my way to Southwest Washington Medical Center in Vancouver, which, fortunately, was only a short drive from our new home. Shortly after I arrived, the medical personnel told me I was having serious gastrointestinal bleeding.

That Friday, December 12, Sammy was on his way home from Western Washington University for his first Christmas break as a freshman. Donna called him from our car as she followed my ambulance to Southwest Washington Medical Center. She and Sam quickly informed the rest of the family via cell phones. When Sam arrived in Vancouver, he picked up Bill, and my two sons came directly to the hospital to see me.

I remained in the hospital for twenty-two days. The first Christmas in our new home was pretty bleak. My kids called it "the Christmas that wasn't." Heather, Sam, and Bill picked up a Christmas tree, expecting that I would be released in time for Christmas. That tree remained in the house, untrimmed, until it dried up.

I was diagnosed with diverticulitis, a condition in which pockets in the intestine become inflamed and lead to gastrointestinal bleeding. I had surgery, including six blood transfusions, on December 15, 2003, to remove fifteen inches of my right colon, but my gastrointestinal system refused to recover. I was discharged on January 3, 2004, after Donna was trained on the intravenous total parenteral nutrition (TPN) I would need at home, as I could not consume or digest food normally.

My system failed to restart by January 25, and I was hospitalized again, so that doctors could try to determine the source of the problem. When they found no direct cause, Dr. James Scarborough, the surgeon who had performed my earlier surgery, removed my gall bladder on my seventy-eighth birthday. I came home after ten more days in the hospital, still on TPN. Finally, around the middle of February, I was able to eat again. My body was still weak, since I had lost more than thirty pounds, but my spirit, my mind, and my will were strong.

This was the greatest medical crisis I had ever faced. I had prided myself on being strong and robust over my entire life. At seventy-seven,

I still played eighteen holes of golf, drank my scotch, and did most of the things I could do at fifty or even at thirty. Now I understood my own mortality.

During our many conversations at the hospital, Donna and I discussed our lives together and what the future might hold for us. My total hospital stay had been thirty-two days; Donna had spent every night with me except for two, when Sam Jr. had been able to stay. We vowed that we had a long, bright future ahead of us and that spending time with our family was the most important priority in our lives. During those conversations, we began to consider the idea of returning to the Seattle area someday, since Brenda, Sharon, and Heather all lived in and around the city with their own families.

On June 30, 2004, Donna and I both retired from Portland OIC and the Rosemary Anderson Middle and High School. I was seventy-eight, and for the first time in my adult life, I would not be getting up in the morning to drive to work. Although we continued to assist in fund-raising activities until December 2004, we ended our formal relationship with the school. It and its work, however, will always remain close to our hearts.

CELEBRATING LIFE

As a kid who didn't have any birthday celebrations, I had grown to understand the importance of commemorating life's milestones. My seventieth birthday had been one such milestone. On January 26, 1996, Donna and I had hosted a party at Green Meadows Golf Course in Vancouver. Nearly a hundred of our family members, friends, and their children had converged on Vancouver. I was fortunate to have old friends from both my army and University of Washington days come to our celebration. The guests included Dr. Charles Odegaard, Dr. Hank Reitan, Jim Ryan, and Colonel Lucian Truscott III. Bill Hilliard served as master of ceremonies, while our children and other family members and friends had toasted and roasted me during an evening of food, drink, and dancing.

As my eightieth birthday approached, we began planning another milestone celebration, spurred partly by my medical crisis two years earlier. This one, at the Riverside Golf and Country Club in Portland,

SAM AND DONNA KELLY AT THE PREMIER OF *PURSUIT OF SOCIAL JUSTICE* AT THE
UNIVERSITY OF WASHINGTON IN JUNE 2008. COURTESY OF THE KELLY FAMILY.

would also be a retrospective on my life. Donna created an invitation
with a picture of me in uniform, from 1951, when I was in Korea at age
twenty-five.

About a hundred friends and family members joined us for my
eightieth birthday celebration. Sammy's band, Riverside Drive, played,
backed up by Heather on vocals and Bill on tambourine. The kids also
created a mix of Donna's and my favorite dance tunes, many from the
1940s, including "our" songs—"Satin Doll," "I Left My Heart in San
Francisco," and many more. Our grandchildren, Cecelia and Malcolm
Blackthorn and Madison North, charmed the crowd, as did our niece
and nephew Kallie and Duke Schaplow (who shares my January 26
birthday).

Again, friends and family from Vancouver and Seattle joined us. Ike
Kelley, my old friend from Denver who once ran for lieutenant governor
of Colorado, arranged for a call from the White House during the party,
surprising everyone, including me, as President George W. Bush sent his
regards via an aide. By this point, few of my army friends survived, but
several members of the University of Washington faculty and staff came
to celebrate with us. Donna and I could not have been more pleased to see

HERMAN LUJAN, MYRON APILADO, SHEILA EDWARDS-LANGE, SAM KELLY, AND RUSTY BARCELO CELEBRATING FORTY YEARS OF THE OFFICE OF MINORITY AFFAIRS AND DIVERSITY IN JULY 2008. COURTESY OF THE KELLY FAMILY.

so many people come together to celebrate the long and, I hope, productive and useful life of this old soldier.

Not long after my eightieth birthday celebration, Donna was diagnosed with breast cancer. She underwent surgery and chemotherapy, supported by the love of friends and family. As she recovered, we began talking more seriously about moving back to Seattle. Donna's mother, Irene, was now in an adult family home in Bellevue, just a few blocks from my brother-in-law, Gary, and his special lady, Robin. Her transfer to this home eliminated one of the primary reasons we had moved to Vancouver in 1991. Our three daughters were married, and two had children of their own. They all lived within fifty miles of Seattle. Billy lived with us, and Sam Jr. had already decided to take a job at Western Washington University in Bellingham after his graduation. So on December 1, 2006, we moved to Redmond, a Seattle suburb, happily anticipating a new home, time with our children and grandchildren, and the opportunity to reconnect with our Seattle friends.

Epilogue: A Life of Service and Friendship

We are completing this manuscript in the spring of 2009. It is the six-tieth anniversary of President Truman's Executive Order 9981, which integrated the U.S. Army, and the fortieth anniversary of the Univer-sity of Washington's Black Student Union protest. I have lived through seven decades of American history, almost a third of the life of the nation itself. My life embodies the enormous changes we have seen in the twentieth century. Along with millions of Americans, I have wit-nessed Illinois Senator Barack Obama wage an improbable campaign that made him the first black president. Senator Obama's vision of one America, no longer divided by race, class, and gender and built on the principle that all have a right to the American dream, is an idea that has dominated my thinking since I was a child in Connecticut. It is a value I have tried to instill in my children. It is an ideal I have tried to model for everyone I meet.

I lived through the Great Depression, experienced Harlem nightlife, and met many legendary people. I experienced Jim Crow when I was forced to ride in the colored section of the train and live in the colored section of town and in colored-only barracks. I fought in Korea, trained for nuclear war, and taught the next generation of young men to be offi-cers. I saw protests and student demonstrations. I was praised by many and called the n-word by others. I worked with Democrats, Republicans, and Black Panthers.

I often say, "I've been black all my life." By that I mean that despite the good fortune of my Connecticut birth and the considerable personal success I have achieved, I still had to face the pain of racial segregation and discrimination through much of my life. My story is a paradox all too common among African Americans: it is simultaneously ordinary and extraordinary.

Surviving and succeeding unscathed, but certainly not untouched, by the pressures I faced over the decades made me, for better and worse, the man I am today. These experiences have enabled me, I hope, to leave a legacy and an example of how you can overcome obstacles with consistency, perseverance, and the courage of your convictions.

I was a dreamer. I always dreamed I would rise above my family's humble circumstances. My dreams, however, were never without doubt. I think often of events in my life over which I had no control but which provided the foundation and the motivation that enabled me to prosper through adversity. My education, reinforced by my family's deeply held values and consistent reiteration of the proud history of African Americans, infused me with a keen interest in the arts, music, and cultural activities. That education also made me heed the call for public service. When Paul Robeson asked me, when I was seventeen, "What are you going to do for the race?" I felt my destiny was determined.

People could never figure out Sam Kelly. I never fitted into a neat little box. They did not understand that you could be militant in demanding change yet not be violent, that you could criticize a university president or a U.S. president even while working within the system. Even though I was often criticized for mau-mauing the faculty during my years at the University of Washington, I realized the weakness of the confrontational, rhetorical approach of shaming or humiliating opponents into doing the right thing. This approach deludes us into thinking that we do not have to do our homework and thus neglect the opportunity to prevail through sharp, intelligent argument.

I consider myself an ordinary man who was fortunate enough to encounter many remarkable people who influence me to this day. I have also accomplished much that I hope makes this world a better place. In the process, I have made my share of enemies, but I believe I have also made far more friends who believed not just in me but in my desire to put all on the line and risk my own life in defense of our country and in pursuit of a just and fair society. I hope the people I have touched and those who have touched me will see that as my true legacy.

Chronology

1926   January 26: Samuel Eugene Kelly was born in Greenwich, Connecticut, to James Handy Kelly and Essie Matilda Allen Kelly.

1932   September: Began attending Mianus Elementary School, Greenwich, Connecticut.

1933   July 27: Essie Matilda Allen Kelly died.

1934   James Handy Kelly married Leah Hockaday.

1942   Began working for Northern Warren Cutex Corporation, Stamford, Connecticut.

1943   Dropped out of high school.

1944   May 18: Inducted into the U.S. Army; first post, Fort Devens, Massachusetts.

1945   August 16: Commissioned a second lieutenant, Officer Candidate School, Fort Benning, Georgia.

        November: Arrived in Yokohama, Japan, to serve with the U.S. Army occupation forces.

1946   November 30: Promoted to first lieutenant.

1947   November–December: Court-martial.

1948   May 9: Left the army as part of reduction in force; in army reserve as first lieutenant.

        Awarded high school diploma, Stamford High School.

        October 1: Returned to U.S. Army, assigned to Fort Lawton, Washington.

1950   November 5: Married Joyce Estella Lyle at Fort Benning, Georgia.

1951   February 11: Arrived in South Korea to participate in the Han River line breakout offensive.

June 2: Awarded first combat citation, Combat Infantry Badge.

July: Awarded first Bronze Star with V device for valor in combat.

July 16: Promoted to company commander, K Company, Nineteenth Infantry Regiment Battalion.

September 22: Given command of M Company, Nineteenth Infantry Regimental Battalion.

1952   May 1: Transferred to Signal Corps Center, Fort Monmouth, New Jersey.

May 5: Awarded second Bronze Star for valor at Fort Monmouth.

June 8: Promoted to captain.

December 18: Son, William Lyle Kelly, was born at Fort Monmouth, New Jersey.

1953   December: Assigned to Parachute Infantry and Jumpmaster School, Fort Benning, Georgia, for airborne training.

1954   February 5: Qualified as airborne officer, assigned to command of D Company, 188th Airborne Regimental Combat Team, Fort Campbell, Kentucky.

December 29: Operations and training staff officer, 508th Regimental Combat Team, Fort Campbell, Kentucky.

1955   July 9: Company commander, H Company, 508th Airborne Regimental Combat Team, Armed Forces Far East.

1956   March 7: Twin daughters, Brenda Joyce and Sharon Yvonne, born in Fukuoka, Japan.

1957   August 21: Began assignment as assistant professor of military science and tactics, West Virginia State College (until June 11, 1962).

December 2: Promoted to major.

1959   June 1: Awarded bachelor of arts degree, with distinction, West Virginia State College.

1960   August 24: Awarded master of arts degree, Marshall University, Huntington, West Virginia.

1962   June 4: Awarded bachelor of science degree, summa cum laude, West Virginia State College.

August 8: One-year assignment with general staff as G-3, plans, training, and operations officer, Seventh Infantry Division, South Korea.

1963   Brigade S-3, First Brigade, Eighth Infantry, Fort Lewis, Washington.

1964   June 17: Promoted to lieutenant colonel.

Served on general staff as G-5, chief of division testing and maneuvers, Fourth Division Civil Affairs, Fort Lewis, Washington.

September: Part-time instructor in European and United States history, Everett Junior College, Everett, Washington; first African American to teach in the Washington State community college system.

1964   G-3, plans and operations officer, Tenth U.S. Army Corps, Fort Lawton, Washington.

1965   September: Began teaching full-time at Everett Community College.

1966   January 1: Retired from the U.S. Army with twenty-two years of active duty and the rank of colonel.

1967   September: Began employment at Shoreline Community College with concurrent appointments as professor of African American history, special assistant to the president, and assistant division chair of social sciences.

1968   September: Chair, Ethnic Studies Division, and assistant to the president for minority affairs, Shoreline Community College (until 1970).

1970   October 1: Founding vice president for minority affairs, University of Washington, Seattle (until 1976).

1971   December 16: Awarded PhD in higher education administration, College of Education, University of Washington, Seattle.

1976   July 1: Special assistant to the president, University of Washington, Seattle; represented UW president on the Committee on Urban Public Universities.

1978   Appointed to the Bellevue Community College Board of Trustees by Governor Dixie Lee Ray (until 1980).

1980   Director of the Black Studies Program, University of Washington, Seattle.

Appointed to the Shoreline Community College Board of Trustees by Governor John Spellman (until 1982).

July 27: Married Donna J. Schaplow, Lake Tahoe, Nevada.

1982   June: Appointed to the State of Washington Board of Tax Appeals by Governor John Spellman (until June 1986).

1985   January 21: Son, Samuel E. Kelly, Jr., born.

1986   Self-employed consultant.

1990   March: Vice President for Governmental Relations, Gamma Vision, Inc. (until January 31, 1991).

1991   April: Moved to Vancouver, Washington. Appointed professor of U.S. History, African American History, and East Asian History, Clark College, Vancouver, Washington (until September 2002).

September: Appointed to faculty, Rosemary Anderson Middle and High School, Portland Opportunities Industrialization Center (OIC), Oregon (until June 30, 2004). Director of Education, Portland OIC (until July 1997).

1997   July 1: President/CEO, Portland OIC (until June 30, 2003).

2003   July 1: Development officer, Portland OIC (until June 30, 2004). President/CEO Emeritus, Portland OIC.

2006   December 1: Moved to Redmond, Washington.

2009   July 6: Dr. Samuel Eugene Kelly died at his home in Redmond, Washington.

U.S. Army Awards, Citations, and Commendations, 1945–65

Good Conduct medal, 1945

Honorable Service lapel button, World War II

American Campaign medal

Asiatic-Pacific Campaign medal, 1948

World War II Victory medal, 1948

Army of Occupation medal with Japan clasp, 1948

National Defense Service medal

Combat Infantryman Badge First Award, June 12, 1951*

Bronze Star with V device for valor and one bronze oak leaf cluster,
    August 11, 1951, and May 1, 1952*

Korean Service medal with four bronze service stars*

Republic of Korea Presidential Unit citation

United Nations Service medal

Parachutist, February 5, 1954

Parachutist Badge, Senior, March 21, 1956

Army Commendation medal with two bronze oak leaf clusters,
    May 28, 1962, and November 4, 1965*

*Awards that meant the most to him.
Source: Verification of Awards Entitlement, National Personnel Records Center, August 23, 2004, Awards Case Number A4HQ9X838EDUJ.

Index

Page numbers for photographs are shown in **bold.**

Abyssinian Baptist Church, 25
affirmative action, 186, 200, 208–9
age discrimination, 209
Aldinger, Paul, 211
Alex, Greg, 171
Allen, Clemoris, 124
Allen, Wade, 7
Ampere Electric, 218
Anderson, Rosemary, 212–14
Antioch Missionary Baptist Church, 6
apartheid in South Africa, 188–91
Apilado, Myron, **223**
Archambaugh, Celeste, 204
Asian American students: and ethnic
    studies program, 191; and faculty
    recruitment, 125, 132; and inclusion
    in OMA program, 141, 150, 155, 165;
    recruitment, 161–62; student associa-
    tion of, 151, 181
Associated Students of the University
    of Washington (ASUW), 185
Association for the Study of Negro
    Life, 127
Atkinson, Fred, 65–66, 70, 71–72
Austin Peay State University, 110

Baker, Bill, 163, 180
Bangkok, Thailand, 110
"The Bankers Club," 53, 58
Barcelo, Rusty, **223**

Barkley, Lola, 18
Battle of Bastogne, 110
Bayard, Ralph, 171
Beaches Restaurant, 218
Bearden, Romare, 18
Beckman, George, 183–86, 188
Becton, Julius, 78, 116
*Before the Mayflower: A History of the
    Negro People* (Bennett), 127
Bell, Kimberly, 166
Bellevue Community College, 166, 203
Bennett, James, 166
Bennett, Lerone, 127
Berg, Rob, 121
The Big White Fog (Lindsey), 25
Black Athletes Alumni Association,
    170–74
Black Panther Party, xvi, 128–31, 171
Black pride. *See* race consciousness
Black protest. *See* protests
Black Student Union: and athletics
    boycott, 171–73; and Kelly, 129–31,
    137; and support of OMA, 181; and
    UW protest, 225
Black Studies and the Academy confer-
    ence (1972), xvii–xviii
Black Studies Department (UW), 191
Black Studies programs. *See* Shoreline
    Community College; University of
    Washington

Black Studies teacher training conference, 129–30

Blackthorn, Cecelia and Malcolm, 222

Blackthorn, Heather. *See* Sanford, Heather

Blanks, Harvey, 171–72

Blufield State University, 16

Bohn, Louisa Harvey, 30, 69

Bonano, Sergeant, 73

Bond, Julian, 150, **193**, 194

Braim, Paul, 81, 86

Brand, Eleanor, 202

Bridgetown Coffee, 218

"Bridging the Gap" Breakfast, 166–67

Brisker, E. J., 124, 130, 136–37

Brown, Margaret, 162

Brown v. Board of Education (1954), 16, 104

Bryant, Cathy, 180

Burke, Maurice, 42

Burton, Tony, 170

Bush, George Herbert Walker, 207

Bush, George W., 222

California, 41, 96; Watts Riot of 1965, 115, 147

California State College, 183

Camp Casey, Korea, 113–14

Camp Stoneman, Calif., 51–52

Cannady, Herman G., 111

Carpenter, Pat and Kathy, 216

Carter, Randolph, 116

Cartwright, Philip, 139, 157

Carulli, Nicholas, 220

Casey, Mrs., 11

Castiliano, Mike, **148**, 200

Central District, 128, 163, 194

Central State College, Ohio, 127

Central Washington University, 210

Chalice, Miss, 20

Chandler, Kirby, 127–28

Chandler, Trevor, 147

Chew, Ron, 166

Chicano/a students: and ethnic studies programs, 191, 200; and faculty recruitment, 125, 132; and inclusion in OMA program, 141, 150, 155, 165; and MEChA, 151, 181–82; and Padelford Hall incident, 183–86; recruitment, 161–63, 196; and student protests, 183–86, 188; tensions with black students, 182

China, entry into Korean War, 78–79

civil rights movement, 104

civil unrest and race riots, 115–16

Civil War, 79–80, 98

Clark, Robert L., 111

Clark College, 211–12, 215

Coe, John, 5

Cold War, 117–18

Collins, Jim, **148**, 155, 162, 163

Columbus, Ga., 49

Colville Indian Reservation, 163

Committee on Urban Public Universities (CUPU), 187–88

Condé Nast Publishing, 68

Connor, John P. "Poopie," 95–96, 101–3, 117

Conrad, Ernie, 139

Cooper, Jesse, 86–88

Cooper, Mark, 170

Corwin, Larry and Dayna, 216

Cos Cob, Conn.: and the Great Depression, 30–33; growing up in, **4**, 5, 7–8, 14–15, 19. *See also* Greenwich, Conn.

"Crawford suit," 31

Crispus Attucks Community Center, 21–22

Cusick, Ron and Yon, 216

Dahlen, Chester, 114
Daily, 179, 184–85
Daimler Chrysler, 218
Dark Cavalcade (Lindsey), 25
DeFunis, Marco, Jr., 176
DeFunis v. Odegaard (1974), 176
Delta Sigma Theta Sorority, 192, 214
The Detroit Riot of 1967 (Locke), 188
Dewey, Billy, 10, 22
discrimination. *See* racial
    discrimination
Dixon, Aaron, 128
Dixon, Elmer, 128
Douglas, Mildred "Dolly," 23–24
Drenkhaun, Ernest J., 7
Dr. Samuel E. Kelly Award, 166
DuBois, W. E. B., 26, 127
Duchamp, Marcel, 18
Dunn, Jennifer, 207
Dunn, N.C., 6

Eastern Nazarene College, 15
East Port Chester, Conn., 19
Edmonds Community College, 210
Educational Opportunity Program
    (EOP): and the alumni association,
    166–67; and donation from football
    game, 172–74; enrollment goals of,
    196; and fundraising, 167–70; name
    change from SEP, 164. *See also* Spe-
    cial Education Program
Edwards, Chester "Chet," 71
Edwards, Harry, 194
Edwards, James Wesley, 86–90
Edwards-Lange, Sheila, **223**
"eight balls," 106
Eisenhower, Dwight D., 105–6
El Centro de la Raza, 183
"elfing," 217
Ellis, Jim, 180

Ellison, Mrs., 10–11
Ellsworth, Jennifer and Don, 216–17
Emmert, Mark, 199
Ethnic Cultural Center, 150
Ethnic Studies Department, UW, 191
Evans, Charles (athlete), 171
Evans, Charles (professor), 135–36, 138
Evans, Daniel J., ix–x, 167–68, 206
Evans, James, 69
"An Evening with Charles and Sam,"
    170
Everett Community College, 116,
    121–22
Evergreen State College, 186
Evers, Charles, 144
Evers, Medgar, 144

Fails, Leroy, 132
Fairfield Army Air Base, Calif., 52
Farrakhan, Louis, 194–95
Farwell, George, 139
Feldman, Jacob and Hannah, 32–33
Fenstermacher, Daniel Earl, 204
Fenstermacher, Earl, 204
"Finger pool," 23
First African Methodist Episcopal
    Church, 74–75, 125, 192
Flaherty, Miss, 11, 30
Flathman, Richard, 183
Fleming, George, 167, **207**
Flennaugh, Robert L., 180
Florida A&M University, 16
Fort Benning, Ga.: marriage to Joyce
    at, 76–77, **77**; and officer training,
    43–46, 74, 81–82; and Parachute
    Infantry and Jumpmaster School,
    102
Fort Campbell, Ky., 102, 110, 114
Fort Devens, Mass., 38
Fort Lawton, Wash.: integration of,

71–74; and Kelly, x, xvi, 70–71, 115–16, 192. *See also* Mercer Island, Wash.; Seattle, Wash.

Fort Leavenworth, Kans., 114, 117

Fort Lewis, Wash., 73, 115

Fort McClellan, Ala.: assignment to, 46; Jim Crow conditions at, 49; and pre-OCS training, 43–44

Fort Monmouth, N.J., 99

Foster, John, 62–67

Fox Hills Cantonment (Staten Island), 40–41

Freccia, Gene, 33

Friends of Portland OIC/Rosemary Anderson School, 216–18

Friends of the Educational Opportunity Program, 206

Friends of the Minority Affairs Program, 131–33, 169–70, 174

Fujii, Michiko, 202

Fujita, Sandra, 180

Fujitami, Jimmy and Bobby, 34

Gamma Vision, 207, 209

Gardner, Booth, 170

Garland, G. S., 80

Gates, Mary, 169–70, 180

Gayton, Carver, 171, **175**

George, Dan, 150

Gerberding, William, 188

Gilmore, John, 162

Giovanni, Nikki, 194, 217–18

Gloucester, Va., 6–7

golf, 15, 32, 58, **207**, 217

Goodman, James, 137, 159–60

Gossett, Larry, 124, 129–30, 136–37, **148**, 162, 166, 180, 185

Graduate Records Exam (GRE), 134

Graham, Gordy, 164

Great Depression, 30–34

Great Migration, 6–7

Green, Eugene, 166

Green Meadows Golf Course, 221

Greenwich, Conn.: and African Americans, 5, 19, 25–26; growing up in, 27, 29–30; Kelly family relocation to, 6–7; race and social class in, 21–24, 32–33. *See also* Cos Cob, Conn.

Greenwich High School, 19–20

Greenwich Playhouse, 25

Gregory, Dick, 194

Hamilton Avenue Elementary School, 19

Hammond, Ira, 171

Harlem, 25–26. *See also* New York City

Harrisburg, Pa., 38

Harry's Fresh Foods, 218

Harvard University, 156, 191, 194

Hauberg, John H., 170

Hayes, L. R., 74

Hayes, Ralph, 165

Heath, Herschel, 122

Helen's, 194

Henley, Ernest, 191

Hill, Wade, 143–46, 173

Hilliard, Bill, 146–47, **148,** 155, 162–64; and athletics boycott, 173; and cabinet briefing incident, 152–53; and Padelford Hall incident, 186; relationship with Kelly, 221; role in OMA success, 180

Hodogaya Golf and Country Club, 58

Hogness, John, 145, 190; and Kelly, 139, 153; and Padelford Hall incident, 183; as UW president, 187

Howard University, 15

Howse, Harvey and Jerry, 22

Humphrey, Hubert H., 111

Hundley, Jean, 147

Indiantown Gap Military Reservation, Pa., 38–39
Infantry Replacement Training Center, Ft. McClellan, 46
Inglemoor Golf and Country Club, **207**
Institute, W.Va., 111–12
Instructional and Tutorial Center, OMA, 149–50
integration of the armed forces, 104–5; at Fort Benning, 44; at Fort Monmouth, 99–101; in Japan, 56, 58–60; in Korea, 95–96; and Little Rock, Ark., 105–6; and Truman integration order, 71–72. *See also* racial discrimination; segregation
interracial relationships, 35, 57, 60, 171, 201
In the Land of the Blind, the One-Eyed Man Is King (Graham), 164
Irmsher, Bill, 147
"Iron Major," 44–45
"I've been black all my life," 156, 225

Jackson, Leonard, 166
Jackson State University, 143–46
James's Store and Post Office, 5–6
Japan, occupation of, 46, 47, 52, 53–54, 58–61; and Japanese civilians, 56–57, 59; Kelly assignment to, 49–51, 52, 173; Kelly return to, 107–10; and living conditions, 52–54, 58–60; and post-war changes, 58–60; racism in, 57–58; segregation and morale in, 55–56. *See also* Yokohama, Japan
Johnson, Campbell C., 69
Jones, Calvin, 171
Jones, Ed, 173–74, 188
Jones, Joe, 171
Jones, John D., 202
Jones, Lt., 56

Jones, William G., 72
Jordan, Mr., 125
"joro-houses," 57–58
Journal of Negro History, 127

Kane, Chris, 216–17
Katz, Solomon, 139, 145, 153
Kellee Communications, 218
Kelley, Ike, 201, 217, 222
Kelley, Mark, 44
Kelley, Vivian, 166, 170
Kelly, Albert (grandfather), 5–6, 205
Kelly, Albert (OCS candidate), 44
Kelly, Brenda Joyce, 112, 192, **201**, 202, 210; birth of, 107–9, 204
Kelly, Donna Schaplow, 200, 210, 212, **222**, 223, and birth of Sam Jr., 203–5; marriage to Sam Sr., 201–2; and Sam Sr.'s medical crisis, 219–21
Kelly, Essie Matilda Allen, 6, 7–8, 10–11
Kelly, Eunice Lyon, 54, 67–68, 75
Kelly, "Frisbee," 205
Kelly, Hilda Cheatham, 5–6, 205
Kelly, James Handy "Pop," 8–10, **9**, 205; in Greenwich, Conn., 6–8, 11, 29; marriages of, 6, 12–14; and racism, 22–23
Kelly, James Richard, III, 201, **207**, 217–18
Kelly, James Thomas Bland "Tee," 6, **98**; career of, 15–16, 102, 111, 129–30, 139, 188
Kelly, John Edward Alexander "Bub," 6, 17–18, **98**
Kelly, Joyce Estella Lyle, 85, 96, 112, **118**, 192, 214; and birth of children, 99, 107–9; courtship and marriage of, 74–77; illness of, 115, 121, 200; as teacher, 113, 121
Kelly, Leah Spencer Hockaday, 12, **13**,

38; as teacher of black history and culture, 14, 25–26

Kelly, "Little Roxanna," 18

Kelly, Myrtle Brown, 17

Kelly, Robert Wade Allen "Tot," 6, 15, 29–30, **98**; career of, 18, 31, 37

Kelly, Roxanna Greene, 18

Kelly, Samuel Eugene, Jr., 210; birth of, 200, 203–5, **205**; at Western Washington University, 220, 223

Kelly, Samuel Eugene, Sr.: and age discrimination, 209; award named for, 166; birth of, 6; and black radicals, 128–31; celebrations of, xv, 221–23; and Charles Odegaard, 151–54, 157–58; and Clark College, 211, 215; court-martial of, 62–66; as doctoral student, 133–35, 155, 195; education of, 11, 19–21, 23–24, 30, 37, 68–69, 110–13; as enlisted man, 38–39; and Everett Junior College, 116, 121–22; as father, 192, 203–5; and golf, 15, 32, 58, **207**, 217; and the Korean War, 76, 78, 113–14; leadership style of, 85–86, 180; marriages of, 54, 74–77, 200–202; as mentor and role model, ix–x, 134–35; nicknames of, 18, 45, 83; and the occupation of Japan, 49–51; and Officer Candidate School, 43–45; patriotism of, 97–98, 106; politics of, 206–7; and Portland OIC, 212–15; pride of, 97–98, 117–18; and the private sector, 208–9; promotions in the army of, 39–41, 42–43, 45–46, 54, 99, 112, 115; and recall to active duty, 69–70; and recruitment of minority students, 131–33; and Reduction in Force, 67–69; retirements of, x, xvii, 116–18, 196, 199, 221; and Shoreline Community College, 122–28; and

University of Washington, 75, 137, 180, 187; and UW Office of Minority Affairs, 138–43, 146–51, 186–88; and Washington State public service, 202–3; and West Virginia State College, 110–13. *See also* Japan, occupation of; Korean War; Office of Minority Affairs; U.S. Army

Kelly, Sharon Yvonne, 112, 192, **201**, 202, 210; birth of, 107–9, 204

Kelly, Thomas, 5

Kelly, William Allen "Willy," 6, 16–17, 37, **98**, 210

Kelly, William Lyle "Billy," **100**, 112, 121, **201**, 202, 205, 220, 223; birth of, 99, 204; education and employment of, 192, 210

Kennedy, John F., 111

Kennedy, Robert, 112

Kent State University, 143

Kilson, Martin, 130, 194

King, Martin Luther, Jr., 104, 124, 160

King's Ridge Golf and Country Club, 15, 32

Knight, Dalwyn, 131–33, 169–70

Knight, Gwendolyn, 18

Knight, Harry, 131–33

Knox, Sergeant, 64

"Kool-Aid" house, 192

Korea, return assignment to, 113–14

Korean War, 75, 78–79; combat patrols and command failures in, 80–82; crossing the Han River, 82–84; and desertion under fire, 91–92; Hill 750 rescue operation, 88–91; landing at Inchon, 92, 94; Kelly as Company commander in, 88–96; Kelly as platoon leader in, 80–88; Kelly assignment to, 78; Kelly return home from, 96–98; Objective Queen, 82–84; Objective William, 82–83, 85

LaFontaine, Ken, 125
Lake Washington Technical College,
    166
Lambright, Jim, 171
Larkin, Luther, 72
Laughton, K. B., 99–101
Lawrence, Jacob, 18
Leonard, C. F., Jr., **118**, 121
Lindley, Ray, 214
Lindsey, Powell, 25, 41
Lindsey, Raymond, 25
Links, 170, 192, 214
Little Rock, Ark., xvi, 105–6
Locke, Alain, 25
Locke, Hubert, 188–91
Logan, Rayford, 127
Lombard, Harry, 103
Los Angeles, Calif., 115
Louis, Joe, 41
Loving v. Virginia (1967), 201
Lude, Mike, 204–5
Lujan, Herman, **223**
Luxey, Jimmy, 10, 22
Lyle, Joyce Estella. *See* Kelly, Joyce
    Estella Lyle
Lyle, William and Mattie, 74–76
Lyon, Eunice. *See* Kelly, Eunice Lyon

MacArthur, Douglas, 60
Madrona Diversified, 208–9
Maeda, Sharon, 170, 180
Maestas, Roberto, 166, 183
Magnuson, Warren, 167
Marshall University, 113, 119, 122, 195
Martin, Jim, 108–9
Martin, Michael, 188
Martinez, Ricardo, 166–67
Martin Luther King, Jr., Memorial
    Park (Seattle), 18, 210
Mates, Amy, 126, 148–49

Matsuda, Larry, 166, 180
Matthias, Mark, 216
Mays, Benjamin, 160
McAdams, John, 95
McAdoo, Benjamin, 150, 170
McAulliffe, Anthony Clement, 110
McCoy Millworks, 218
McCune, Mrs., 11
McFerrin, Joe, II, 219
McIntosh, Bill ("Mac") and Helen, 208
McIntosh, Brian, Blair, and Blake, 208
McKenzie, Loratius L., 111
McKinney, Herman, 166
MEChA, 151
medical crisis in the Kelly family,
    219–21
Mercer Island, Wash., 113, 122, 171–72,
    192, 206
Merriwether, Ray, 170
Miamus Elementary School, 19, 22
Michalek, Dick and Gwen, 216
Miller Analogies Test (MAT), 134
Mills, Lamar, 162, 171
Minor, "Red," 110
minority affairs programs, 137–39,
    156–57, 160, 203. *See also* Office of
    Minority Affairs; Shoreline Commu-
    nity College
minority enrollment, 141–42, 176; UW
    efforts to increase, ix–x; and UW
    graduation rates, 164, 196. *See also*
    Office of Minority Affairs
Mitchell, Herman and Napoleon, 23
"A Model for Emerging Black Studies
    Programs Viewed in Historical Per-
    spective" (Kelly dissertation), 195
"Momma Dottie," 56–57
Moore, Rodney, 167
Morales, Rosa, 185
Morehouse College, 160

Morishima, James K., 186
Morrell, Karen, 164
Mount Ebenezer Baptist Church, 6
Mount Zion Baptist Church, 8
Multicultural Alumni Partnership, 166–67
Muñoz, Carlos, Jr., 183
Myriad Systems and Services, 208

"NAACP meetings," 105
National Committee for Advanced Teacher Education (NCATE), 126, 129–30
National Council of Negro Women, 170
National Defense Education Act (NDEA), 16
National Endowment for the Arts, 18
Native American students: and ethnic studies program, 191, 200; and faculty recruitment, 125, 132; and inclusion in OMA program, 141, 151, 155, 165; recruitment, 161–63; student association of, 151, 181
Nat Turner Literary Society, 123
Negro History Week, 127
Nelson, Sophia, 111
Nesbitt, Bob and Dawn, 216–17
New Lebanon Elementary School, 11, 19
Newman, Constance Berry, 207
Newschwander, Charles, 202
New York City, 18, 24, 25–26, 41
Nike, Inc., 218
North, Madison, 222
Northern Warren Cutex Corporation, 37, 68
North Seattle Chrysler Plymouth, 208
North Seattle Community College, 166

Northwest Center for the Retarded (Seattle), 192
nuclear weapons, 46, 117–18

Obama, Barack, xv, 225
Odegaard, Charles, 170, 183, 186; and black activists, 145–46; and Kelly, ix–x, 138–43, 151–54, 157–58, 181, 194, 221; and support of minority programs, 160–62, 164, 167; support of OMA, 182, 187, 199
Ode to Marcel (sculpture), 18
Office of Minority Affairs (OMA): and alumni association, 166–67; and community outreach, 193–94; creating the model for, 124, 155–57; finances and budget of, 147, 152, 155, 167–68, 173–74; formation of, 130; and fundraising, 169–70, 174, 206; and Kelly, xvi–xvii, 138–43, 187–88; Louis Farrakhan attack on, 194–95; and Padelford Hall incident, 183–86; programs of, 147–51, 162–66; racist attacks on, 177–79; staff selection for, 146–47; and student recruitment, 161–62. See also Asian American students; Chicano/a students; Educational Opportunity Program; Native American students; University of Washington; white students, disadvantaged
Oliver, Emmet, **148**
Olivotto, Guglielmo, 72
Olympia, Wash., 203, 208
Omega Psi Phi Fraternity, 112–13, 192
Operation Angry Arm, 115–16
Opportunities Industrialization Centers (OIC), 188
Owens, Jim, 170–74

Pacific School (Seattle), 192
Padelford Hall incident, 183–86
Padilla, Gary, 185
Parachute Infantry and Jumpmaster
    School, 102
Partlow, George and Bobby, 22
Partlow, Mrs., 22
Patch, Lloyd, 94
Patterson, Edwin H. "Pat," 107–8
Pearl Harbor, 34
The Peculiar Institution: Slavery in the
    Ante-Bellum South (Stampp), 127
Peoples, Gertrude, 180
Peternick, Leonie, 147
"Poker Club," 172
Poore, Jeanette, 119
Port Chester, N.Y., 8–10, 27, 29
Port Chicago mutiny trial, 41, 72
Portland, Ore., x, xv, 221–23
Portland Community College, 218
Portland Opportunities Industrializa-
    tion Center (OIC), 26, 212–13, 215;
    fundraising efforts of, 216–18; and
    Kelly, xvii, 213–15, 216, 221; student
    and faculty growth at, 216, 218–19
Portland Trail Blazers, 218
"Pot Slinger's Day Off," 7
Powell, Adam Clayton, Jr., 25
Powell, Adam Clayton, Sr., 26, 206
Powell, George V., 180
Pratt, Ed, 130
Precision Castparts, 218
prostitution, 57–58
protests, 159–61, 179; army awareness
    of, 104; of black militant students,
    122–24; campus athletics boycott,
    171; college demonstrations, 143–46,
    225; Padelford Hall incident, 183–86;
    South Africa divestment debate,
    188–91

Puget Sound Minority Affairs Consor-
    tium, 133

race consciousness, 14, 25–26, 95;
    Kelly commitment to, 206. See also
    Robeson, Paul
race riots and civil unrest, 115–16
racial discrimination, 70, 156, 225;
    in the army, 57–58, 60–61, 86–88,
    101; education as escape from, 14;
    encounters with the police, 29–30;
    in Greenwich, Conn., 5, 16, 21–23,
    32–33; toward Japanese, 34; on UW
    campus, 156–57, 173, 177–79. See also
    integration of the armed forces;
    reverse discrimination; segregation
racial equality and justice: and faculty
    diversity, 176–77; Kelly commitment
    to, 97–98, 175–79. See also affirmative
    action; reverse discrimination
Raritan Arsenal, N.J., 42
Ray, Dixy Lee, 203
Read, Eliot C., 170
Redmond, Wash., 223
Reduction in Force program (RIF), 67
Reed, Featherstone, 167
Reed, Walter, 6
Reitan, Henry "Hank," 133–35, 221
Republican Women for Nixon, 170,
    206
Reserve Officer Training Corps
    (ROTC), 111
Resident Release Project, 164–65
reverse discrimination, 16, 176
Rhoades, Cecil, 69
Rice, Norm and Constance, 167
Richmond, Va., 49
Ridgway, Matthew, 79
Rising Valley Baptist Church, 6
Riverside Drive, 222

Riverside Golf and Country Club, 217, 221–23
Riverview Community Bank, 218
Robeson, Paul, 24; and Kelly, xvi, 159, 206, 226
Rosemary Anderson School. *See* Portland Opportunities Industrialization Center
Rosenfield, Mark, 216
Russell, Millie, 147–48
Ryan, Jim, 139, 221
Rye, Eddie and Andrea, 125

SAFECO, 170
Sale, Roger, 165
Sanchez, Juan, 184–86
Sanford, Heather, 200–202, 205, 210
Sanford, Teddy, 117
Sanggukuhara Club (Japan), 58
Scarborough, James, 220
Schaplow, Donna. *See* Kelly, Donna Schaplow
Schaplow, Duke, 222
Schaplow, Gary, 201, 223
Schaplow, Irene, 210, 223
Schaplow, Kallie, 222
Schauss, Lieutenant, 90–91
Schill, Bill, 133–35
Scott, Hazel, 25
Seale, Bobby, 150
Seattle, Wash., 113, 192, 212; Central District of, 128, 163, 194; Kelly return to, 221, 223. *See also* Fort Lawton, Wash.; Mercer Island, Wash.
Seattle Community College, 209
segregation, 6; in the army, 38, 47–48, 48–51, 55–56; and the civil rights movement, 104; and "separate but equal" policy, 110. *See also* integration of the armed forces; racial discrimination

Sheraton Portland Airport Hotel, 218
Sherbourne, Tommy, 117
Shoreline Community College: Black Panther students at, 128–31; Black Studies collection at, 126–27; and fundraising, 131, 169; hiring minority faculty and staff at, 132; and Kelly, 157, 159, 203; minority affairs program at, 124–26, 141–42; minority enrollment at, ix, 131–32
Sigma Pi Phi Boule, 192
Silva, Peter A., 39, 42
Sloat, Mary Garrish, **21**
Smith, Al, Jr., 133
Smith, Don K., 172
Smith, Wayne, 107
South Africa divestment debate, 188–91
Southwest Washington Medical Center, 220
Special Education Program (SEP), 136, 152, 163–64. *See also* Educational Opportunity Program
Spellman, John, 202–3, 206, 209
Spratlen, Lois Price, 148
Spratlen, Thad, 148, 186, 188
Stamford, Conn., 27
Stamford High School, 30, 37, 68–69
Stampp, Kenneth, 127, 130
Stanford University, 138–39, 156, 194
Stanley, Milford, 56
Stinson, William H., 165
Stokes, Charles, 123
Storer College, 16
Strong, Luther, 212
student protests. *See* protests
Sullivan, Ed, 27
Sullivan, Leon, 189–91, 212
Sullivan Principles, 189–91

"Target ball," 23
Taylor, Sergeant, 95

Tennessee State University, 110
Tiger Mountain State Forest, 202
Truman, Harry S., 71, 225
Truscott, Lucian, III, 114, 221
Tualatin Valley Shopping Centers, 218
Tucker, Sergeant, 85–86
Turnipseed, James, 39–40
Tweedy, Isabella, 186

Ulbrickson, Al, 139
"Uncle Tom's Cabins," 47
University of California, Berkeley, 156
University of California, Los Angeles, 134
University of Massachusetts, 156, 194
University of Nebraska, 189, 194
University of Pittsburgh, 16, 139, 156, 191, 194
University of Washington, 135–36, 143–46, 166, 187, 200; admission requirements, 161; and apartheid, 189–91; athletics programs, 170–74; Black Panther students at, 128–29; Black Student Union, 129–30, 137; and Black Studies, 123, 136–37, 188, 191; Board of Regents, 157, 164, 169–70, 175, 180–81, 190; Ethnic Studies Department, 191; faculty diversity at, 176–77; minority enrollment program, ix–x; minority graduation rates at, 164, 196; Padelford Hall incident, 183–86; president's cabinet, 138, 151–55, 161, 181; resistance to integration, 156–57; Special Education Program, 136, 152, 163–64. See also Educational Opportunity Program; Office of Minority Affairs
Upward Bound Program, 165
U.S. Army: 2nd Infantry (Indianhead) Division, 78; 4th Infantry Division, 115–16; 7th Infantry Division, 113–14; 10th Corps, 115–16; 11th Airborne Division, 102, 114; 19th Infantry Regiment, 24th Division, 79–80; 21st Infantry Regiment, 24th Division, 95; 24th Infantry Division, 79–80, 95–96; 25th Infantry Division, 87; 40th Infantry (Sunburst) Division, 96; 92nd Division, 95; 101st Airborne Division, xvi, 105–6, 110; 188th Airborne Infantry Regiment, 103–4; 445th Port Company, 38–39; 492nd Port Battalion, 52, 59; 506th Battle Group, 110; 508th Regimental Combat Team (Red Devils), 107–8; 610th Port Company, 52, 59
U.S. Army: airborne operations, 85, 96, 101–2, 103–4, 107–10; Command and General Staff College, 114, 117; Far Eastern Command (FECOM), 74; integration of, 44, 71–72, 95–96, 99–101, 225; Kelly family entry into, 37–38; and Little Rock, Ark., 105–6; and military justice, 41, 57–58, 64–67, 91–92, 99–101; military police, 48; mobile force deployment of, 110; National Guard, 115; Officer Candidate School, 42–46; Operation Angry Arm, 115–16; post-war demobilization of, 59; and racial discrimination, 48–51; Reduction in Force program, 67; Reserve Officer Training Corps (ROTC), 111; and segregation, 38–41, 47–51, 104–5; Signal Corps, 99. See also Japan, occupation of; Korean War
U.S. Army, black soldiers and officers in: advancement opportunities for, 45–46, 55, 116; camaraderie of, 104–5; conduct under fire, 86–88;

and integration, 44, 56, 58–60, 71–72, 95–96, 99–101, 104–5; leadership, 39; pride of, 95, 97–98; as professional soldiers, 106; and segregation, 38, 47–51, 55–56
U.S. Constitution, 129
U.S. Government, 129, 208–9; and funding minority programs, 160, 164–65, 167, 169, 187–88, 207
U.S. Navy, 52
U.S. Supreme Court, 16, 104, 176, 201
UW Out of South Africa Committee, 189–91

Vancouver, Wash., x, 211–12, 220, 221; Kelly relocation to, 210, 219. *See also* Portland Opportunities Industrialization Center (OIC)
van den Berghe, Pierre, 178–79
Vietnam War, ix, 143, 179

Waldo, Robert, 139, 142, 177
Walker, Major, 64–65
Walker, Walton Harris, 79
Wallace, William J. L., 111
Walter Reed Army Medical Center, 6
Ward, Jimmy, 23
Washington, James, 18
Washington Department of Natural Resources, 202
Washington State Board for Community College Education, 132–33
Washington State Board of Tax Appeals, 202–3, 208
Washington State Legislature, 167–68
Watts Riot of 1965, 115, 147
Waugh, Bill, 128
Wayne State University, 188
Wesley, Charles Harris, 126–27
Wesleyan College, 194

Westchester Golf and Country Club, 15
Western Washington University, 186, 220, 223
West Virginia State College, 112–13, 192; and James Kelly, 16, 102, 111; and Sam Kelly, Sr., 69, 110–13, 119
Weyerhauser Company, 202
Wheeler, Mark, 171
White, Richard, 122–24, 130, 203
White House Rose Garden ceremony (1990), 207
white students, disadvantaged: inclusion in OMA program, 141, 154, 187; recruitment of, 161–62, 175–76; and tutoring and counseling, 164
Wilberforce University, Ohio, 127
Wilkens, Lenny, **207**
Wilkins, Roy, 112
Williams, Ronald, 42
Williams, Wayne R., 188, 190
Willoughby, Ruxford, 71–72
Wineberry, Jerry, 185
Winslow, Miss., 16–17
women, 14, 58; and interracial relationships, 16–17, 33, 57, 60, 73, 171, 201
Woo, Ruth Yoneyama, 170
Woodard, Robert, Jr., **207**
Woodson, Carter G., 26, 127
Wooten, Andre Stratman, 123
World War II, 34, 46, 110; African Americans in, 95, 98

Yale University, 156, 191, 194
Yates, Jack, 6
Yokohama, Japan, 56–57; Kelly assignment to, 52–54; segregation in, 54–56. *See also* Japan, occupation of
Young, Artee, 188
Young Man of Harlem (Lindsey), 25